Interviews with **Dwight Macdonald**

Conversations with Public Intellectuals Series
Douglas Brinkley and David Oshinsky, General Editors

Interviews with

Dwight Macdonald

Edited by
Michael Wreszin

University Press of Mississippi
Jackson

www.upress.state.ms.us

The University Press of Mississippi is a member of the Association of American University Presses.

Copyright © 2003 by University Press of Mississippi
All rights reserved
Manufactured in the United States of America

Frontis: Courtesy of Manuscripts & Archives, Yale University

11 10 09 08 07 06 05 04 03   4 3 2 1
∞
Library of Congress Cataloging-in-Publication Data

Macdonald, Dwight.
    Interviews with Dwight Macdonald / edited by Michael Wreszin.
      p. cm.—(Conversations with public intellectuals series)
    Includes bibliographical references and index.
    ISBN 1-57806-533-X (alk. paper)—ISBN 1-57806-534-8 (pbk. : alk. paper)
      1. United States—Intellectual life—20th century. 2. Popular culture—United States—History—20th century. 3. United States—Politics and government—20th century. 4. United States—Social conditions—20th century. 5. Macdonald, Dwight—Interviews. 6. Intellectuals—United States—Interviews. I. Wreszin, Michael. II. Title. III. Series.
    E169.1 .M1363   2003
    973.93—dc21   2002033076

British Library Cataloging-in-Publication Data available

Books by Dwight Macdonald

Henry Wallace: The Man and the Myth. New York: Vanguard, 1948.
The Ford Foundation: The Men and the Millions. New York: Reynal & Company, Inc., 1956.
The Root Is Man. Alhambra, California: Cunningham Press, 1956.
Memoirs of a Revolutionist: Essays in Political Criticism. New York: Farrar, Straus, and Cudahy, 1957.
Parodies: An Anthology from Chaucer to Beerbohm—And After. New York: Random House, 1960.
Against the American Grain: Essays on the Effects of Mass Culture. New York: Random House, 1962.
Poems of Edgar Allan Poe: Selected with an Introduction by Dwight Macdonald. New York: Thomas E. Crowell Company, 1965.
Dwight Macdonald on Movies. Englewood Cliffs, New Jersey: Prentice Hall, 1969.
Politics Past: Essays in Political Criticism. Formerly published as *Memoirs of a Revolutionist*. New York: Viking Press, 1970.
My Past and Thoughts: The Memoirs of Alexander Herzen. Edited and abridged by Dwight Macdonald. New York: Alfred A. Knopf, 1973.
Discriminations: Essays and Afterthoughts, 1938–1974. New York: Grossman Publishers, 1974.

Contents

Introduction	ix
Chronology	xxi
Ex-"Revolutionist" Visits Yale *Jeffrey F. Thomas*	3
Macdonald Interview: Just a Big Family *Peter M. Perez*	5
Dwight Macdonald Interview *Mike Tracey*	7
Today Show with Dwight Macdonald *Hugh Downs*	14
An Informal Discussion on Film *UC, Santa Barbara*	18
Dwight Macdonald Interview *Roy Newquist*	22
Unpublished Response to a Questionnaire *Esquire*	33
Portrait of a Man Reading *Book World*	38

Interview with Dwight Macdonald *Jack Graves*	45
Please, High Culture: An Interview with Critic Dwight Macdonald *F. Anthony Macklin*	48
Brooks Shot Right out of Saddle by Critic's Blazing Crossfire *Jeff Simon*	70
Conservative Anarchism: An Interview with Dwight Macdonald *Paul Kurtz*	77
Interview with Dwight Macdonald *Esther Harriott*	90
Notes from Interview with Dwight Macdonald *Alan Wald*	104
Interview with Dwight Macdonald *Paul Avrich*	113
Interviewing Dwight Macdonald *Diana Trilling*	115
Dwight Macdonald Interview *Shirley Broughton*	159
Index	175

Introduction

It is two decades since Dwight Macdonald's death in 1982 and nearly forty years since his influential essays on mass culture and politics appeared in the 1950s and 60s, and yet his name crops up regularly in the *New York Times* and contemporary journals of politics and culture.[1] Why is this so? Because he was always deeply engaged in the enduring problems of human existence. He really needed to know how to live, how to remain human in an increasingly dehumanized world. He always asked the important questions in a clear, precise prose: Just how do people lose their humanness? How are they made into things? What is the process? How may we tell good from evil? Striking at the root, his observations remain a seminal source for those who would try to grasp our history and what has made us what we are. Surely after 11 September 2001, when it was constantly asked: "Why did this happen?" Macdonald's careful discussions of how dehumanization had become a worldwide menace lends a crucial perspective to contemporary discussion. In September 1944, in his *Politics* article, "Notes on the Psychology of Killing," he wrote about the brutality of the war: "The Killers are removed and not conscious of the killing. . . ." Young men were trained to be efficient at mindless brutality and, worse yet, to glory in the work. There was an "anatomy of mayhem" whereby they were taught to hate total strangers and revere the State's commands. The research for this article was based on United States military manuals.[2] When the art critic of the *New York Times*, reviewing an exhibit at the Jewish Museum, is prompted to ask "how mass murder and mass murderers in just half a century could become the iconography of Conceptual provocations, snappy videos and other art diversions," it is obviously time to return to the critical insights of Dwight Macdonald.[3]

Like one of his heroes, Randolph Bourne, Macdonald was a marvelously witty, acerbic, and penetrating critic of culture and politics here and abroad. Hannah Arendt observed, twenty years after the demise of his influential journal *Politics*, that Macdonald had an "extraordinary flair for significant fact and significant thought." But more than his acute sensitivity to what was important was his ability to shape debate on controversial issues. He was a veritable catalyst of controversy. It was, as Daniel Bell noted, his insistence on calling attention to the "changes that were taking place in the moral temper, the depths of which we still incompletely realize." So honestly did he confront what he described as the "barbarism and rationalized lunacy" of America's social relations, not to mention its foreign policy, that he was frequently called an American Orwell. His writing reminds others of Twain or Mencken. Macdonald's prose style is in their class.

Macdonald was a rebel in the tradition of Henry David Thoreau, Randolph Bourne, and more recently Albert Camus, Noam Chomsky, and Vaclav Havel. It is the tradition of the rebel who says NO to the intolerable absurdities of life and by doing so makes an affirmative statement.[4] Naysaying was Macdonald's stock in trade. During and immediately following World War II, when he was editing *Politics*, he defended himself against charges of negativism and insisted that the times called for "technicians of vilification . . . we need specialists in abuse, expert mudslingers." When an English editor introduced one of his anti-American articles by assuring his readers that Macdonald was a "good American," Dwight wrote to complain that he was not a good American, "patriotism has never been my strong point." He was "a critical American." Many, myself included, felt that Macdonald erred in his opposition to the United States' participation in World War II, but some of his articulate admirers have argued persuasively that it was a "creative mistake," because it freed him to openly criticize all sides in the war. When many of his Trotskyist comrades at the time declared themselves in "critical support" of United States policies, Dwight complained that it was mostly support and damn little criticism. "In politics," he wrote, "the mask molds the face. You become what you do and say. You don't become what your reservations are." Dwight Macdonald was one of a very small band who at the time spoke out against the atomic bombing of Japanese cities.[5] He held up the front page of *Politics* in August 1945 in order to denounce the "atrocious action" proclaiming that it "placed 'us,' the defenders of civilization, on a moral level with 'them,' the beasts of

Maidanek."⁶ He was among the first to try to grasp the meaning and implications of the Holocaust and the menace of totalitarianism. He knew, along with Randolph Bourne, that "WAR IS THE HEALTH OF THE STATE."

At the present moment, spring of 2002, with a press described twenty years ago as being on bended knee, it is little wonder that a small band of thoughtful Americans look for a Dwight Macdonald. With a left fragmented and without confidence, strong and forceful criticism is increasingly necessary. However it is confined, as it was in Macdonald's time, to the little magazines, and even these have long since lost their cachet. Bourne in 1917 referred to himself as a "voice in the wind" and Macdonald often felt the same. He kept a careful record of what he considered his failings. He never, as he put it, "wrote a book in cold blood", meaning that he did not have a big book to his credit. His work was confined to intellectual and cultural magazines as well as several published collections. But from the beginning with his work in the Trotskyist press and the *Partisan Review* and throughout the longevity of *Politics* (1944–49) followed by twenty years in the *New Yorker*, and then the movie reviews and the political columns in *Esquire* of the 1960s, an educated elite waited for his analysis and commentary. A younger generation of radicals, Theodore Rozack, Noam Chomsky, Staughton Lynd, Todd Gitlin, all expressed their indebtedness to Macdonald. His essay "Responsibilities of Peoples" (March 1945) denounced the concept of "collective guilt" and had an important impact on Reinhold Niebuhr and Albert Camus. It remains a seminal article that is frequently reprinted. His influential essay "The Root Is Man," challenging contemporary Marxism as a viable basis for any radical movement, which appeared in *Politics* in 1945, was seen by many as a main inspiration for the New Left's "Port Huron Statement." The most recent edition was brought out in 1995 by a group of young radicals in New York City. In the 1980s Staughton Lynd recalled Macdonald's writing in *Politics*: "There was more good sense and fresh thinking in this one magazine . . . than in all the left journals from that day to this." Noam Chomsky opened his provocative 1967 essay "The Responsibility of Intellectuals" by citing a series of articles Macdonald had written for *Politics* in 1944. He found in rereading them more than twenty years later that they had lost none of their power of persuasiveness.

Dwight Macdonald's life story is the story of an American awakening. It is an account of an upper-middle-class white male, schooled in the elite institutions of the establishment, who started out with all the prejudices and provincialisms of his class—anti-Semitism, racial bigotry, sexist patronizing—and through the force of his inquiring mind managed to jettison a footlocker full of dandyish pretensions and become one of the most penetrating critics of politics, society, and culture in twentieth-century America.

It is, indeed, a remarkable story. Born of upper-middle-class parents in New York City in 1906 he attended only private schools, went away to Exeter at the age of fourteen, and from there to Yale University where he graduated in 1928. He was an extremely precocious child, who wrote to his parents several times a week, often instructing them on how to read what he was reading. He would present lists of poems, stories, and books and demand that they be prepared to discuss them when he came home on vacation. He was remarkably disciplined and constantly prepared lists for his own private reading that he felt must be read on schedule. He was elected class poet at Exeter. He studied Latin and Greek: "I have decided I should get a good foundation in the Greek and Latin classics before tackling modern literature. . . ." He did not get the highest grades in his classes. He told his younger brother not to worry about grades since courses and grades were a necessary evil and that one should pursue one's interests and concentrate on self-education. Following his own advice he won several literary awards for his writing in school and college publications and edited two of them. As he had at Exeter, he associated with a small group of aesthetes. They called themselves the Hedonists, and their patron saints were Baudelaire, Oscar Wilde, George Jean Nathan, and Henry Mencken. The club members had little in common with most of their classmates. For many years he did not think highly of Yale as an educational institution. The only good thing he could say about it was that the faculty and administrators did not prevent his use of the library. He sent his sons to Harvard. He was not political in college but he was a dissenting critic of the curriculum. He ridiculed compulsory chapel and publicly denounced some of his professors as incompetent. These were indeed early examples of his naysaying. He often imagined that he and his cohorts in the Hedonist Society would upon graduation establish their own version of Brook Farm where they could escape the vulgarity of everyday life, converse, write, and live quiet but productive literary lives.

Real life was a different story. In his senior year he traveled to Manhattan and interviewed several executives in advertising and retail. His interviews with businessmen made an initial impact on him. They seemed to be doers and he was sick of what he saw as ineffective academics. He accepted a slot in the executive training program at Macy's. But it was not long before he experienced disillusionment. He felt he had no talent at all for business and that he would have to return to graduate school, ending up a member of the academy. He was saved from that horrendous fate by Wilder Hobson, a trombone-playing classmate, who worked for *Time* and persuaded Henry Luce to hire Macdonald. He worked at *Time* and was in on the founding of *Fortune* magazine. Macdonald did remarkably well writing profiles of corporate leaders although he found them "pretty dull fellows." There were pieces on prep schools, on giant Japanese crabs, on mental breakdowns.

During this period he met Nancy Rodman at the literary and political salon hosted by Selden Rodman, Nancy's brother and a co-editor with Alfred Bingham of the quasi-socialist journal, *Common Sense*. It was Nancy Rodman, a Vassar graduate and New York debutante, who radicalized Macdonald. She had a very strong social conscience inherited from her mother. She fed Dwight some of the classics of radical literature including Trotsky's autobiography as well as *The Communist Manifesto* and Lillian Symes and Travers Clement's *Rebel America: The Story of Social Revolt in the United States*. It was Nancy who wondered why he continued to write about relatively trivial matters in the midst of a devastating depression. There is no evidence that Macdonald, prior to meeting Nancy, had any serious interest in politics, although he did vote for Al Smith in 1928 and for Roosevelt in 1932.

After he married Nancy in 1934, Macdonald began writing on serious matters. He did a piece on the Communist Party for *Fortune*, which while full of waspish mockery nevertheless praised the party for its critique of capitalism. He then undertook a series of articles on the United States Steel corporation. While doing the research, he became sympathetic to the radical union leaders and increasingly contemptuous of the steel executives. When he insisted on leading off the final article with a quotation from Lenin's *Imperialism* and a full scale assault on the steel management, the editors drastically bowdlerized the piece and Macdonald walked out on a $10,000-a-year job. It was reminiscent of Sherwood Anderson's departure from a business firm to become a full-time writer.

With his departure from the Luce organization Macdonald grew closer to the prevailing American radicalism of the thirties. At first he was a fellow traveler of the Communist Party, and he helped organize a unit of the Newspaper Guild at *Time*. He raised funds for the Share Croppers Union and signed petitions and wrote letters for the imprisoned black Communist, Angelo Herndon. It is pretty certain that he voted for Earl Browder in 1936. In 1937 he joined Phillip Rahv and William Phillips on the editorial staff of the revised *Partisan Review*, which had severed its relationship to the Communist Party. Macdonald became one of its most astute editors with a remarkable ability to recruit well- known contributors. He also wrote several important articles. Both Dwight and the journal grew close to the Trotskyist Socialist Workers Party, and it was not long before Macdonald was writing for their publications. Macdonald's main attraction to the Trotskyists was their antiwar position. However, when Germany attacked the Soviet Union, the party became lukewarm in its antiwar stance. Dwight was infuriated with the editors and after a series of name-calling letters and articles he left the journal and set about establishing his own periodical, *Politics*. The first issue appeared in February 1944, and it ran until the winter 1949. *Politics* was a remarkable enterprise. Macdonald called it a one-man operation, since he not only edited the magazine, but often contributed a large portion of its material, worked on the layout, and was involved with the entire production. However, without Nancy it would never have happened. She inspired his departure from *Fortune*, and she encouraged his split with the *Partisan Review*. Dwight readily conceded that without Nancy the magazine would "have been improbable if not impossible." Nancy's deep moral conscience, her inordinate need and desire to help others according to her well-formed political convictions, gave Dwight, the journal, and those who worked and contributed to it a bedrock of integrity not to mention its financial stability, since her inheritance provided a good deal of the funds. But it was, indeed, Dwight's magazine, and while its circulation was never more than five thousand, it was read by many more as it was passed from hand to hand among those of the radical community. It was particularly appreciated by conscientious objectors to the war and also by radical servicemen who reported reading it abroad. It was more than just a magazine: it became the center of a unique international intellectual community of like-minded readers and contributors and assorted activists who were unhappy with the status quo. It proved to be a place where they could find a refuge and provide solace for one another as well as a defense against what they saw as an increasingly terrifying world. They were bent on dedicating themselves to a critical analysis of that world and, even more, to advocating ways and means to encourage a change.

Despite his previous Trotskyist connections, Macdonald wanted a freewheeling journal that would hew to no ideological line. He had been anti-Stalinist since the Moscow Trials, and he had resigned from the Worker's Party because of its undemocratic and authoritarian discipline. Trotsky was so irritated by Dwight's constant criticism that he is alleged to have complained that "every man has a right to be stupid on occasion but comrade Macdonald abuses it."[7] For Dwight in 1944 the only consistency would be his unremitting exposure of the hypocrisies of the Allied position on the war, a forceful negativism directed against the status quo of the bureaucratic State and against all the forces of modern life that were contributing to the process of dehumanization, alienation, "thingification." That was Macdonald's dominant sensibility, and it is what drew admiring comrades into the orbit.

From the start Dwight managed to recruit and introduce to the American intellectual scene a cadre of Americans and Europeans who became some of the most influential participants in the controversies of the Cold War Era: C. Wright Mills, who named the journal, Paul Goodman, Louis Coser, Daniel Bell, John Berryman, Meyer Shapiro, George Woodcock, and many more. Three major and internationally influential essays by Europeans appeared in the early editions of *Politics*: Albert Camus's "Neither Victims nor Executioners," Simone Weil's, "The Iliad or the Poem of Force," and Bruno Bettelheim's "Behavior in Extreme Situations." Andrea Caffi, Nicola Chiaromonte, Victor Serge, and Nicola Tucci were important contributors.[8]

Dwight Macdonald and his journal reflected what amounted to the deradicalization that occurred in the liberal leftist community following World War II and during the rise of the Cold War. Stalinism had proved far more lethal to American radicalism than the conservative movement in America. The Cold War accompanied by increasing nationalism and chauvinism undermined Macdonald's hope for an independent resistance to both superpowers. By 1949 he had lost his faith in the possibilities of any large-scale radical movement. His pacifism declined as his own anti-Stalinism increased to the point that he too favored the Berlin airlift and even the United States's intervention in the Korean War. But he saw the terrible irony of contemporary events wherein the U.S. Army, "a most reactionary organization whose purpose is mass slaughter," had now become, with the airlift, "the protector of the popularly elected government of Berlin. Only a few years earlier they had firebombed Dresden and killed hundreds of thousands." There was, Macdonald wrote, a logic to both actions, "but it is not a human, not a rational or ethical logic. It has the logic of a social mechanism that has grown so powerful that human beings have become simply its instruments." This continued to be his overriding concern—the dehumanization and the mechanization of society, and despite his own tilt toward the West, he took little comfort in the rapid development of the national security state. Dwight Macdonald would have been outraged by the current military budget of the United States and particularly by the argument that dropping bombs and food supplies on the same people turns a war into a humanitarian enterprise.[9]

With his loss of faith in potential political action, Macdonald finally decided, in 1949, to abandon *Politics* and turn his attention toward literary and cultural criticism. Criticism became for Macdonald a substitute for politics because his devastating critique of mass culture amounted to an indictment of American society. At one point during this transition he wrote to Nicola Chiaromonte that if "the United States doesn't or cannot change its mass culture (movies, radio, sports cult, comics, television, slick magazines) it will lose the war against the USSR. Americans have been made into permanent adolescents by advertising, mass culture—uncritical, herd-minded, pleasure- loving, concerned about trivia of materialistic living, scared of death sex, old age. . . . We have become relaxed, immersed in a warm bath, perverted to attach high value to trivial things like baseball or football (kids' games really) and we don't function when we get out into the big cold world where poverty, the mere struggle for existence is important and where some of the people are grown ups."

In the next fifteen years Macdonald wrote influential articles on literary and cultural topics in which he described what is currently referred to as the dumbing down of the society. Many of these articles appeared in the pages of the *New Yorker, Partisan Review*, and *Commentary*. His first major success was his extended ridicule of Robert Hutchins and Mortimer Adler's Great Books project (*New Yorker*, 1952) as a mass culture entrepreneurial operation fueled by all the technology and marketing sophistication that he held responsible for spreading spurious culture and driving out the genuine article. "The way to put over a two-million-dollar cultural project is to make it appear as pompous as possible." The Great Books project was, for him, the perfect example of "mid-cult," even more menacing than "mass cult." Dwight had coined the terms and along with Clement Greenberg's "kitsch" they became the prevailing pejoratives used by the opponents of what Dwight called the "spreading ooze."[10] This was followed by his denunciation of the Revised Standard Version of the Bible for its desecration of the language of the King James Version so as to make it more accessible to the common man (*New Yorker*, 1953). He said reading it was like discovering a parking lot where there had once been a great cathedral. In much the same vein was his devastating assault on the third edition of *Webster's New International Dictionary* (*New Yorker*, 1962) lamenting the loss of cultural authority, the erosion of standards, the rise of permissiveness, ignorance, and the lack of respect for tradition, history, and the culture of the past. Dwight called these demolition jobs his "reactionary essays," which prompted his biographer to describe him as a "rebel in defense of tradition."

Interspersed with the explicitly cultural analyses were Dwight's attacks on works admired by many leading critics. Particularly notorious was his acerbic dismissal of James Gould Cozzens's novel, *By Loved Possessed*, touted upon publication as a most likely Pulitzer Prize winner. Dwight's ridicule of the work was unrelenting as was his caustic commentary on the critics who had praised the novel. Cozzens's style, he wrote, was so artificial and unnecessarily complex that it "approaches the impenetrable—indeed often achieves it." The love scenes reminded him of "a *Fortune* description of an industrial process." Colin Wilson's *The Outsider* received rave reviews in London and New York. Dwight refused to take the young Britisher's account of modern alienation seriously and dismissed Wilson's tortured sensibility as pretentious ignorance. But once again the main target of his criticism was the critics, such as Cyril Connolly, Philip Toynbee, and Elizabeth Bowen, who had praised the volume. For Macdonald this was one more illustration of what he saw as a terrible decline in intellectual and aesthetic standards.

Like George Orwell, Macdonald feared the corruption of culture by capitalist commercialism as much as he feared the corruption of politics by Stalinist totalitarianism. While he remained a democrat in politics, he called himself a cultural conservative. He defended classical principles and standards and evaluated the arts and literature on the basis of his classical education and tastes. He, like Orwell, thought that the degradation of politics in the forties and fifties was directly connected to the decay of language. When it came to culture, he made it his business to defend the achievements, standards, and traditions of the past. Despite the obvious conservatism of his cultural perspective (today the postmodernists would say elitism) his attack on mass society and mass culture had important political implications. It was ironically seen by conservatives during the Cold War as an assault on American values and thus subversive and unpatriotic. In effect Macdonald was using cultural criticism as a substitute for traditional political criticism and again attacking and irritating the defenders of the status quo.

Perhaps the most politically effective of Macdonald's articles was his review of Michael Harrington's book, *The Other American: Poverty in the United States*, in the *New Yorker* of 19 January 1963. It was the longest review in the history of the magazine. Despite his fear of the State he came out squarely for a federal tax program that would address the poverty stricken. "Until our poor can be proud to say 'Civis Americanus sum!', until the act of justice that would make this possible has been performed by the three-quarters of Americans who are not poor—until then the shame of the Other America will continue." He also was a harsh critic of Senator McCarthy and McCarthyism during those deplorable years. He ripped apart William F. Buckley and Brent Bozell's apology for the senator likening it to a "brief written by Cadwalader, Wickersham & Taft on behalf of a pickpocket arrested in a subway restroom."

By the time of his Harrington review Macdonald was already well on his way back to the political barricades. He was speaking on college campuses about the relevance of anarchism. He was publicly defending Morton Sobell, convicted at the time of the Rosenbergs, for not having received a fair trial. He was denouncing the Bay of Pigs and voicing great skepticism at the time of the Cuban Missile crisis. But it was Lyndon Baines Johnson's interventionist policy in the Dominican Republic and Vietnam that brought Macdonald back into full participation with the activist left. Where his previous anti-Stalinism had tended to blunt his criticism, he now saw such a political stance as irrelevant. Communism was no longer the danger. It was unrestrained American power. While never a supporter of Ho Chi Minh, the North Vietnamese, or the National Liberation Front, he denounced American intervention and wrote scathing criticisms of Johnson and his administration month after month in a regular political column in *Esquire*. He helped organize and participated in a protest at a White House arts festival. When a radical group called for the impeachment of Johnson, he heartily endorsed it. He advocated draft resistance and refusal to pay income taxes to support the war. He enthusiastically supported the younger generation of radicals and was a visiting celebrity at the time of the student uprising at Columbia. He even went so far as to raise money for the Students for a Democratic Society and was proud to speak at the Columbia Counter Commencement. In 1968 Macdonald wrote to one of his former instructors at Exeter that the youth of the sixties was "the best generation I have known in this country, the cleverest, the most serious and decent (though I wish they'd READ a little). . . ."

Macdonald's positions alienated him from many of his old colleagues on the left who found it hard to stomach the mindlessness they saw among the student revolutionaries. But Macdonald felt these critics had been far too accommodating to the status quo and not activist enough in their proclaimed opposition to the war. By this time, suffering from bouts of severe writer's block, Macdonald was often teaching on campuses throughout the country as a visiting professor of politics, culture, and literature. He had a remarkable ability to make contact with the young and was much admired as an instructor. He particularly enjoyed teaching police officers at the John Jay College of Criminal Justice—he liked their street smarts. But it was his provocative essays that brought him interviewers who were delighted to talk with him about books and politics, art and culture.

There is some irony in this. Macdonald loved to converse and to argue and detested small talk. But he was a writer first and not a facile speaker. He was also an editor and often did not have the opportunity to edit the interviews; and most have not been edited here. His son recalled Macdonald's spirited conversations, his "high-pitched, red-in-the-face, shaking-away, giggling, wheezing laugh that only a dog could hear." Michael Macdonald could think of few rationalists as capable of such "boyish spontaneity." The interview with Diana Trilling about the Columbia student revolt captures some of that youthful enthusiasm. His students note that he was seemingly nervous and awkward at the podium during a lecture. His forte was at the seminar table in conversation. There he was stimulating and provocative. The interviews reveal Macdonald's commitment to his role as a serious critic and intellectual commentator, which is why he was so important and often influential and why he remains so today. His good friend, the noted historian John Lukacs, wrote that Macdonald, when writing, "knew that the choice of every word was not only an aesthetic but a moral choice. In this sense alone he was an American moralist." Lukacs called him the "American Orwell," and there was much of the defiant independence that allowed both to be known as critics against the grain. As Czeslaw Milosz, a poet who surely understands the menace of human inertia and accommodation, recently recalled, Macdonald was "a totally American phenomenon" out of that tradition of "the completely free man, capable of making decisions at all times and about all things strictly according to his personal moral judgement."

Notes

1. The *New York Times* in a six-month period in late 2001 to early 2002 had nine references to Macdonald not counting reviews of his recently published correspondence. There are many more references in newspapers throughout the country in the same period.
2. The full text of this article may be found in Dwight Macdonald, *Memoirs of a Revolutionist*, New York, 1957, and again in his *Politics Past* (formerly titled *Memoirs of a Revolutionist*), New York, 1970. Most of the quotations in this introduction are taken from my biography, *A Rebel in Defense of Tradition: The Life and "Politics" of Dwight Macdonald*, New York, 1994, and my edited collection of Macdonald letters, *A Moral Temper: The Letters of Dwight Macdonald*, Chicago, 2001.
3. Michael Kimmelmann, "Evil, the Nazis and Shock Value," *New York Times*, 15 March 2002, pp. E33, 35.
4. I use the term "rebel" in the same sense as Albert Camus; see the opening paragraph of the first chapter of his *The Rebel*, New York, 1956.
5. To see how few, look at Paul Boyer, *By the Bomb's Early Light: American Thought and Culture at the Dawn of the Atomic Age*, New York, 1985, chapter 19.
6. Maidanek was the site of one of the more horrendous of the Nazi death camps.
7. This alleged Trotsky remark has been cited over and over again but without any verifiable source. Trotsky did call Macdonald stupid on more than one occasion, but the felicity of the quotation strikes me as Macdonald's version not Trotsky's.
8. Chiaromonte was the model for the character Scali in André Malraux's novel *Man's Fate*. See Gregory D. Sumner, *Dwight Macdonald and the "Politics" Circle*, Ithaca, New York, 1996, p. 29.
9. See Michael Stern, Letter to the Editor, *New York Times*, 14 March 2002.
10. It was Macdonald who was responsible for getting Clement Greenberg's influential article, "Avant-Garde and Kitsch," published in the *Partisan Review* in 1939.

Chronology

1906	Born on 24 March in New York City to Dwight Macdonald Sr. and Alice Hedges Macdonald.
1916–20	Attends the Barnard School.
1920–24	Attends Phillips Exeter Academy.
1924–28	Attends Yale College.
1926	Death of Dwight Macdonald's father.
1927–28	Serves as Chairman of the Board of the Yale Record.
1928	Spends six months with Macy's executive training program in New York City.
1929	Becomes an editor and staff writer for Luce publications—works on *Time* and as an associate editor of Henry Luce's new magazine *Fortune*.
1930	Publishes six numbers of a literary magazine, *Miscellany*, with Yale classmates, George L. K. Morris, Geoffrey Hellman, and Frederick W. Dupee. Begins writing serious film and literary criticism.
1934	Marries Nancy Rodman.
1935	Dwight takes leave of absence from *Fortune* for an extended trip to Italy and Majorca.
1936	Resigns from *Fortune* in dispute over the editing of his articles criticizing the United States Steel Corporation and its chief executives.
1937	Becomes an editor of the revived *Partisan Review* with Phillip Rahv and William Phillips; his initial article is a quasi-Marxist critique of the *New Yorker*. Publishes a three-part article criticizing the Luce publications in the *Nation*.

1938	Birth of a son, Michael Dwight. Begins writing for *The New International*, a Trotskyist publication. Writes *Fascism and the American Scene*, a Trotskyist publication.
1939	Joins the Trotskyist Socialist Workers Party. Becomes the acting secretary of the League for Cultural Freedom and Socialism and signs its cable to French President Daladier protesting the imprisonment of French pacifists.
1940	Writes *Jobs, Not Battleships* for the Socialist Workers Party. Sides with Max Shachtman's Worker's Party in its split with James P. Cannon's SWP.
1941	Resigns from the Worker's Party over issues of intellectual freedom and party organization.
1943	Resigns from the editorial board of the *Partisan Review*, protesting what he sees as a shift away from political commentary to a narrow focus on literary criticism as well as lukewarm criticism of the war and U.S. foreign policy.
1944	Begins publishing *Politics* and in the first issue writes "A Theory of Popular Culture."
1945	Birth of a second son, Nicholas Gardiner.
1946	Writes "The Root Is Man," an anti-Marxist critique for *Politics*.
1948	Publication of *Henry Wallace: The Man and the Myth*.
1949	Discontinues publication of *Politics*, confessing to a "stale, tired, disheartened and . . . demoralized" feeling.
1951	Joins the staff of the *New Yorker*.
1953	Publication of *The Root Is Man: A Radical Critique of Marxism* and his critique of the Bible modernization in his article "The Bible in Modern Undress" for the *New Yorker*.
1954	Divorced from Nancy Rodman Macdonald; marries Gloria Lanier.
1955	Publication of *The Ford Foundation: The Men and the Millions*.
1956	Lives for a year in London as a staff writer and roving editor for *Encounter*. *Memoirs of a Revolutionist* is published. Is appointed to give a course at the Salzburg Seminar.
1957	Death of Macdonald's mother, Alice Hedges Macdonald.
1958	In "The *Encounter* Row" Macdonald complains of the editorial control wielded by the Congress for Cultural Freedom. His

	article "America, America" is rejected by *Encounter* and published in *Dissent*.
1960	Publication of "Masscult and Midcult" in *Partisan Review*. Becomes film critic for *Esquire*. Publication of *Parodies: An Anthology from Chaucer to Beerbohm—And After*.
1962	Publication of *Against the American Grain*
1963	Appearance of his influential review of Michael Harrington's *The Other America: Our Invisible Poor*.
1964	Publication of "Fellini's Masterpiece," a review of 8½ in the *New Yorker*.
1965	Publication of *Poems of Edgar Allan Poe*.
1966	Drops the *Esquire* film column, tired of watching poor films.
1967	Begins writing polemical column, "Politics" for *Esquire* in which he consistently denounces the Johnson administration and the Vietnam War.
1968	Macdonald visits and defends the student rebellion at Columbia University and writes of it in the *New York Review of Books*.
1969	Publication of *Dwight Macdonald on Movies*.
1970	Reissue of *Memoirs of a Revolutionist* retitled *Politics Past*. Selected for membership in the National Institute of Arts and Letters.
1973	Publication of *My Past and Thoughts: The Memoirs of Alexander Herzen*, edited with a preface by Macdonald.
1974	Publication of *Discrimination: Essays and Afterthoughts*.
1974–80	Several visiting professorships and speaking engagements throughout the country.
1980	Last publication, essay review of a study of Buster Keaton in the *New York Review of Books*.
1982	Dwight Macdonald dies 19 December in New York City.

Interviews with **Dwight Macdonald**

Ex-"Revolutionist" Visits Yale

Jeffrey F. Thomas / 1958

From *Yale Daily News*, 11 April 1958. Reprinted by permission of the *Yale Daily News* Publishing Co., Inc.

Dwight Macdonald, 1928, is a tall, substantial man with a short goatee, mustache and reflective eyes behind horn-rimmed glasses. Sitting in the dull brown living room of the Trumbull College guest suite yesterday afternoon, he cheerfully discussed Yale, his own life, and the world in the tones of a retired "revolutionist."

Mr. Macdonald has been visiting Yale for five days as a Hoyt Fellow. He has found the duties of his stay informal ones: "I've just been living here since Monday, appearing at meals, and talking to students." He has addressed one class of Political Science 50 on Marxism.

Writer, editor, reporter and critic, he has moved within the field of letters since his undergraduate days at Yale, when he was managing editor of the *Yale Literary Magazine*, chairman of the *Record*, and columnist for the *News*. He described his column, "The Inquisitor," as "mostly criticism of Yale." "I devoted a lot of issues to comparing the curricula of Yale and Harvard, much to the detriment of Yale."

Mr. Macdonald looks upon his alma mater with a sort of affectionate distaste. "I think that Yale has improved a good deal since I was here, but, of course, that isn't saying much. What impresses me is that there's a lot more attention paid to the individual student and his courses. When I was here, I thought I was majoring in English, and it wasn't until my senior year that I found out I was majoring in history."

He attended a Scholar of the House meeting Wednesday evening, and extols the program, while complaining that "the chief defect of the papers was that they were too academic" and that their authors "were too timid about giving opinions," a fault he attributes to most American scholars.

Ruminating on his years at Yale, and on his impressions since then, he concluded, "I'm just a disaffected Yaleman. I should have gone to Harvard, I suppose." To explain this apparent disloyalty, "I guess I should point out that I've got a son at Harvard."

During his five days at Yale Mr. Macdonald has done some research in Sterling Memorial Library for an anthology of parodies which he is editing. The anthology will cover the entire range of literature, "from Aristophanes on down," and "I'm also only including parodies I think are funny."

He terms Sterling Library "the most hideous building I've ever seen, except for the library at Northwestern (University)." He considers Yale's pseudo-Gothic architecture "the worst thing about Yale," and maintains "if you have to imitate something, why choose that?" He advocates more use of the native Georgian style. "I think New Haven is a very dismal city, anyway," he concluded.

Long known for his leftist political views, he says that he is now "more aware of the values of tradition in politics and culture than 20 years ago." He explains, "I was a Trotskyist and a Marxist in the 30s but not any more." His present political leanings are "a blend of conservatism and anarchism. I think the main danger comes from the state—I'm for breaking down large bodies."

At present Mr. Macdonald is a staff writer for the *New Yorker* magazine. The author of four books, he seems fondest right now of a scathing review of James Gould Cozzens' much ballyhooed *By Love Possessed*, published in *Commentary* magazine. "It's a grotesque book, really," he declares. "It takes a real literary scholar to puzzle it out." He clearly delights in debunking the celebrated novel, for he has by no means retired completely from the field of revolution.

# Macdonald Interview: Just a Big Family

Peter M. Perez / 1960

From *Yale Daily News*, 5 May 1960. Reprinted by permission of the *Yale Daily News* Publishing Co., Inc.

Anarchist-novelist Dwight Macdonald, 1928, paused to vituperate the architecture of Sterling Memorial Library and the neo-Gothic style of most Yale buildings. He then erupted into a lengthy damnation of Robert Moses, ex-Park Department boss and newly-appointed director of the 1964 World's Fair.

"Moses is the opposite extreme of an anarchist. He's the typical planner. He breaks up communal links. No one man has done more to make New York an impossible city to live in," he stated acidly. "He has torn down the slums to put up those horrid, huge barracks. The slums had their own links—the local bar, the cop on his daily beat, the stores and churches."

The radical paused to tug on his red suspenders which contrasted sharply with the grey of his conservative tweed suit, his horizontally-striped grey and white shirt, and sober black bow tie.

Mr. Macdonald then explained his tirade against Moses. "You see, anarchy represents the philosophy of the individual. Anarchists are advocating a decentralization—a community small enough so that the individual can make himself felt. This is what Moses is opposing. He builds vast river drives so that more people can crowd into New York and asphyxiate us all with car fumes. He even tore down that lovely aquarium so he could build a tunnel to Brooklyn or some place like that," he explained. "You know he never did use the aquarium land for the tunnel—the ruins are still there," he quipped.

Stroking his Van Dyke beard, he turned to the question of anarchy as a form of civilization in the world today. Conceding that the abolition of all law would make the situation only worse, he pointed out that the anarchists desired another form of government—"a group cooperation where people decide things together."

Speaking in terms which had a utopian ring, he emphasized that people would have to radically change their thought to understand anarchy. "You have to imagine the family on a bigger scale. They don't kill or club each other. They work things out.

"Anarchy is not political action, but political inaction. Anarchy is not the collectivization of Russia or China. Their system destroys the individual."

Commenting on the super-state of the Soviet Union he pointed out that it is precisely the growth of the state rather than its withering away that distinguishes communists and anarchists. They differ over the means of accomplishing this new civilization, not the ends.

Plunging more barbs into recent national issues, Mr. Macdonald next discussed segregation and the civil defense drill of two days ago.

Labelling the Montgomery bus strike and recent lunch counter sit-downs as "in the anarchist tradition of free cooperation," he mocked Eisenhower's inept handling of the Little Rock incident. "Groups such as CORE and the NAACP are doing something for themselves on a local level," he emphasized.

He sank back in his chair and reflected for a moment. Then he continued, "You know sending those troops to Little Rock really set the cause of desegregation back quite a bit."

The conversation turned back again to Yale and the recent civil defense drill. "The whole idea of a warning signal and shelters is ridiculous. What good will they do?" he queried. "But you know I think the number of anarchists in this country is growing. Last year only 50 of us protested the civil defense drill in New York. There were over 1,000 of us Tuesday and 500 of us remained after the police told us we were under arrest," he remarked with obvious pleasure. "They really couldn't arrest all of us—they only brought three patrol wagons."

Dwight Macdonald Interview

Mike Tracey / 1961

From *Motion: The University Film Magazine*,
Summer 1961. Reprinted by permission of
Motion Publications.

MIKE TRACEY: *In an article in* Encounter *about four years back you made a distinction between the "professional" critics in America and what you called the "amateur" critics in England who are amateur because they make off-the-cuff judgements. What sort of critic do you think you are?*
DWIGHT MACDONALD: I think I am an amateur. Of course I am a professional in the sense that I am making my living by some form of criticism, but I like the idea of a broad range of interests and not crossing the T's and dotting the I's and not going in for linguistic analysis and so on.

MT: *Film criticism in England recently has been terribly involved in this form versus content and committedness argument: Americans don't seem so interested. I don't think you've ever mentioned these things at all.*
DM: If you carry form versus content very far in either direction it is a false argument, it seems to me. I know when I was first around *Partisan Review* in 1938 this question of form versus content was always being talked about and nobody could ever come to any conclusion as to what was form and what was content. It is ridiculous to talk about the political or ethical content of film and not pay attention to the rest and it's also ridiculous to do the other thing which is done over here and even more in France, to talk just about the lighting and the camera etc. of some really cheap little Western or detective story. This is nonsense. Several far out form critics praised *Elmer Gantry* very much—but I don't think it was very good even to form. I just thought it was a typical

overblown technicolour production and very badly acted by Jean Simmons and Burt Lancaster.

MT: *Is there such a thing as an uncommitted critic do you think?*
DM: What do you mean by an uncommitted critic?

MT: *Well, when a critic decides what a film maker has tried to do and then says how successful he has been in doing that and not worrying about the aim itself. For instance, if you were to talk about* Triumph of the Will *one could say it was an extremely well-made film and make no other comment.*
DM: *Triumph of the Will* was a superb film from the point of editing. Riefenstahl is really good. I think it is the most marvellous anti-Nazi propaganda. Don't you feel that?

MT: *Anti?*
DM: The intention is to glorify and so on but the reality is not. When I saw all those people shouting Heil Hitler and Sieg Heil I thought this is menacing and sinister; those close-ups! Those porky, beefy, mis-shapen faces of the Nazi leaders. They are the faces of a bunch of crooks and murderers. You can see that. Don't you think so?

MT: *Well I saw it 20 years after Nuremberg which makes a difference, but I was still terribly impressed by its sheer power....*
DM: Of course there is power but it is as if a gang of crooks were in control of the whole thing. There were some shots of Goebbels and Streicher and Goering which you couldn't possibly admire. Nobody but a Nazi could admire these people. Were you impressed by Hitler?

MT: *I am impressed in one sense. The simple fact that he could make those people do that sort of thing is ... inspiring. If I were a German ... well I wouldn't like to say just how I'd have felt or still feel ...*
DM: People were hypnotised, that's all. Riefenstahl shows this. She is so good a director that she produces truth even when she wants to produce lies.

MT: *To return to your own criticism, you once said, I think: "The artist is one who can make the likely out of the fortuitous." You always seem to emphasise credibility.*
DM: Yes, you are right but I think this credibility seems to be a little bit too modest a word. What about Coleridge's definition of poetry that it embraces a "willing suspension of disbelief." You certainly do have to suspend your dis-

belief in order to be affected by a work of art. Once you begin to say to yourself, "These are just actors and just fellows behind a camera," then you don't have any emotional rapport with the film.

MT: Hiroshima Mon Amour, *a film you admired so much, produced just this feeling in me; the posing, the poetic dialogue. . . .*
DM: There is a great problem in dialogue in films and as I see it, it can either be solved the way it is in *Shadows* which is to make it as realistic as possible, to have people interrupting each other, to have people mumbling, to have people repeat themselves over and over again; or else you do the opposite as they did in *Hiroshima* with the very stylised dialogue, particularly at the beginning. I think that alright too, you can have one or the other. I know the script has been attacked even by people who liked the film. I rather liked the artificiality. In that sense I suppose I am rather on the form side than the content side. *Citizen Kane* is one of the greatest experiences of my life and I have seen it about six times and the last time I saw it. . . . I was just as fascinated as I was the first time because it's an extremely artificial film and extremely good for the same reason.

MT: *What do you think of* Sight and Sound?
DM: First of all there is none like it as good and complete in America certainly, I don't know about France.

Sight and Sound tends to be too soft on films: I think that would be my main objection to it. I think that they are at their best when they are presenting documentary stuff like long interviews with directors and so on. I think that they are at their worst when they are trying to criticise and appraise films.

MT: *Don't you find that they are a little boring when they do this complication stuff?*
DM: Oh yes! Those round-ups of the Polish, Mexican, and so on. First of all they are always uncritical, they always exaggerate the importance of it. This is an interesting thing about criticism of films especially that the critic tends to exaggerate the importance of what he is criticising because if he didn't he would really be out of a profession. I have noticed and God knows these daily critics, the ones in New York that have to produce four or five times a week—if they really applied any modestly serious standards what would happen?

This business of repeating the plot has become a mania with reviewers. If you notice I practically never do repeat the plot. Maybe in some films like

Hiroshima where I write a great deal about it it is necessary to repeat it just to be understood. I don't see why anybody wants to know the plot. The critic should be something much more than just a person to give you the facts. The theory in most criticism, especially the dailies, is that the critic tells you what kind of film this is without ever saying what he thinks about it; but my conception is just the opposite.

MT: *You often use similes from other arts in your film criticism. I've found these are usually misleading.*
DM: I see nothing wrong; on the contrary, criticism should always bring in other arts. Why not? It is getting another line, another angle on it like engineers do. Of course it can be very absurd and just to conceal any real analysis. I think that *Hiroshima Mon Amour* and *L'Avventura* have a novelistic quality. Their structure is determined the way certain novels are determined, more by the mood of the moment which sort of suggests other things to the writer which he then puts in for no particular reason. You see the difference if you compare that with the ordinary play or the ordinary Hollywood movie where the plot is so important. In a good novel, after Trollope anyway, even in Trollope, the plot is not the determining thing; *Hiroshima* and *L'Avventura* are more freewheeling, much less predictable.

MT: *I will give that some of the way but in* Hiroshima *the main fault about it was to me that these things were terribly familiar. It was "deja vu," in a poetic dress but just cliche. For instance take the scene in the cafe. This was terribly melodramatic.*
DM: But it was terribly funny too. This shows what a great artist Resnais is. It was funny the way this ridiculous Japanese gigolo comes over and in English tries to scrape up an aquaintance with her. It is true that the poor architect looked at her with burning eyes and I think that the weakness of the film is his character. He is too passive and much too much just a mere foil for her. I thought it was marvellous to bring in this perfectly accidental and realistic bit of the Japanese man-about-town trying to pick her up.

MT: *All right, this was novelistic in one sense but the first ten minutes of the film is plain propoganda and very effective as such. How does this tie into the rest of the film?*
DM: It didn't. You could have cut all of that off—I suppose that is the really great structural weakness of the film. It was only connected in a purely intellectual way in the sufferings of the Japanese people under the atom bomb

were analogous to her sufferings in the cellar and having her hair shaved and that the moral is that men are related to each other as brother individuals and not related as hostile members of vast nations. That seems to be the point there, but I agree it takes an awful big wrench to get it in but I forgive him because that I think he did the first ten minutes so brilliantly.

MT: *I've got a quote here I'd like to get an American opinion on: "The British film industry is a world-wide laughing stock. It is becoming a poor man's Hollywood with neither the financial or technical expertise of the American industry nor the possibilities for artistic individuality present in France or Poland." What do you think? Is this exaggeration?*
DM: No I think there's a lot in that. I think the British do fall between Hollywood and the continent. It is true that they don't have the slickness or if you want to be flattering you can say the technical proficiency of Hollywood and at the same time they don't seem to have the flicker you often get in European films of an individual artist trying to say something to you. So in that sense I think it is true. It is certainly true of a great many of those inane comedies like *Carry on Nurse.*

MT: *You see those,—they come to America do they?*
DM: Yes, in fact I think *Carry on Nurse* is the one that has been playing to packed houses all over America. It has been making an enormous amount of money in America.

MT: *It makes me squirm. What about more serious British efforts?* Saturday Night and Sunday Morning *for instance?*
DM: As far as I know I am the only critic in London who didn't like the film and the only reason, here we get into this form and content I suppose, and the reason I didn't like it was because I felt that as a piece of movie making it was not particularly interesting. I saw that other film called *We Are the Lambeth Boys,* which was one of the dullest documentaries I have ever seen in my life. Did you like them?

MT: *Yes.*
DM: Well I think the reason you all liked both these films is because they show lower class, working class, life without any pathos or comedy melodrama, just straight—and this is a very unusual thing. It's a new thing over here, but not to somebody from America where we don't have this class problem particularly and anyway we have had this sort of thing since Dreiser, for

three generations or maybe even before that. It is of no interest to me that this is a realistic picture of working class life. Why is it any more interesting than upper class life?

He doesn't do much with the medium, he does it almost entirely by dialogue and some of those dialogues seem to go on forever. When those two guys are fishing and talking over their philosophies of life . . . this is not what you do. Look what Resnais does in a fifth of the time. The cinema is something which shows you visual things—it doesn't just go back and forth like a faithful dog from this speaker to this speaker to this speaker.

MT: *Why not? Bergman does the same thing because he wants to analyse people.*
DM: Bergman gives you a hell of a lot more to look at all the time. Bergman is rather over-rated, but in *Wild Strawberries* he gives you wonderful things to see whereas Reisz doesn't give anything at all. What do you remember from *Saturday Night and Sunday Morning* except the extremely expressive face of Albert Finney? Now another director could have got all kinds of cross currents, all kinds of subtleties, peculiar things out of him. Whereas he was just a very good picture of a straight slam-banging, self-confident ordinary worker—that's all he was!

MT: *I don't know if it's because we are much further away, but I think you're a bit too hard on Hollywood.*
DM: I know, everybody over here thinks this. I think you probably have, the French have it particularly, a certain nostalgia and sentimentality about things American and so on and if you live in America you don't feel this. There is a tendency to accept all kinds of films which I would think are just more of Hollywood's boring things, and to see all kinds of undertones in it. André Gide's reaction to detective stories is an example. When he was liberated in Algeria by the Americans the first question he asked was where can I get a copy of *Red Harvest* by Dashiel Hammett? I've heard that it's fantastique. That is all he thinks of!

MT: *Sometimes I get the feeling that you think there is a psychological block which prevents Americans making good films, but it seems to me that their hands are tied by economic circumstances.*
DM: Yes, of course I should have made that clear. The ironic thing about Hollywood is that the growth of the so-called independents, where the stars

and the directors get their own finance and make the film for themselves, has made so little difference. Of course my explanation is that they have been used to working in the old manner and they are still unconsciously writing the same way and I think that only the new generation of people . . .

MT: *Mankiewicz says that he can always make the pictures he wants to . . .*
DM: I don't see any difference between his pictures and the rest. Well I mean they are slicker and he is a more clever director than others but still·they are esentially just the same kind of thing. I think that *Suddenly, Last Summer* was, in fact, over directed.

MT: *People must often say to you "Well you know, people only go to the cinema to enjoy themselves and relax." Millions found* Ben Hur *enjoyable—then don't you think that your criticism is really in a sense a little out of place? Nobody would think of giving a book of Erle Stanley Gardner to Cyril Connolly to review. As a serious film critic why don't you just ignore* Ben Hur *and why not just criticise serious films? I can appreciate films on different levels—you don't seem to be able to—you have the same standards for everything.*
DM: First, I do like what you might call good-bad films—like Hollywood's good-bad girl. Some B movies are often far more entertaining, and better done, than more presentation films. *The Sundowners* and *Tunes of Glory* are two recent examples.

Second, the reason that I took up *Ben Hur* was that almost all the other critics in America praised it to the skies. It was extraordinary. The *New Yorker* was the only one that was contemptuous of it so I thought from that point of view it would be interesting. Anyway I am not only a critic I am a journalist that means you think of news that will arouse attention and make people talk and God knows this did. Of course it was because I put in that remark about the Jews being responsible for the crucifixion of Christ—I said it was, therefore, not fair to blame it on the Romans, to make them the fall guys so to speak, and it was not that way in the Bible and I was also tactless enough to say it is because there are no ancient Romans around now but lots of living Jews. Well really you should have seen it! I had something like 150 letters all taking the same line that I was a Fascist or that I was identified with the people who killed the Jews.

This is the sad thing about the critic's life that he makes some remark like this, which I think is perfectly justified, and instead of what he said about the movie, this sort of thing arouses all the passion. This is the trouble with our whole mass culture, that people react on much too primitive a level to things.

Today Show with Dwight Macdonald

Hugh Downs / 1962

Transcript of *Today Show*, 20 November 1962, from the Dwight Macdonald Papers, Manuscripts and Archives, Yale University Library. © National Broadcasting Company, Inc. 2001. All rights Reserved. Reprinted by permission of Yale University Library and the National Broadcasting Company.

HUGH DOWNS: *The distinguished gentleman on my left/right is . . . a distinguished gentleman. He is Dwight Macdonald, author of a new book of essays called* Against the American Grain, *and more famously film critic of* Esquire *magazine. He's here this morning as our film critic. Welcome, Dwight, and start shooting.*
DWIGHT MACDONALD: Thank you, Hugh.

One of the chief ways Hollywood has been competing with television is through "spectaculars," a kind of movie that is enormous in every way: enormously long, enormously expensive (the 35-million-dollar *Cleopatra* will make or break 20th Century Fox) and enormously boring.

It is not a bad art form in itself. Michelangelo's frescoes in the Sistine Chapel of the Vatican might be called a spectacular—or Homer's *Iliad* or Milton's *Paradise Lost* or Tolstoy's *War and Peace*.

Some very great movies have been spectaculars—such Russian silent films as Eisenstein's *Potemkin*. The greatest American director, D. W. Griffith, made two famous spectaculars. One is *The Birth of a Nation*; its battle scenes have never been equaled—they look like Brady's photographs put into motion. The other is *Intolerance*, the most spectacular spectacular of all time. But Griffith worked in the heroic past of Hollywood, when American movies were the most creative in the world, the time of Chaplin, Keaton, Stroheim and Mack Sennett. Today we have to look abroad for interesting films—to Bergman in Sweden, Kurosawa in Japan, Fellini and Antonioni in Italy, Resnais and Truffaut in France.

I have recently seen three current spectaculars—*The Longest Day*, *Mutiny on the Bounty*, and *Barabbas*—and I find they are often best when they are *least* spectacular, when two or at most three people are shown in close-up. Just like TV. This is odd because the justification of the spectacular is that it can give the audience something *big*, something that TV cannot.

It is true that, on the TV screen, crowds look like those confused blurs I used to see in Biology One when I looked through my telescope at the busy inhabitants of a drop of water. It is also true that one can indeed see such scenes much more clearly in a movie spectacular. But they rarely have much impact, visual or emotional. This is because, while geniuses like Griffith and Eisenstein could make twenty extras look like two thousand, our present directors perform the miracle in reverse: they know how to make a crowd look like a cocktail party.

That old warhorse, *Mutiny on the Bounty*, has now been remade as a spectacular ("filmed in ultra-vision 70" whatever *that* means). Two normally competent actors take the lead parts: Trevor Howard is Captain Bligh and Marlon Brando is Lieutenant Christian. But I prefer the old non-spectacular version, with Charles Laughton as Bligh and Clark Gable as Christian. It concentrated on the real interest of the story, which is not all those sails and natives and storms but rather the clash between two strong-willed individuals. Here we see the basic dilemma.

MGM spent some 25 millions on the picture. They could have saved 20 millions by sticking to the struggle between Bligh and Christian and leaving out what might be called The Spectacular Clutter. Storms are dull because one wave looks about like another, especially if both originate in a studio tank. The enormously expensive scenes in the South Seas were equally boring, in spite of the hordes of native extras. Or perhaps because of them. You see? The director just didn't know how to handle crowds.

Such illusion of reality as the director leaves intact is disposed of by the script—as Captain Bligh's speech before they first land in Tahiti: "Let any man provoke an incident which interferes with our mission and I shall give him cause to curse his mother for having given him birth." This melodramatic ranting is inconsistent with the actual character of Bligh.

The best of the three—or anyway the least bad—was Darryl Zanuck's *The Longest Day*, which is about the D Day landings in Normandy. It is about something that is still important to us. The best part of the film was the scenes in the German High Command, which were beautifully directed by Bernard Wicki. I wish I could say the same for the corresponding scenes in the American command, for which Mr. Zanuck in person was responsible.

Whatever his talents as a producer, Mr. Zanuck is not much of a director. Compared to those businesslike Germans, our commanders show up here as Boy Scouts, given to he-man posturings and corny heroics. Also, the Germans were portrayed by actors who were both skilled and unknown to American audiences, so that one could believe in Werner Hinz as Rommel or Paul Hartmann as Rundstedt. But Mr. Zanuck made the mistake—for good box-office reasons of course—of using stars like John Wayne, Henry Fonda, and Robert Ryan. They are *not* good actors and their faces and mannerisms are by now so familiar that it is impossible to see Mr. Fonda as a real person called "Brigadier-General Theodore Roosevelt." He is Forever Fonda.

But the great trouble with *The Longest Day* is a very simple one: it goes on for three hours. The first hour was exciting—except for the scenes when John Wayne and the other stars were doing their all-too-familiar stuff. But then I began to get battle-wise—and battle-weary. One burst of a burp-gun is not very different, emotionally, from another. And there is a certain monotony in grenades exploding. I stumbled out of *The Longest Day* as dazed and exhausted as if I had actually landed on Omaha Beach. Not enough emphasis, not enough selection and—above all—not enough omission.

Finally, we have *Barabbas*. The Roman-Christian spectacular has been with us a long time, since the Italian *Cabiria* (1913), the Cecil B. DeMille *Ten Commandments* (1923), and the first MGM *Ben Hur* (1926). I can't honestly say it's improved with age. The second MGM *Ben Hur* (1960) ran for almost four hours. It seemed eight. I felt like a motorist trapped at a railroad crossing while a long freight train slowly trundles by.

Barabbas was produced in Italy by Dino De Laurentiis, who for some peculiar reason seems to be trying to become the Italian Louis B. Mayer. It is based on a novel by Pär Lagerkvist, one of those Nobel Prize authors nobody has ever heard of before or since. The hero is Anthony Quinn, a good actor who here proves that mind cannot triumph over matter. Almost anybody else—say Primo Carnera—could have taken his part, which is that of the simple-minded bruiser with the usual golden heart who after three hours of bewilderment comes to believe in Christ's message. Here again the only faintly interesting scenes were the unspectacular ones, such as the confrontation of the Roman patrician with his two slaves.

Di Laurentis has said, "Barabbas changed the history of the world." But the new four-volume interpretation of the Bible gives less than a column to him. Not clear whether he was a bandit and murderer or a resistance leader against the Romans. And not clear in the movie either. He seems to be just a good-natured fellow with more muscles than brains. I really don't think he changed the history of the world—or even of the spectacular. We are treated to a half hour or so of the horrors of the Roman sulphur mines. There is the usual sadistic emphasis on brutality and torture that these so-called "religious" films always go in for, the usual endless dwelling on degradation.

Going to a Biblical spectacular means investing between three and four hours of one's life in looking at scenes which are either boring or repulsive—and often both. The moving and lovely story of Christ, as told in the New Testament, is butchered to make a Roman Holiday. Only a Nero or a Caligula could really enjoy these blood-drenched "religious" epics. I feel less strongly about non-Biblical spectaculars. The worst you can say is that they are very long and not very interesting. But if you have a lot of spare time—why not. You could be doing worse things in worse places.

An Informal Discussion on Film

UC, Santa Barbara / 1964

> Unpublished interview conducted while Macdonald was a visiting professor at the University of California, Santa Barbara. From the Dwight Macdonald Papers, Manuscripts and Archives, Yale University Library. Printed by permission of the Yale University Library.

> Comments by Dwight Macdonald from an informal discussion on film in Santa Barbara, Spring, 1964.

C: *What do you see as the distinctions between a reviewer and a critic?*
DM: The reviewer's job in the daily press is essentially that of a tipster. Like the guy who gives you a tip on the horse races, the reviewer tells you that you will or will not enjoy this or that. But the job of the critic, which is much more important, is to try to explain why he likes or why he does not like a given work of art. A critic must make clear why he has reached certain conclusions. Even if one disagrees completely with the conclusions, if his method has a certain depth and if he is intelligent, sensitive, experienced in the art, then the reader will get something out of what he writes. One reads a critic for the process by which he reaches his conclusions, not only for the conclusions themselves.

Another distinction between a reviewer and a critic is that often a reviewer is considering a work in terms of a season or the last couple of seasons, whereas the critic is considering it in terms of a much longer time span. In the case of a play, a critic must consider a comedy, for instance, in terms of Sheridan and Wilde or Ibsen and Shaw. A play reviewer has to write his stuff in two hours. Why can't they wait at least a day? Why does everyone have to have it the next morning? It means that the poor reviewer has to knock out his review in two or three hours, so that one finds a constant over-estimation. In movies too, for that matter, there is always going to be something that is better than anything else you have seen that season. But if you look at plays in a broader sense, you are lucky to find one in a single season that can be taken seriously on the Ibsen-Shaw-O'Neill scale. The same applies to movies, which are a very brief art. In fact it is extraordinary that movies only began as an art form about 1910—maybe not even then. One might even say they did not begin until *The Birth of a Nation*. So that now, about 50 years later—just in my lifetime—it is possible to bring everything in the art to bear on a single movie without being unfair.

Q: *You say that a play critic might keep O'Neill or Shaw in mind. Who would a film critic keep in mind?*
DM: Griffith, Chaplin, the great silent Russian and German directors and so on.

Q: *It is pretty hard to keep up with modern innovators, isn't it?*
DM: Well, I think we have had an amazing renaissance in the last six or seven years. For the first time we have gotten back to the level of the great silent directors. There was a long period of inferior films, though there have been a few great ones; but now, we have so many—whole schools of them.

Q: *But Sheridan was part of a tremendously developed tradition. How can you go back to Griffith and, as a critic, try to keep him in mind when you would not even sit through an evening of his films?*
DM: What do you mean I wouldn't! He's extraordinary! I am not one of those antiquarians, either, like William K. Everson—one of those silent film buffs (they have a special name for themselves—Foofs!*) But when I see *The Birth of a Nation* or *Intolerance*, I think Griffith's photography, his simplicity, his drama and his cutting, his use of actors is still good. In some ways it is dated, of course. The captions are ridiculous, but you don't have to make apologies for that, and certainly not for Keaton and Chaplin. If they couldn't still be looked at, then, of course, what they did was not great art. I think, too, that Keaton

---

*Friends of Old Films

is rather underestimated, compared with Chaplin. Keaton is the equal of Chaplin, and *The Navigator* and *The General* are better films than any one film Chaplin ever made. Keaton's *Sherlock, Jr.* has one of the great scenes in all of films. Our hero is a projectionist, dreaming about his girl, and his spirit gets up, walks down the aisle of the theatre, climbs up on the stage, walks into the movie being projected, and becomes part of the movie. What follows then, any surrealist would have been proud to have thought up.

Q: *In our local film society, I think of every one of the members as a critic, potentially. It is interesting to me that a few of these people, for whom one has equal respect, have completely opposite opinions of any given film. I am wondering if there aren't many different opinions of every film—perhaps all of them valid? For instance, we are interested in knowing what the members of our society would like to see. If I ask someone in our society if he would like to see a given film, and he says "no," then I feel that I may have learned something. But then I ask someone else, whom I respect and who knows something about films, and he says the exact opposite. What conclusion can you come to? I know how I feel about it, but is that enough?*
DM: I think you *should* show films that you like yourself, otherwise I don't see how you would have enough enthusiasm to go on with your job. The same with a critic. It would be no fun being a critic if he couldn't say what he thought about a film.

Q: *Don't you think it possible to enjoy something and not like it?*
DM: I think you're describing the "good-bad" movies, and Hollywood makes a lot of them. One often sees a very well-made comedy or dance film. It is really no good, but it is very enjoyable. Also the enjoyment is of a lower order than that provided by a film like *Jules and Jim* or $8\frac{1}{2}$ or any of the really first-rate movies. . . . Sometimes, too, people may feel that they do not "like" a film, but feel interested in it and feel that they should know something about that kind of movie. And the second time they see it or a movie like it—assuming that it is a good movie—they may find themselves more able to take it in. There is no question that a really original work of any kind is often very difficult—that's why it is "original." The function of a critic should be to help people discriminate, but how many people read the critic? Instead they read the reviewers!

Q: *Would you comment on compromise versus taste?*
DM: It's often said that the industry "gives the audiences what it wants," but I

think this is a very weak excuse. The fact is that Hollywood, at least, gives the audience what Darryl Zanuck and Louis B. Mayer want. I think their taste is low, vulgar, and childish. It is true that they often do find the same taste in the audience. But the reason they make these films is not really to give the audience what it wants, but to give it the kind of films *they* like (certainly, you can have a good film—even from Hollywood). Griffith proved that, even at the very beginning. He was the biggest money-maker for years. And I think that audiences—in America, anyway—took much more in the way of experimentation and real art in the silent period than they have since. The fact is that Hollywood began to go downhill very sharply, partly as a result of sound but even before that, when the banks got into the act and movies became a big industry.

When the movies were under the control of people like Chaplin and Griffith and Sennett and Keaton who were essentially working with haywire—putting something together without really knowing what they were doing—millions of dollars didn't ride on every decision. The audience at that time was willing and able to take all sorts of new things, whereas after the experience of a lot of Louis B. Mayers and Irving Thalbergs, the audience was molded by their prejudices. It is a circular process. An audience may respond to good things or it may respond to bad things. The more junk an audience gets, as it does year after year in television, the harder it is to break out of this peculiar circle. Everything bad seems to condition an audience to accept more of the same.

Dwight Macdonald Interview

Roy Newquist / 1964

From *Counterpoint*, compiled and edited by
Roy Newquist, Chicago: Rand McNally, 1964.

RN: *As critic, and as stylist, few figures in the literary world are rewarded with the esteem accorded Dwight Macdonald. Look, for example, at the number of times he is mentioned by the writers contained in this book—and further, to his continuing work for the* New Yorker *and* Esquire—*and still further (entering the royalty zone) to* Memoirs of a Revolutionist *and his brilliantly edited* Parodies. *To begin with I'd like to ask Mr. Macdonald to fill in at least a rough biographical sketch of his life and career as a whole.*

DM: I was born on Riverside Drive in New York City in 1906. I've always lived in New York, went to private schools there, Collegiate and then Barnard. From fourteen to eighteen I attended Phillips Exeter Academy. This was the most important educational part of my life; I had always known that I wanted to write, but this is where I began to write. They had an extremely good English department and a marvelous library, and I actually became a writer and critic while I was there.

I went to Yale and was graduated in 1928. At that time Yale really wasn't very much; I think it has improved a great deal since then. I got more out of Exeter. After finishing at Yale I got the naïve idea that I'd make a lot of money in retail trade, and retire at the age of thirty and write, so I enrolled in Macy's training course. They had a training squad for college graduates, and they paid me thirty dollars a week. At the end of six months I was graduated and they offered me the job of selling neckties at thirty-five dollars a week. They said they liked me very much, but they didn't think I was executive material. I certainly wasn't.

Then I did what I should have done originally. Through a friend, Wilder Hobson, who had been my roommate at Yale, and who was then at *Time*, I got an interview and took a test for getting a job there. I passed it, and became the first editorial employee of *Fortune*, which was just beginning in 1929. I was on *Fortune* all through the Depression, up to 1936, in fact. It was very educational for me because I did a great deal of writing. I was a staff writer and sometimes I'd do two or three short articles a month. I learned from *Fortune* how to deal with data and organize facts.

Then I resigned from *Fortune*. I really had had enough of it, and I was also becoming more and more left-wing. I wrote a big article in 1935–36, a four-part article on the United States Steel Corporation which was very critical of it. *Fortune* went along, but on the last article I began with a quotation from Lenin about monopoly capitalism being the last stage before socialism and therefore the steel corporation was leading us toward socialism. They balked at an acidulous profile I did of Myron C. Taylor, then the Steel Corporation chairman, and I resigned.

I was very political by that time. When I was at Yale I'd had no interest whatever in politics—I wasn't even a liberal, but at *Fortune*, when I saw the Depression and the reaction of the business community to the Depression, and then to Roosevelt, I came to realize how incompetent big businessmen were, how stupid and provincial. This made me begin to think all kinds of basic thoughts about American society. Until the Moscow trials came along I was sympathetic to the Communists, but I decided that the trials were frame-ups and became a Trotskyite which I remained for six or seven years. I was a sympathizer for the most part, a member for only two years. In 1938 I became one of the editors of *Partisan Review*. Three of us from Yale, F. W. Dupee, George L. K. Morris, and William Phillips and myself joined forces with Phillip Rahv, who were the old editors under the Communists. We took the magazine away from the Communists and ran it as an indepedendent revolutionary socialist literary magazine. I stayed with this for six years, then resigned to start my own magazine called *Politics* in 1944.

Politics came out once a month, and I wrote at least a quarter of each issue, edited, published it, and raised the money for it. I kept it up for five years, until 1949, when I became just plain tired of politics as a whole. Also, there was no hope for this kind of radical politics any more. The war was over, no revolutions had taken place, and the two big imperialist powers, the United

States and Russia, had complete control of the situation, so there was no possibility of the fundamental revolutionary change that I, as a Marxist, favored. So I gave the magazine up. Then I had to make a living. I had been living partly on my savings from *Fortune* and my then wife had a small income. I became a staff writer on the *New Yorker*, am still there, and three years ago I added the job as movie critic of *Esquire*.

RN: *Are you still interested in politics?*
DM: For many years I wasn't but I think that politics has become more interesting again in the last five or six years. Not that there's anything fundamental to be done in this country; there is no chance of basic change. But I think the rise of the Negro movement is important; it concerns me very much, and I'm completely on the side of the Negro. The pacifist business interests me very much, too. But I don't write about politics. I did write quite a long article on poverty a year or so ago for the *New Yorker*, and this got quite a lot of attention because it was one of the first things written on that kind of poverty. I read in the paper the other day that reading it stimulated Kennedy to begin plans for the "war against poverty" that Johnson is now carrying out.

RN: *To turn to a specific book you did, I'm curious to know how you put together that superb anthology of parodies.*
DM: I've always been interested in humor—and in parodies in particular—and I suggested the idea of doing an anthology to Jason Epstein at Random House, my publisher and friend. He said, "Fine," and it took me about two and one-half years of on-and-off work to turn it out. I do a lot of speaking at colleges, and whenever I'd end up at Yale or Harvard or Wisconsin or somewhere else I'd take a day or two off and browse around in the stacks. This is the only way I know of doing an anthology, though of course, you begin with other anthologies. I wonder what the first anthologist ever did, the poor ———.

Well, in this case there was only one anthology that was any good—Walter Jerrold's one of English nineteenth century parody, published about 1907 by Oxford. But it was fun to do, and I suppose that if I'd taken five years I'd have had even more good stuff in it.

RN: *One article you did that caused quite a furor was your piece on the* New York Times *book review magazine. Could you discuss your reasons for writing it?*
DM: I've been angry at the *Times* book review section for about thirty years

now. I mean, every time I read it I'd get irritated. Not that they'd ever injured me personally. They had asked me to review in the past, and I can't complain about their reviews of my books. My anger sprang from the fact that it's on such a low level and it should be so much better. I get angry rather easily, and I get personally angry when institutions or individuals aren't up to their job. This is how I felt about the *Times*. The chief villain of my *Esquire* series was Lester Markel, the fabulous editor of the Sunday sections. I had two interviews with him, and I must say that he couldn't have been more amiable or charming. We got along beautifully, except that I kept taking notes. I've found that people often make this mistake with me. We get along, and they say to themselves, "This fellow seems all right so I'll talk freely." They do, I take it down, it comes out, and Oh, God. I really liked Markel, yet everything he said confirmed my low opinion of his Sunday book review section. Americans are sure that if they can "sell" themselves personally to a journalist he will write favorably of them. But I can like a man and still think he is, professionally, a disaster. And print it, too.

RN: *Do you think that the book review situation in general has improved in the past few years?*
DM: Yes. There are two obvious examples. One is the *New York Review of Books*, which is a very hopeful thing. The reviews are too long, to say the least, but the level is high. The other is the remarkable renaissance of the *New York Herald-Tribune* book section. A year or so ago this was even worse than the *Times*—the same sort of stuff, but only half as much coverage. Now they have a new editor, as you know, and they have made great strides on their Sunday section, also. I think the *Tribune* book section is a very hopeful try.

RN: *I'll turn to the movies, now, into the field you cover for* Esquire. *What do you think of the quality of movies today?*
DM: I was fortunate in coming into the field three and one-half years ago, when movies were really getting interesting. It began with Ingmar Bergman, and then came the French new wave, the Italians, and Japanese. Movies are now an interesting, developing lively art form. What happened in movies was basically this: We had the primitive period, fifty years ago, when movies began—Griffith was the greatest, of course, and there were in the twenties the Russians and the Germans. The silent period ran up to 1930—Chaplin, Keaton, Erich von Stroheim, and Griffith. Murnau and Pabst in Germany

and above all the great Russian school headed by Eisenstein, Pudovkin, and Douzhenko.

Then came sound and as so many experts predicted, it had a terrible effect upon the art of the cinema. In all countries, even Russia. Stalin came into power at the same time and imposed his socialist realism nonsense, outlawing all experiment as "formalism." The decline in Russia was so great that the Russians never have come back even to the level of Hollywood.

In this country, the great silent directors were completely out, and we had a long period of a rather mediocre sort of photographic stage play. Some good movies were made, but in general the medium wasn't interesting. It seems to me that only in the last four or five years has a whole new aesthetic been worked out. They have discovered, finally, how to use sound in a realistic and non-theatrical way, and the great directors, like Renoir and Truffaut in France and Fellini in Italy have worked out new and original approaches to the film. I think I can safely say that movies are now more interesting than the stage or even the novel, and it's wonderful to be on the critical end of an art that is in flower.

A few years ago, at a party, you would talk about novels or plays, but now you constantly run into people who have recently seen a particularly good movie five or six times, and know every nuance. You can talk to someone for a half-hour about one scene in a Fellini film. Perhaps the movies are developing scholars as well as fans.

RN: *How would you define your obligation as a movie critic?*
DM: I think the main obligation I have is to myself to express what I think about the work I'm reviewing. I don't think the critic has any obligation to the public to try to figure out whether they'll like something or not, and explain it to them in those terms. If he does that, he's not writing criticism at all—he's turning out a tip sheet. (It's done this way in daily newspapers all the time.) The only obligation a critic has to the public is to make his ideas clear and to write as well as he can. It's up to them if they find something useful and persuasive in your work; if they don't it's too bad for them and too bad for you. As to approaching the work of art, I don't think that criticism should be "constructive." I think it's impertinent of a critic to second-guess the director of the movie, something which my friend the late James Agee, an excellent critic in other ways, persisted in doing. He always tried to show how it could

have been better done. Agee was really a frustrated director. He would have made a very good director, too.

I think the obligation to a work of art is simply to relate it to other and similar works of art. I would say that the difference between a reviewer and a critic is in the inclusiveness of the standard by which works are judged. A reviewer judges a book or a play on the basis of the season. This may be a service to the public, but it leads to grotesque judgment because it tends to overestimate the book or the play which may be mediocre and yet look, on this narrow comparison, like a work of genius if the season is bad. The critic had to judge on a much broader standard.

I don't mean that the theater critic should go back for comparisons to Shakespeare and Greek tragedy, but he should at least go back to modern masters like Shaw and Ibsen. In the case of the movies which are, after all, quite young, I think it's perfectly legitimate to draw comparisons with anybody and anything in their history, beginning with Griffith and Chaplin. In fact, when it comes to some of the comedies that are made now—frank imitations, for instance, of Mack Sennett and Buster Keaton—I'm afraid the present variety must be discredited. For instance, Jacques Tati is so much like Keaton it seems weird—the same frozen business—but he hasn't the charm and magic Keaton had. He seems somewhat psychotic to me, and makes me uncomfortable.

RN: *How do you feel about the general level of criticism and review in all fields?*
DM: Well, we always have the inferior kind of hack criticisms that magazines like the *Saturday Review* or papers like the *New York Times* specialize in. But we also have some extremely good critics who write for the little magazine—and, of course, there's always Edmund Wilson.

As far as theater—well, Robert Brustein of the *New Republic* is good, but this is back to the little magazines. John Simon is good, in the *Hudson Review*. As for the newspaper reviewers, Walter Kerr is much the best of them; he actually seems to know something about theater. Unfortunately, there isn't much to criticize in theater—they have so little to work with.

Movie criticism—most unfortunate. Maybe the newspapers have to pay too much attention to local theater advertising.

The most insidious thing in movie criticism—and this applies just as much to France and England as it does to this country—is what I call the "insider" approach. You get the feeling that these critics accept everything that certain people do because they are part of an establishment. It's impossible to find criticisms of certain directors, certain producers, but actually nobody is perfect and the best people in the business make gaffes. There's a confusion now, for example—they think that any film that is the opposite of a Hollywood film is good. I've seen some terrible French noncommercial films.

RN: *Obviously, despite the fact that you spend a great deal of time at the movies, you read a great deal. What do you find in current literature that you most admire, and what, conversely, do you most deplore?*
DM: Well, I think that Faulkner was the last of the major twentieth-century novelists. We had the extraordinary outburst beginning with Dreiser, then after World War I with Anderson and Fitzgerald. I don't think we have had anything comparable to that, since.

I think we have two extremely talented novelists in Saul Bellow and John Updike. Both have done extremely good things. Norman Mailer is a great disappointment to me, at least recently, because he's turned from being a novelist into being some sort of man of action; he's living his life instead of writing it. He's of more interest right now to a psychiatrist than to the public because he's using his writing as some sort of therapy. His new novel running in *Esquire* degrades art to wish-fulfillment, and this is a shame because he has such a great talent.

You see, a whole historical period ended around 1930, sometime in the 1930s, the classical avant-garde that began with Rimbaud and James and Proust, then embraced Joyce, Eliot, Stravinsky, Picasso, and so forth. This period produced all of our really great works of art in every field.

Well, every movement has to come to an end, and it's extraordinary that this movement lasted almost fifty years. To some extent history intruded, because what happened in the 1930s was that the political thing came to the fore, and writers became very political. The Second World War didn't do much good because, unlike the aftermath of World War I, there was no flowering of the arts.

In other words, for a generation or two we haven't been able to create or invent a general movement, anything to approximate the classical avant-garde. There are very few current writers, painters, and musicians who are on the level of the antediluvian giants like Stravinsky and Picasso. Samuel Beckett, for example, is a peculiar sort of carry-over from Joyce. He was Joyce's secretary, but think of how limited he is compared to Joyce. His latest novel, *How It Is*, has been reduced to such a plane of abstraction, repetition, and minutia, there's almost no content left in it.

RN: *Now, if you were to give advice to the young writer, what would that advice be?*
DM: I think the most important thing a young writer must keep in mind is his way of making a living from writing. We've got to consider the relationship of the professional writer to the people who employ him. What he should try to do is use the magazine, or the publisher, or the producer, whomever he writes for, to meeting his purposes and not their purposes.

A good example of this is William Faulkner's career in Hollywood. There was a time, you know, when he spent three or four months of each year in Hollywood, writing scenarios. I've seen some of these movies, and they're no better than the usual Hollywood film.

Now, Faulkner had no illusion about these scenarios. He did his work and led a very sober and nonparty life. He saved his money and went back to Oxford, Mississippi, to write good novels. He didn't try to reform movies, which he couldn't have done. He did a competent job but somewhere along the line kept himself detached, separated what he had to do from what he really wanted to do. No one was cheated. In other words, the young writer has to find, at some point, a way of making a living that coincides both with what he wants and with what a publisher wants. He can't expect to be subsidized. No one is in business for his health.

Sometimes, of course, it's best for the writer to work completely outside the field, far from the written word. At other times it's advisable to work as closely as possible in the field—for a magazine, as a critic, or some sort of journalist. Then the problem becomes one of keeping your talent your own. Edmund Wilson is a very good example of somebody who has made his living by writing all his life and who has also been able—in any extraordinary way—to do just what he wanted, and to be very well paid for it. His whole relationship with the *New Yorker* is an example of this. His writing for the *New Yorker* is not different from his other writing; he doesn't write *New Yorker* style. The subjects he takes up for them are the ones that interest him, even to writing boring articles about Indians. I don't know why he's so fascinated with Indians, but he got away with it, and now I hear he's writing a whole book on French Canadian culture.

RN: *Now I'm going to get personal. You have been alluded to as a snob, and I wonder what you might want to say in your own defense.*

DM: Well, it's true that I'm often accused of being a snob. But I'm not a social snob—I'm quite a democratic fellow, really. But I admit that I am a snob in an intellectual and cultural sense. I think it is important to stand up for certain standards and not to relax these standards at all, not even for the very worthy cause of democratizing culture or bringing a great many people into contact with great works of art. Mind you, I'm not at all against that. As many people as possible should take an interest in reading and writing and theater and good cinema and music. I'm not in favor of closing libraries or public art galleries, and I'm in favor of free education.

What distresses me is the assumption that somehow or other "democracy" means that everybody has to get into the act, that everybody must be cultured and take a serious interest in good art and good literature. I don't see any reason for making this assumption. I don't see why interests shouldn't be completely voluntary. It has nothing to do with real democracy. You can have two completely distinct cultures, as I think is actually the case right now. An elite culture, for people who care about these things, and a mass culture for people who don't. Both sides are happy.

But this business of making concessions to the public in order to interest them, I don't understand why this should be done at all. This is where real snobbishness comes in, it seems to me. The assumption is that you somehow cannot be a really dignified human being without deep cultural interests. I don't agree. I can respect somebody even if he hasn't the faintest interest in "culture."

Historically, a very small percentage of the population at any time—and I'm talking about Renaissance Italy and Periclean Athens and so forth—were really interested in art, music, sculpture, literature, history, and philosophy. I would say less than 20 percent, and why isn't that a perfectly good state of affairs? In the past, up to 1800, it was not only just a small percentage of the people in general, but even a small percentage of the only people who had any contact with art (namely, the ruling classes) who were interested in culture. Seventy or 80 percent of the population were peasants or other lower-class people who were completely outside the cultural marketplace. Only the upper classes—the clergy and the nobility—had anything to do with culture, and very often they were much more interested in hunting than they were in art.

Why is it necessary to have this broad diffusion? The avant-garde movement I just spoke about turned its back on the masses and on the cultural marketplace, which is precisely why they were able to create such great things. They appealed to a very small and sophisticated audience, and therefore they were able to be original, to be imaginative, to do the very best work they could do. They didn't have a lot of ignorant democratic louts looking over their shoulders and telling them they couldn't understand it.

When I was at Yale, I'd guess that less than 15 percent of my classmates ever went to the library for any reason that did not relate to an assignment. I used to go to the library all the time because I was interested in books; I like to read books. But here were these sons of rich families who were paying a lot of money for their education, and they wouldn't read a word they didn't have to read. And if these rich boys, coming from homes with "every advantage" including books and educated parents, were still apathetic about culture, how can one expect any real interest from the great majority of Americans who never even finish high school? And why try to stimulate this interest artificially? I think it is the right of every American *not* to read books or go to museums or attend concerts. This is a free country, isn't it?

RN: *I shouldn't say this—but I couldn't agree with you more. My final question is really ethereal: If you could imagine yourself in the position of a critic or reader fifty or a hundred years hence, looking back to the work of Dwight Macdonald, how would you like to be regarded?*

DM: My God, what a question! I suppose I'd like them to think I was a good fellow, really—but it's more than that.

I would like them to think that I had some critical intelligence and that I wrote well. There might be some connection between the two; I think there is. I don't think you can conceive of a really good critic who doesn't write well. Bernard Shaw was the best all-around critic that we've had in the last century—the greatest practicing critic, that is.

On further reflection I don't care very much what posterity thinks of me. In fact, I don't have that concept at all. I want my work to be admired—but right now, not after I'm dead.

I'd like my work to communicate with some people who share my taste or come to share my taste. It isn't a question of how many people, either, because when I was running my little magazine *Politics*, which had a top circulation of a little over 5,000, I had the most satisfactory audience I've ever had. I got more letters than I could possibly answer, and even now, fifteen years after it folded, I seem to be better remembered for *Politics* than for my work for bigger magazines.

So I guess I don't care about either large audiences or posterity. After I'm dead, what possible pleasure could I get from having a chapter, or more likely a footnote, given to me in some history of American literature? I would trade all of that for more of the fun of success here and now: for more communication, more of making an effect on people's minds. Furthermore, these things work themselves out. I won't put anything over on posterity, I'm sure.

Unpublished Response to a Questionnaire

Esquire / 1967

From the Dwight Macdonald Papers, Manuscripts and Archives, Yale University Library. Printed by permission of the Yale University Library.

What papers do I read to keep up with things? Two are central, for symmetrically different reasons: the *N.Y. Times* and the *N.Y. Review of Books*.

The *Times*: 30 minutes reading, and clipping, every morning—the one great teeming indispensable spate of grist for my little journalistic mill—my window on the world for so many years; or perhaps my peep-hole, but where a larger? Why don't they winnow out more of the chaff? It would destroy one of the *Times* most stimulating qualities for me—every man his own editor, a do-it-yourself kit. But it would also save my time and might give the amateur reader—I assume non-journalists also read it—a better notion of the, or a, truth than the factual hodgepodge now slopped out in long, grey formless columns under the American pragmatic motto of "All the News That's Fit to Print." They have been edging that way of late with more "background" series which, of necessity, select and arrange the raw data from *some* point of view. And there are other gains such as the editorials, a little better written and a lot more liberal and sophisticated than they used to be—there was, as my grade-school teacher used to write on the report cards, "room for improvement"—and the noticeably higher level of the Sunday magazine and book review sections since Lester Markel's thirty-year grip was pried loose and he was given, as the *Times* might and perhaps did put it, more general editorial responsibilities, or, in the vernacular, was kicked upstairs. (I like to think my articles have played some modest part in Mr. Markel's elevation.)

The *New York Review of Books* generalizes, for me, with the same usefulness as the *Times* particularizes. It's the periodical I feel closest to, intellectually and politically, as reader and as contributor, and I look forward to its new number every other week as I used to eagerly await the liberal weeklies before the Moscow Trials. Its enterprising, sophisticated editors get the most serious and interesting critics, scholars, and experts to write without any concessions including length (the editors might be a little less permissive here I think) reviews or articles in their special fields of competence or commitment, from Gombrich on art to Stokely Carmichael on Black Power, to take extremes in subject matter and brain power—people whose ideas one respects or doesn't but in either case wants to know more about. In its four years, the *Review* has established the kind of intellectual center of consciousness for this country—at last—that half a dozen weeklies have long been providing in London. Like all of them, it has a well-developed letters column, like some of them it has a definite political line; its articles on Vietnam by Draper, Stone, Morgenthau, and others have been especially remarkable. I also like the no-nonsense format: a tabloid size newsprint with heads and authors' names as uniform and modest as the *New Yorker*'s. And it's equally simple illustrating policy which it has held to from the beginning: in each issue a half dozen superb caricatures by David Levine of the authors reviewed, combined with fantastic and grotesque 19th-century engravings, mostly by Grandville; somehow the combination works.

I also read the columnists in the *N.Y. Post*. Always Pearson-Anderson and Evans-Novak (informed political gossip that is sometimes of great importance, as the former's expose of Senator Dodd); Clayton Fritchie (what editorials should be: a general idea concisely stated and supported by research); Flora Lewis (if only for her recent series from Greece); James Wechsler and Harriet Van Horn (*sympatico* always, often also enlightening); Art Buchwald (funny half the time, a .500 b.a. tops in the league, Ty Cobb never made it); Jules Feiffer (.750 in my book and who's this Cobb?); and always a glance at Murray Kempton's latest subversion of the goo-goo, bleeding-heart liberal syndrome, his heart bleeds exclusively for the bad guys like Hoffa and even more dubious clients and it is often boring as any mechanical reaction to a mechanical stimulus is, but he often can't find any certified public enemy to bleed over and is reduced to reasonable polemics; and in any case he is a master of the column form, always providing a beginning, a middle and an end in 900 words, plus many a lagniappe of wit en route. I sometimes dip into Max Lerner's column—which a *Post* editor once told me was the most popular of all, and I believed him—for what you might call a test boring but I always find I agree with him and, worse, can't imagine any one who wouldn't. I've also read some of William Buckley Junior's recent "On the Right" columns and I must retract what I wrote in my column here [*Esquire*, September 1967, p. 45] about his furious fulminations, or some such phrase: he seems to be sobering up, perhaps affected by the soothing atmosphere of the *Post*—he's quite sensitive to the dominant political ambiance, one of his most endearing qualities—and the columns I've recently "caught" have been moderate and almost reasonable in tone; no worse than a bad cold, really.

I. F. Stone's Weekly Newsletter: a four-page *multim in parvo* job by one man who knows everybody in Washington, as a correspondent there for decades for the *Nation* and other magazines, reads everything, including the *Congressional Record*, and who has extreme, sensible and humane opinions about Vietnam and other issues. His *Weekly* is a scandal sheet, printing information, always with attributions to the source, which somehow escaped the respectable press, the best muck-raking journal I know of—odd how that term, invented by the first Roosevelt, after Bunyan's "man with a muck-rake," as a pejorative term at once became an accolade—perhaps because we have always had so much muck to rake.

Newsweek v. *Time*: both have data you don't get in the *Times*. . . . but both to be used with caution-distortion, slanting not only easier in their condensed items but also harder to avoid because of more insistent demands of dramatic effect drama in their short, snappy mini journalism. Only value is their long "take-out" or "cover" stories sometimes—and their weekly *specialites de la maison*, a few topics they pick out for special research. *Newsweek* superior to *Time* in every way: style—less contorted, political bias less blatant (also more congenial to me on Vietnam, admitted, but I think my opinion can be sustained objectively)—and coverage of the arts—more knowledgeable and sophisticated. Also its critics now sign their names, a great advance over Luce's "collective and anonymous journalism" because if a writer signs his stuff he is more likely to take care with it, also to make a more determined stand against that sabotage of their best ideas and phrases editors feel it their professional duty to insist on—else why editors? When the writer is anonymous, they don't insist, they just do it—I speak from six years' experience of "collective journalism" on *Fortune*.

The *Nation* v. the *New Republic*: I've been prejudiced in favor of the latter because it made a clean break with Communism after the war and the former didn't but (1) Communism is no longer a central issue for me after LBJ's crusade in Vietnam, and more important, (2) I've been reading both for the last year and I find the *Nation* livelier, better-written, more varied and unpredictable, hence more serious, in its editorials and political articles; also its book reviews are better (no great feat).

The *Village Voice*: Nat Hentoff's column on the press usually interesting, also the letter column, and while Mekas on films soars ever more wildly into the vast insane of the underground, Sarris, now that he's gotten over his *auteur* measles, has his feet on the ground and is both impressively informed, as always, and also judicious, as not always. (To think I once compared Sarris, in print, unfavorably to Mekas! We live and learn—and change.) But I like especially the *Voice*'s reportage, some of the best going, as in Stephanie Harrington's interview with a Black Power fanatic, Joe Flaherty's "The Hawks in May: A Day to Remember," and, a really impressive, the best report on and analysis of that sniper's massacre from the library tower of the University of Texas last year.

The *New Leader*: Good for informed, analytical articles on politics in Latin America and Asia, also for translations of "underground" texts, literary and political, from Yugoslavia and the Soviet Union; consistently strong critical departments: Raymond Rosenthal (books), John Simon (movies), John Goodman (music), James Mellow (art).

The *New Yorker* I read for such Talk of the Town items as the fine reportage on the Newark and East Harlem riots and for such recent articles as Jacob Brackman's clever and scholarly treatise on "The Put-On" and Jonathan Schell's "The Village of Ben Suc," as closely and subtly observed a piece of reportage from Vietnam as I know, all the more moving because of its restraint—for once the magazine underkeyed, no-comment house style pays off. That Mr. Brackman and Mr. Schell are both under twenty-five is encouraging.

Commentary is, for "keeping up" purposes, much the best of the monthlies and quarterlies, in fact it is the best for any purposes, including just reading. *Encounter* is its only rival and while it always has one or two interesting things, it also has a lot of stuffing; *Commentary* seems freer and bolder editorially, more journalistically alive and less of a repository of the right names. I know I should read *Dissent* and *Liberation* and *New Politics* (if it still exists) and doubtless other radical magazines more than I do, but I had an overdose of that kind of reading matter in the old days that seems to have put me off it for good.

Portrait of a Man Reading

Book World / 1968

Unpublished manuscript from the Dwight
Macdonald Papers, Manuscripts and Archives,
Yale University Library. Printed by permission
of the Yale University Library.

Q: *What do you like to read most?*
A: Biography, history, and novels. I'd have to put novels second. And then, of course, when you're really sick of words, detective stories. And never science fiction. I've read Sherlock Holmes about 8 times, I guess. I'm sort of worn out. And I like the English style better than the tough guy style. Raymond Chandler is the one exception because Chandler has humor and also a kind of romantic nuttiness about him that I like very much. I never read science fiction. It bores me and it's not about people. That's the same reason I have no interest in science of any kind. I've never had any interest in either science or religion.

Q: *Have your likes and dislikes remained the same over time or have they changed?*
A: I never even went through an adolescent period of religiosity. I'm just interested in people and in human things.

Q: *What about particular authors?*
A: My favorite American author has always been Edgar Allan Poe. Not because I think he's the greatest or the best, by any means, but simply because something about Poe from the time I was a schoolboy always appealed to me. I think it's partly the fact that he was extremely rationalistic. It's a great pleasure to me to see somebody using his mind—completely just using his

mind—in order to dominate his material and sometimes to do very strange things with it.

Another reason that I've liked Poe as I've grown older is that he was a money writer like myself. He was a journalist and had to make his living by writing. I've a great sympathy with Poe.

Q: *Outside of science fiction are there other types of writing you dislike?*
A: I don't like the kind of lady novelist that Virginia Woolf and Dorothy Richardson represent. I prefer Mary McCarthy, George Eliot—whom I really don't consider a woman writer at all. I dislike this oversensitive subtlety of Virginia Woolf. Sometimes novelists get so sensitive that they lose all sensitivity, really. I've always been very fond of Jane Austen and Gogol, especially *Dead Souls.* Herzen's *My Past and Thoughts,* a book I'm reading right now for the second time, is a very great book. It's just been reissued with a really excellent introduction by Sir Isaiah Berlin.

Q: *You are not a specialist scholar. What rule (if any) do you use to decide what to read? Do you just read what comes to hand?*
A: I suppose, to be quite frank with you, I read almost exclusively books that are in my library already or else that are sent in to me by publishers. I do a lot of rereading of novels and history—de Tocqueville and people like that. I do get quite a lot of books sent to me—more political than literary things.

Q: *Any books which influenced you at times in your life? As a writer? A political person?*
A: Certainly, reading Marx influenced me to become a Trotskyist. That and Trotsky's autobiography. That was in the middle of the 30s. But of course the books that have influenced me in that immediate sense have probably not been terribly good books. For instance, the reason I read Marx was because of books—which I couldn't bear to think of now—like John Strachey's *The Coming Struggle for Power,* Palme Dutt's *Fascism,* and things like that.

Q: *But you did lose interest in politics, or so you say in* Memoirs of a Revolutionist? *Did books have any affect on that change in you?*
A: Events did it. It was the fact that there wasn't any revolution and the war was over and the world was settling down into a period of stasis. There was nothing much for my particular kind of radical interest—I now realize it was essentially radical—to work on. Of course, since Vietnam I've come back into politics with a big bang and now I'm suporting the SDS and left-wing things.

Q: *Did you read Marx and Trotsky before you read the anarchists?*
A: Oh yes, for all the American radicals I knew in the thirties, the old left, Marx and the whole Marxist canon was the only thing going. Only a very small bunch of odd people ever even heard of anarchism. It wasn't like England. In England, they've always had a certain continuity of interest, or for that matter on the continent too. We didn't read G. D. H. Cole or the English Guild Socialists. I was strictly organized around Russia too. Because of the Moscow Trials. We knew much more about Russia than we did about the U.S. I came to anarchism much later when I was editing *Politics*, and I suppose you might say that reading Proudhon especially, even more than Kropotkin, really pushed me a great deal farther towards an anarchist position than I'd ever been before. I began to call myself an anarchist. I became more and more dissatisfied with Marxism in the late 30s and 40s and even with Trotskyism after having gone through the Trotskyist movement for two years—I'd been a member between 1940 and 1942—and I came to realize that there was something basically antidemocratic and authoritarian in Marxism itself. It was natural to think of something else and then I became very much interested in the anarchists and still am. I still think that anarchism as a philosophical guide to political action is very good.

Q: *Much of your life as a writer and reader has been tied to the history of little magazines. Have they changed since you began at* Partisan Review?
A: Are there any little magazines anymore? I must say I don't keep up with them all. There must be a crop of them in the Village. You see the little magazines I knew that survived are all big boys now like *Partisan Review*. No I can't think of any. There's *I.F. Stone's Weekly*, but that isn't literary. I read the liberal weeklies and the news magazines and things like *Commentary*. I used to read *Encounter* before I realized it had been financed by the C.I.A. They've taken me off their free-list as a matter of fact. There's no love lost there.

Q: *Do you recall when you began to read and what it was you read?*
A: My first literary memory is of reading a book called *Buddy and Brighteyes Pigg*, about two guinea pigs, by Howard R. Garis, the one who created Uncle Wiggily. It was one of the Uncle Wiggily Longears series. He had this series about these pairs of animals and I became infatuated with the guinea pigs for one reason or another—I guess I was around 8 or 9 then—and I remember having an argument with my parents. I insisted on collecting the whole

series—there were about 15 in the thing—and saving up my 25¢ a week or whatever it was I got—to buy them and my parents told me, "You will not want these in a few years," and I remember saying, "Of course I will!" The next step up was O. Henry and Kipling which I read when I was 10 or 11. I still think Kipling is one of the most underestimated geniuses of the last 100 years. I still reread a lot of Kipling. I welcomed Eliot's essay praising Kipling, but it didn't really help his reputation. Neither did Orwell's essay which I welcomed as well. I think Kipling is coming back now—perhaps as a result of those essays to some extent. But I've always felt that Kipling was a very much underestimated writer because of his political views. I remember imitating O. Henry at an early age. Then I graduated to Thackeray and Dickens; we had a complete set of Thackeray and Dickens.

Q: *Did your parents push you to read in general and to any authors in particular?*
A: No, my parents weren't literary at all. In those days, you know, middle class families used to buy these sets. We had a set of Mark Twain, Dickens, and Thackeray and the *Encyclopedia Britannica,* and that sort of standard thing. Robert Louis Stevenson, too. It took me a long time to get to serious reading. I seem to have been a very late developer. Because I remember collecting Stevenson the way I did *Buddy and Brighteyes Pigg.*

Q: *But you say in* Memoirs of a Revolutionist *that you were rather an aesthete at Philips Exeter?*
A: Oh sure by that time, but really after all, I was by then 15. One should really be more advanced by that age. After I got to Exeter, where I really began to be educated, there was a sharp jump up in my literary tastes. I discarded even Lord Dunsany about whom I was crazy when I first went to Exeter. Then I leaped into another somewhat better fire or frying pan—you know, Oscar Wilde, other decadent sort of stuff. James Branch Cabell, I'm afraid, was also one of the ones I turned to. And Mencken, of course.

Q: *Were you considered precocious at Exeter?*
A: Oh, yes. I was in the avant garde of the school. There weren't many of us but more than there would have been at any other school in this country or in England I daresay. The faculty encouraged us a great deal. In fact several members of the English department were very important in that way. They patronized us, lent us their books, gave us tea and cookies in the afternoon

and literary conversation. This was very important, much more than what happened in the classroom. Especially the idea of having someone with hundreds and hundreds of fairly new books with nice covers and who was willing to lend them to you. This was a great thing.

Q: *At Yale you wrote a letter in the* Daily *to the president raising questions as to the competence of William Lyon Phelps to teach a course in Shakespeare. How do you feel in this age of professional academic literary criticism about the older less rigorous, gentlemanly ways?*

A: It's never occurred to me for one second that I should change my view of Phelps. Oh, no. You can't talk seriously about someone like Phelps. That extreme of Robert Louis Stevenson and William Lyon Phelps, that sort of ladies club culture is certainly no more interesting than whatever would be the opposite extreme. Allen Ginsberg, perhaps? Well, he has talent. I almost got fired because of that Phelps letter. It really was an editorial in the Yale *Record*, the English magazine I edited. The printer took it up to the dean. The printer was so shocked by the editorial he took it up to the dean, in advance. The dean called me in and said if you print this in your next issue you'll be out. So I naturally didn't print it. A marvelous illustration of the difference between these two periods that doesn't have anything to do with literature comes up. Mark Rudd wrote a letter to the president of Columbia University and addressed him as "Dear Grayson". . . etc.

Q: *How did your days at* Fortune *magazine affect your reading?*

A: Well, it taught me to read quickly and get the essence of something without spending time to go through to its style. In writing *Fortune* articles most of the material came from interviews and not reading. Reading became a surcease from the boredom of writing about American business.

Q: *How did reviewing movies for* Esquire *affect your reading?*

A: It didn't change my reading much. I didn't see that many movies. I only went to those I was pretty sure that I'd want to write about. I never saw more than 2 movies a week—about 10 a month. You do get blunted if you read or see too much. Some of my colleagues go to the movies the way kids would often look at TV in its early days, if their parents let them—hour after hour. This results in relativistic taste. Not that I like scholarly criticism. Taste does not equal scholarship. But they tell you some film is better than so much of the other junk they've seen. The critic's final job should be to tell what is or isn't interesting to him and to give his reasons.

Q: *What sort of social critical writings do you read today?*
A: I don't read Marxism today. God, No!! I can't imagine reading economic and theoretical Marxist stuff. Hobsbawm, of whom I've read a little, is excellent. History is better than sociology or economics for generalizations about society. The greatest of the troubles of economic and sociological literature in America today is that it is thin and lacks historical sense. Tracing the development of institutions—giving the historical view—really explains more than the cross-sections our academics take.

Q: *Who do you read, or recommend reading, to redress the ahistorical bias?*
A: Simone Weil, of course is one. Hannah Arendt has been a great influence on me, especially *the Origins* . . . I like Arendt when she's historical and not when she's abstract as in *The Human Condition*. *On Revolution* is excellent as was the Eichmann book.

Q: *Do you read today's classical liberals?*
A: You mean Milton Friedman. I read him in *Newsweek* and he's not so bad. He's for the "negative income tax" and that, of course, is splendid. In general, I'm not interested in economic analysis so much as I was anymore.

Q: *What are you reading right now?*
A: Yes, I'm rereading de Tocqueville and the new edition of Herzen's *My Life and Thought*. Anthony Powell's *At Lady Marley's*. I'm an admirer of his earlier things; this novel is one before the Music of Time series begins. Almost all my reading is in bed. Yglesias' *In the Fist of the Revolution* is another and I liked it very much. I didn't like Jan Myrdal's *Confessions of a Disloyal European* at all. He seems to be one of nature's losers. He's irritating, snotty, and neurotic, and it seems out to make everyone dislike him. Arrogance can be appealing; certainly it's not a major sin to my mind, but Jan Myrdal is so dislikable. I'm also rereading Bourne's *History of a Literary Radical*. He's one of my culture heroes and has been ever since I read him at the start of World War II and saw his reactions to the beginnings of the 1st. He's a marvelous writer and should be as major as Veblen in our political writing. Despite the chapter Christopher Lasch devoted to him, I'm surprised Bourne is not more of a figure. I'm sure that I've read more books at the moment than those I've mentioned. I must

say there is a curious way in which a book becomes comprehensible 10 or 15 years after you've first read it. It becomes comprehensible, even without rereading, in a way it was not at the first. Two examples are "The Wasteland" and *Ulysses*. I read them in the late 20s and they bewildered me. I could not make sense of either of them. I knew *Ulysses* was a considerable work but its surface was very difficult for me to pierce. But then about 10 years later both of them had completely changed for me. They were different when I tried them again. Now I understand the greatness of "The Wasteland" about which I had been supercilious before. Though I must admit I still have the same feelings about *Finnegans Wake*. It is just a tour de force and though I am able to understand a few pages more each time I look at it I've never been able to see it whole.

Q: *Who are today's leading midcultists and highbrows?*
A: Ten years ago it would have been easy to name the kings of the middlebrows. You'd have said Clifton Fadiman, Max Lerner. (How influential is *he* today?) Stuart Chase was up there, but he's been a backnumber for so long. I'm not sure we have middlebrows in that splendor any more. There are no more low-brow influential novelists like Zane Grey or Fanny Hurst. Harold Robbins just doesn't have the style that Grey had. I'm a great admirer of the very highbrow Nabokov as a novelist and autobiographicist and polemicist. The exception is *Pale Fire* which simply doesn't come off. Stravinsky's obiter dica are completely admirable as is Auden as an all-round intellectual who seldom disappoints.

Q: *Are there any political writers you read consistently?*
A: There are many good political journalists. Clayton Fritchey and Evans and Novak do excellent columns. But can you name a real political writer? If Hannah Arendt wrote regularly about contemporary politics she'd be interesting and worthwhile for she always is when she does. There is no one like Gombrich who writes on art with the same authority in political writing. Fairlie is a right-wing Menckenesque debunker and I haven't been a great admirer of Mencken since I was 17.

Interview with Dwight Macdonald

Jack Graves / 1970

From the *East Hampton Star*, 10 September 1970.
Reprinted by permission of John Y. C. Graves.

Dwight Macdonald, an East Hampton resident for the past two summers, wrote an essay in 1944 entitled, "Masscult & Midcult," a long, arresting analysis of American culture.

In 1944, Mr. Macdonald thought that the low level of popular taste could be raised by integrating the masses into High Culture, but revising the essay in 1953 he found himself forsaking his original theory in favor of drawing a sharp line between Mass Culture and High Culture, such as exists in England.

By 1962, when the essay was revised once again, he was certain that these lines would have to be drawn up if High Culture were to survive in America because of the insidious middle stratum termed "Midcult," which was both derived from and opposed to High Culture in that it passed itself off as the real thing.

Into this category, which he believed had won the allegiance of the vast middlebrow audience, he placed such works as Hemingway's *The Old Man and the Sea*, Thornton Wilder's play *Our Town*, Archibald MacLeish's play, *J.B.*, and Stephen Vincent Benet's poem, "John Brown's Body."

Visited at his home one day recently, the well-known critic was found in rolled jeans, work shirt open at the front, and bare feet. "My ideas have changed one way since that book," he began. "First of all, I think what I called Masscult, the low-grade stuff, has obviously become less and less of a threat. Even the movies are a little more sophisticated.

"And as for Midcult—the distilled culture—I underestimated the resistance of serious work to this sort of thing." He cited as examples of artists who had not pandered their work to popular taste the film directors Fellini, Bergman, the poet Robert Lowell, and the writers Norman Mailer, Saul Bellow, and Philip Roth.

"These people seem to have no difficulty in demanding an audience. Actually, the fact is, I don't think a good writer can sell out. It must be so boring to write to make money. If a writer values money and prestige that much he must be a dull fellow . . . if a man's an artist, I don't see how he can do it without falling asleep, you know."

Mr. Macdonald's "for instance" was Norman Mailer, a writer whom he greatly admires and who at the same time makes money and has developed a charismatic persona usually associated with Masscult.

Waving a limp cigarette back and forth as he spoke, the mustachioed and goateed Mr. Macdonald said of Mailer: "The quality of every one of his books is different. He's always trying something new. He exploits the market, he can't help it, for his own perverse reasons.

"So, I don't think it makes any difference if you do want to make money." Edgar Allan Poe, a personal favorite of his, wrote for money, Mr. Macdonald said.

"Poe didn't make any, but that was because he stuck to his principles. He was a very bad businessman and was screwed by his publishers." Being a money-writer, however, didn't dampen Poe's genius, Mr. Macdonald pointed out.

"He invented the detective story—'Murders in the Rue Morgue,' 'The Purloined Letter'—and science fiction, long before Jules Verne."

He continued: "If you're good, you can't sell out. You can't help but put your genius into it. Dickens is a good example. He was wildly popular, popular for his melodramatic and sentimental stuff, perhaps. One really doesn't know why.

"There are no rules for talent. I can't say Mailer resists anything . . . he has more brains than Hemingway . . . he's monkeyed with himself, and yet he remains tremendously objective about it. He has a need to get himself into dangerous, humiliating situations in order to fight his way out, at least that's my theory.

"I think this tension is necessary for him. I would think some of Byron's escapades were helpful to him.

"And yet there's Emily Dickinson and Saul Bellow. Bellow would die of shame, I'm sure, if he got into any of the messes Mailer does," Mr. Macdonald said with a laugh.

"I think *Portnoy's Complaint* was Roth's best book. He must have done it to sell, but that makes no difference. The language in the book is the freest vernacular since Ring Lardner.

"There's no difference in *Portnoy* between the writing and the thinking. I think it's a very serious book. It says a lot. But I do hope it's the last of the Jewish mother business with the poor castrated son."

In "Masscult & Midcult" Mr. Macdonald often expressed a yearning for a "cultural community" or "intellectual elite" in America to preserve High Culture.

Did this mean membership in that community would be reserved to a select few? "No, no," Mr. Macdonald said, waving his cigarette, "My basic idea was that at any time in history a maximum of 20 percent of the population are really interested in these things.

"Anybody can be in the 20 percent. I think there's been much too much professionalism in America. Some of the best contributions to criticism have been by hobbyists, especially in England where generalists . . . informed amateurs are still appreciated.

"Let's have two colleges: Yale One and Yale Two, or something like that. Yale One would be for the minority who want to learn, who are crazy about books, who want to get into movies . . . Yale Two would be for the great majority, who want a pleasant education and want to socialize.

"This separation would benefit the ones who are serious about philosophy, arts, and letters. They wouldn't be held back by survey courses. I don't mean by this to give the others nothing; it's nobody's obligation to be interested.

"And it's not a class thing: working people often go in for the arts and the letters, while many of the rich are Philistines. That's the way the world is, it's not a question of talent, but a question of interest, don't you think so?"

Please, High Culture: An Interview with Critic Dwight Macdonald

F. Anthony Macklin / 1972

From *Film Heritage* 7.3 (Spring 1972), pp. 13–34. Reprinted by permission of F. Anthony Macklin.

INTERVIEWER: *You have not been writing a regular column now for five years or so. Do you miss writing regularly on film?*
MACDONALD: No, I don't or else I would not have stopped the column. It became irksome to do it month after month after six years. I guess I have a six-year span of attention. Also, it's a bore to have to explain the same thing all over again about bad films. Most of the films I reviewed—and *Esquire* allowed me to be a most selective reviewer—were fairly bad, and bad films have a kind of similarity since they are not the expression of an individual but are imitation products by craftsmen, consumer goods not art. In comedy, one of my specialties, I found that I was laying down the same rules and making the same objections way back to comedies like *Hallelujah the Hills*, *What's New Pussycat*, and *Zazie*. Then years later along would come *It's a Mad . . . World*, *Kiss Me Stupid*, *Help!* and *How to Murder Your Wife*—all of them doing just the same thing. It got rather tedious.

INTERVIEWER: *Would you consider this a writer's block or is it something else?*
MACDONALD: Oh, this part isn't at all writer's block. No, that's another thing. What I have said so far is that *one*, after six years I got tired writing about movies, and *two* most of the movies were bad, and bad movies tend to resemble each other. Once you have laid down the principles, why keep on saying the

same thing over and over again? And *three*, it seems to me that I was lucky in the sense that the movies from '60 to '63 or '64 really were on a very high level. I think that this was the peak of the whole post-war period, and then after 1964 I noticed a very distinct falling off even by great directors, and so that was another reason that I gave up the column. You see it is much easier in one sense—and much harder in the creative sense that counts—to review bad films because it's shooting fish in a barrel. Simple enough to show how they are bad, to make fun of them, but that palls after a while. At least it palled on me, because taking candy from a blind man finally gets tiresome. I'm not that much of a sadist. The real fun is finding something that extends you, something you don't know what to make of, something that is new. And that seemed to me to be quite failing when I gave up the column. The *fourth* reason probably was indeed some form of writer's block. As I get older I find it not more but less easy to write; perhaps because I've been doing it so long professionally—44 years to be exact.

INTERVIEWER: *When you moved into politics in 1967 was that new and original? Does anything work against that block?*
MACDONALD: Back into politics actually: from 1938 to 1949 practically all my writing—and there was a lot of it—was political. But it's true I liked changing the subject after six years of movie reviewing. I found doing the politics column easier at first. Not easier intellectually—it was harder that way, but easier in the sense that I wanted to do it—I found the subject interesting, challenging.

INTERVIEWER: *What surprises me is that one of the things that brings you out of retirement is a film such as* Getting Straight.
MACDONALD: That's an accident. I didn't review it as a movie; rather as a cultural document. Seymour Peck of the *Times* asked me if I wanted to see it and write not really a review but a cultural analysis of what it means when Hollywood takes a serious subject. And I was very much interested in the whole "New Left" and the youth rebellion, so I thought that would be fun. When I saw the movie, I was so horrified by it. It seemed to me so typical of what Hollywood does do with serious subjects that I felt first sick, then angry, then articulate. The thing doesn't even pretend to be a movie. Do you think so?

INTERVIEWER: *It's certainly inept. In the last five years, have there been any films which stimulated you?*

MACDONALD: I haven't seen very many films, I'm afraid. I've been out of New York a lot of the time, teaching and living in the country—bought a half-acre with cottage in East Hampton three years ago. I've seen a couple of films I thought were quite good, but certainly not anything great. One of them is Polanski's *Rosemary's Baby*. I have a weakness for ghost stories and detective stories—also I think Polanski is an extraordinarily skillful director. I didn't like *Repulsion*, but it was one of the most amazingly adaptive, economic, and skillfully done films I've seen in a long time, and the same way with *Rosemary's Baby*. The only other one I can think of offhand that I really admired—not as a great film but as a good film—was oddly enough Antonioni's *Blow-Up*. I thought it was a great relief from *Red Desert* and *The Eclipse* because it had humor and also got out of that airless business of Monica Vitti's *angst* that I could never understand. Why was she always so unhappy? The Sorrows of Monica. Also *Blow-Up* got into a certain kind of social comment on the British mod scene. And also I thought it was a very nice little detective story. The fact that it all hinges on the blow-up of this picture—and the question of reality, too, I thought was dealt with in a rather light, but clear way, but the kind of way I like to have things like this dealt with. I even liked the tennis match at the end. It was a bit overlabored perhaps; still I thought it was so graceful and well-done. And the fact that he goes back and can't find the body, and did it happen? and is reality just what you see on a film? Lots more ideas, really, than in his other post-*L'Avventura* films though they took themselves much more seriously. Maybe that was the trouble.

INTERVIEWER: *What about visually?*

MACDONALD: I thought it was very good visually—well, of course his things always are. It was cut much faster than he usually does. It didn't have that great photography of *L'Avventura*; was that that fellow who died—Di Venanzo?

INTERVIEWER: *Aldo Scavarda did* L'Avventura. *Di Venanzo did* La Notte *and* Eclipse.

MACDONALD: Well, he was extraordinary. But anyway, I rather liked *Blow-Up*. Let's see, there was a third one. I saw 2001—Kubrick is always something.

INTERVIEWER: *You thought it was overblown, though.*

MACDONALD: I must say I think it is a pretentious film. I liked the first part, with the "Blue Danube" business; [laughs] I never knew the "Blue Danube" has so many variations in it. I thought that was great, having it blasting out, and making that the theme of going to the moon. Pan Am and all the parody of the current airplane clichés are projected a few years into the future. But I must say when it got into the big stuff of going beyond the moon . . . Except for HAL, the computer, who was absolutely marvelous, I thought, the one human being in the whole film. I really understand him, quite well, and I was fascinated by him.

INTERVIEWER: *I notice one of the things that you do as a critic is that you do evolve, and you do change your mind. Have you changed your mind on 2001? Because I have a feeling that you may have.*

MACDONALD: Yes, I dismissed it too much in that footnote.* Actually I've seen it since then. I think it's more than I thought it was. But not as much as some do—it's become a cultist film. I ran into a chap down South—I was giving this talk on movies at Wake Forest University. And afterward there was a party, and this youngish ex-student said he'd seen it twenty-three times, and I got the impression that he's not alone, not just the potsmokers either, because they see it without knowing what they see. (The first time I saw it I got a small high just by breathing the air.) He was impressed with the symbolism, especially that ending. The Louis XVI decor. And he tried to explain it to me and I still didn't get it. It seemed vaguely pretentious to me—a cop-out—they needed a "strong," "cosmic" ending. And after the prologue and the parodic moon-flight—both very good—I got the feeling it could go on forever and not arrive anywhere—like the spaceship itself. Ingenious, beautiful "technical effects" which were often visually amazing like that ten minutes when the ship is going through Alpha Centauri or whatever, and you have all kinds of reverse printing, different colors fantastic landscapes, as your ship swooshes through it. But after three minutes I got bored—typically—my critical bent is classical and I get restless if I can't find any form to a work—and this sequence, like others in 2001 could have gone on forever, an esthetic logic, as far as I could see.

INTERVIEWER: *It seems that the very best critics often have a problem with ambiguity. Would you agree?*

---

*In a footnote in *On Movies* Macdonald wrote: ". . . Kubrick, the one great hope of the younger Americans, spent three years on perfecting the photographic effects of an over-long and over-blown space fantasy called 2001."

MACDONALD: What do you mean, ambiguity? I don't think there's anything ambiguous about the end of 2001. There's something confusing and pretentious about it, but ambiguity to me can either be conscious or unconscious; I think it's unconscious here. I think the science fiction story is fudging the whole thing because after the ending it's not very clear what it's supposed to be except it's very important. But conscious ambiguity, which Henry James and Conrad went in for, seems to me to be a very deep and important thing.

INTERVIEWER: *Do you think there's any ambiguity in* Blow-Up? *It seems to me that there are critics that somehow don't get through to a film. Now maybe it's not ambiguity, maybe it's something else.*
MACDONALD: You think *Blow-Up* didn't get such good reviews?

INTERVIEWER: *Yes.*
MACDONALD: I think that's because they thought, as they did with 8½, that it was too much on the surface. Some of Bergman's movies, like *The Seventh Seal*—one of my least favorite movies—are tremendously admired by high-brow critics because they have what they call "depth" or "scope" or even just "seriousness." Whereas films like *Blow-Up* and 8½ are rejected because they're rather light-hearted, "superficial," and "obvious." That tennis game was objected to by practically everybody, because it was too obvious. Well, I don't mind the obvious if it works formally. I don't see why one should.

INTERVIEWER: *I think* The Seventh Seal's *reputation has greatly declined. I don't think many people stand up for it now.*
MACDONALD: Well, I didn't like it even when it was considered a great film. I remember I walked out half-way through it; I simply couldn't stand any more heavy-breathing symbolism. No film that begins with Death and a medieval knight playing chess for a human soul on the seashore can be taken seriously. You see, my kind of—well, not my only kind of art—but one kind I like very much is something that seems to be light and worldly, and even frivolous, and yet really is quite profound. I mean Mozart's music, Jane Austen's novels, Tiepolo's painting, *The Importance of Being Earnest*—that kind of thing, as against Beethoven and Wagner—not that they're not great, too, in their own heavy way.

INTERVIEWER: *When you did write that footnote about* 2001, *you seemed to suggest that you thought* Bonnie and Clyde *was a better film.*

MACDONALD: That's true on the whole. I'd forgotten about *Bonnie and Clyde*. Yes, that's a film I was quite surprised by, because I don't like Penn's work in general. I think he is often a rather over-blown, pretentious director—real Hollywood *kitsch*, as in his ghastly *Mickey One*. But in *Bonnie and Clyde* he had a very good script by those two *Esquire* guys—Benton and Newman—which I think restrained his baroqueness somewhat in the same way that Mankiewicz' script in *Citizen Kane* might have restrained Welles. The dialogue was excellent, and the general motivations were really of the period, I thought. And also, Beatty in some way or other absolutely surpassed himself; I've never seen him good before, or perhaps since either. I saw him in *Mrs. McCabe* . . .

INTERVIEWER: *McCabe and Mrs. Miller*—
MACDONALD: A terrible film, that. But anyway, I thought *Bonnie and Clyde* was a very good film, and I liked the violence in it, too, because I thought that for once you realize the effects of violence, that it hurts people. Now this is what a lot of critics and moralists objected to; they said this is wallowing in pain and cruelty for its own sake. But the trouble with most of the violence is that you don't really feel that these people are real. They're like the girls in a pornographic novel or movie, who are simply objects—you never think of them as people—but in this movie, you really felt that that scene when they all are rounded up in a field and they drive around wildly trying to escape like partridges, you remember, when the deputies are shooting them, it's shocking because you feel they really were hurt.

INTERVIEWER: *It's another film that's obvious, though, isn't it?*
MACDONALD: I suppose so. I'm an anti-romantic, that's true. I tend to have rather classical and, therefore, rather surface or formal reactions to things.

INTERVIEWER: *Do you think* Bonnie and Clyde *made any changes in film? Do you think that it was an influence?*
MACDONALD: It certainly wasn't an influence on *Mr. Micawber* or whatever it was—that *McCabe* thing. I mean that was the lushest bit of pretentious, soft-focus romanticism, and underwater photography, muzzy plotline and dialogue . . . I could never understand it. For one thing, I couldn't hear what was being said. Maybe it was intentional—part of the "mythical" effect—and to think the reviewers praised it as "realistic." It was about as realistic as *Beau Geste*. But I suspected bad projection.

INTERVIEWER: *They said it was rereleased in a much better print; the initial print was different from the one that they eventually released.*
MACDONALD: Well, I saw it about a year after it came out.

INTERVIEWER: *That wasn't the excuse then.*
MACDONALD: He mumbles so much that it was impossible—well, it's just as well, I guess.

INTERVIEWER: *You don't see* Bonnie and Clyde *as a romantic motion picture?*
MACDONALD: It didn't romanticize, though it certainly made into humanly sympathetic characters, people who I gather were not such in real life. And why not? Bonnie and Clyde—especially Clyde—were believable in the film—and that's all you should ask—historical truth has nothing to do with esthetic truth. I would say that it isn't romantic; it has humor and it has a realistic—not nostalgic—sense of the historical period which a romantic film wouldn't have. The chief exception was that family reunion when they go back to her mother, and have a lot of noble Carl Sandburg visual sentimentality about the great American frontier country. But that's one of the few lapses in it.

INTERVIEWER: *Have you seen either of Peckinpah's newest movies or* Clockwork Orange?
MACDONALD: I'm going to see them, whenever I'm back in town. I haven't seen them, no. I wish they weren't all about violence. On *Bonnie and Clyde*, and the critical reactions to it, I suspect the trouble was that they felt it was too direct, too much on the surface, you got the point right away, and it didn't have any avant-garde symbolism and all the stuff that Mekas' new American cinema had. Thank God. I'm reminded of Bernard Shaw, as a music critic almost a century ago, when he was talking about Mozart. Mozart was one of his favorite composers. He considers he was greater than Beethoven and even Wagner—though Shaw was one of the first Wagnerians, of course. He said that the English musical public considered Mozart to be a composer of [laughs] "tuneful little trifles fit only for persons of the simplest tastes." And he said he could understand why that was—because Mozart's stuff was easily accessible—even tuneful. Mozart wrote what seem to be completely conventional melodies that anybody can really enjoy, and so the average Philistine who is looking for deeper meanings in music would just dismiss them. Shaw's point was that, on the contrary, if you know anything about music, Mozart's

simplicities are extremely complex and also, that he was a great musical architect. He enjoyed an 1892 performance of Mozart's music so much that, when he noticed the Philharmonic's next program featured Beethoven's *Seventh*, he reflected: "You feel you cannot really listen to such clumsy and obvious sensationalism after Mozart" [laughs]. Shaw's impish exaggeration explains, to some extent, the initial putdown of *Bonnie and Clyde* and *Blow-Up*—and, above all, 8½—see my "Fellini's Obvious Master-Pieces," the longest and, I think, best review I did for *Esquire*.

INTERVIEWER: *How much do you think a film is victimized by its audience? How can you tell when a "midcult" audience, perhaps, is coming to a film? How do you separate the audience's reaction from the film itself?*
MACDONALD: But I don't see why one should bother about it. What do you mean, separate them? That's a sociological, social-cultural question. Of course I always saw films in the screening place, although most of the critics there were obviously middle brow, too. But I must say that I've never been influenced by the reaction to a film. I can see no difference in looking at the movie; I think that that's different than with a play, where live actors interact with the audience. I have no human connections with my fellow spectators— dreamers, really—as we watch the shadows flickering across the screen. Several times I saw a film when there was nobody except myself in the projection room. I wasn't conscious of any difference from the atmosphere of a whole big audience laughing or gasping or rustling in boredom all around me. Usually at the wrong places, of course—that is irritating sometimes but not distracting, as in the theatre, because there is no human collectivity responding to a movie—just X number of isolated *voyeurs*.

INTERVIEWER: *You do often come out like you're trying to puncture the inflation of something like the reaction to* Monsieur Verdoux *when it was rereleased in this country.*
MACDONALD: Well, sure, but this isn't on the basis of going to a screening— that's not the same audience thing I mean—in the *Verdoux* case I was reacting against the critical over-enthusiasm of Agee, Warshow, and others as expressed in print.

INTERVIEWER: *Do you see any serious changes in motion pictures in the last five years?*
MACDONALD: I really haven't seen enough recent films to say. I suppose one thing that's pretty obvious is this extraordinary business of cruelty, rape,

sadism, violence; it's certainly gone much farther than when I was writing about movies—when I was objecting to things like *Cape Fear* with Gregory Peck and Robert Mitchum. I'm sure that would look very mild compared with *Straw Dogs* and *Clockwork Orange*, at least judging from the reviews. I must see them and see whether the violence is distanced. You know, John Simon apparently thinks that it is in *Straw Dogs*. I have gone hopefully to a number of movies like *Klute* and *The French Connection* recently—this was down in the country—and *Mr. Micawber—Mrs. McCabe* whatever it is.

INTERVIEWER: *That one really got to you.*
MACDONALD: And all those three films were so depressing to me. *The French Connection* was a little better, but not much.

INTERVIEWER: *It's not a pleasure anymore?*
MACDONALD: I couldn't understand why people would pay two dollars, even in the country, to see those kind of things, and why the critics go on about them.

INTERVIEWER: *What was your reaction to Jane Fonda?*
MACDONALD: I thought she was very good. But you know, one Fonda doesn't make a summer. She was overwhelmed by the sickness of the film, and also the pretentiousness, and that fancy cutting—you never knew where the hell you were; you'd think you were looking at *Last Year at Marienbad*.

INTERVIEWER: *Some of the films you've liked*—Rosemary's Baby, Blow-Up, 2001, *and* Bonnie and Clyde: *it doesn't seem that acting is that crucial to those films. I wonder, what do you think about film acting? What part does it play for you? There hasn't been much done on it, you know. Stanley Kauffmann probably pays the most attention to the acting going on. Does the performance concern you much?*
MACDONALD: Actually in my reviews I used to pay quite a lot of attention to acting. Mastroianni, for instance, I think really was very important in 8½. With a different actor it might not have been as good a film. Theoretically from Griffith on, the great directors always used the actor as a chair or a table—just a visual element.

INTERVIEWER: *I hate to think of that today, though. I wonder whether that's still true today.*
MACDONALD: Well, for instance, I think that what I thought was a cheesy movie in general was not saved, but tremendously improved by Dustin Hoff-

man, namely, *The Graduate*. I think Hoffman is an extremely good actor, really. I saw him also in another movie that I didn't like at all—*Midnight Cowboy*.

INTERVIEWER: *What did you think of Voight in that picture.*
MACDONALD: Who?

INTERVIEWER: *Jon Voight, who played Joe Buck, the one who wasn't flashy, the one who didn't caricature his part.*
MACDONALD: Oh, I thought he was very good, too. But I wonder if he could do anything more than that; I don't know.

INTERVIEWER: *I heard he's done Shakespeare.*
MACDONALD: Oh, really? You mean the tall blond, who actually seemed like a cowboy? If he can do Shakespeare too, he's an actor—that is, somebody who can successfully pretend to be somebody else. Like Hoffman who was so repulsive and hopeless, and yet one did empathize with him. You saw him as a person, in spite of Schlesinger's over-emphatic, sensationalistic directing. All those sweaty close-ups! The British over-use the close-up—they're not a very visual race, at least in our time—they douse their movies with close-ups the way people with defective taste buds use ketchup.

INTERVIEWER: *Hoffman is one of those people who is not willing to be typed. He makes mistakes, but he does take so many different kinds of roles, and there aren't many actors who do that.*
MACDONALD: He's like Olivier in that he has confidence in himself as an actor. So I agree with you, in that sense, that a good actor can make a poor film not good but better. Olivier did that in *Wuthering Heights*.

INTERVIEWER: *I'd be interested to hear what you think about Hoffman in* Straw Dogs *because there, he may be miscast, but he almost salvages his role, nonetheless, even though it's not right for him. I was wondering about your essay, "Masscult and Midcult," which seems to me to hold up very well today. If you were updating it, would you make any changes?*
MACDONALD: I published three versions of the thing—each longer than its predecessor, and each different in approach—between 1944 and 1960. By the 1960 version, in *Partisan Review*, I had come to realize that the danger didn't come from mass culture, as I'd thought in 1944 when I was still something of a Marxist, but from what I call "midcult." But now I would say that I over-systematized even that point—looking back after another twelve years. I was

right in seeing that midcult does present a more subtle—and therefore more deadly challenge to serious art than masscult did, but I underestimated real, or high, culture's vitality, its ability to at least survive.

INTERVIEWER: *Midcult is fraud, isn't it?*
MACDONALD: It's fraud because they're counterfeiters—they're very knowing and sophisticated and they produce a facsimile of the real thing that takes the middlebrow audience in the way Clifford Irving took in the editors at *Life* and McGraw-Hill. *McCabe and Mrs. Miller* is an example of a relentlessly "advanced" film—in a technical way—with a whole vocabulary of soft shots and marvelous color photography and stylized acting and so forth which is just a lot of junk, really. That sort of a film—*Klute* was another—is much more damaging to movies than Tom Mix was in the old days.

INTERVIEWER: *Why?*
MACDONALD: Because the enemy outside the gates is easy enough to repel, but when you have fifth columnists *inside* culture, inside high culture, then it becomes more difficult tactically. Because so many people are going to be seduced by this, and after all, why bother to encourage serious movies and books when you can get an imitation of the real thing which is much easier to produce—and easier to appreciate too, because midcult also can be appreciated very easily by the educated ignoramus.

INTERVIEWER: *Of course this essay on midcult was before perhaps its greatest living representative, Dick Cavett.*
MACDONALD: [laughs] Oh well, he was, and is—he was very sympathetic, very intelligent, I thought the one time I was on his show. Midcult maybe, but in the higher range certainly. And also he'd done his homework. He knew the right questions to ask.

INTERVIEWER: *Oh, had he? Who had done it?*
MACDONALD: Well, of course, I know. But even David Susskind, who is, by the way, the predecessor of this one, and much the same type, although I think Dick is much better.

INTERVIEWER: *Cuter.*
MACDONALD: I think Cavett is more spontaneous and has more brains. But Susskind—whose "Open End" thing I was on twice—also was remarkable for

having extraordinary quotes and questions on cards, which, of course, were done by researchers. But anyway, what I was going to say was (you asked me whether I would think of change since I wrote the last version of "Masscult and Midcult") I think I had too mechanical a view of the incursions of midcult in the cultural field. As long as you have a relatively free, pluralistic society, as we do in this country—that is not a political totalitarian society—as long as you have that and a lot of money around, which we still do, it seems to me that in all fields, even including movies, it will always be possible and has been possible for people to make their own kind of things. Less so in movies, perhaps, but even in movies now. Certainly Stanley Kubrick, for instance, can make any kind of movie he wants. I haven't seen *A Clockwork Orange* and I've heard it's very good, but if it isn't, it certainly isn't because of any concession to Hollywood or that kind of stuff. And certainly in other fields it's even more striking.

A whole group of minority audiences has sprung up since the last war—the last declared one, that is—everywhere except in television, and so really, somebody like Norman Mailer, to the extent that he has "sold out"—I think he is much more complicated than that, personally, but he certainly has been doing a lot for big amounts of money because he has to make all this money for the movies and his children and wives and general life style. But anyway, for somebody like Mailer, this is a free choice on his part. It's not because that's the only way that he can make a decent living. So I think that I was wrong to think that the bad will always drive out the good. It's true in general, but it's not true in so many specific exceptions; in other words, I think there's much more of a future for the serious things in all the arts than I thought fifteen years ago.

INTERVIEWER: *Really?*
MACDONALD: Just for this reason, that there are so many different crannies and nooks and that there is also an audience for serious work. Look in the movies, the whole business about little movie theatres. They're enormously increased since the war, since 1945. So much so that directors like Antonioni and Fellini can make enough on the American market to finance their films. And without making concessions.

INTERVIEWER: *You suggested that Mailer "sold out."*
MACDONALD: No, I don't think he did sell out. I said it was a much more

complicated thing. In fact, his piece on the moon has some absolutely brilliant material in it. I wouldn't call that a sell-out. I just meant that he certainly had done things for money that he wouldn't have done if he hadn't been paid big money by *Life*. He wouldn't have done that book.

INTERVIEWER: *You stressed the idiosyncratic in that essay, in relation to highcult. What would you make of someone like John Frankenheimer, who's always bothered me in that he experiments, he changes, he does something different every time.*
MACDONALD: Like Tony Richardson, or that awful Joseph Losey, who also does all that, too. I've seen a few Frankenheimer films, but I think that kind of change is not real. That is to say he changes, but he does it as a child picking up a toy, playing with it, and when he gets bored, throwing it down. They exploit techniques in order to hide the fact that they don't have anything really to say, not to *say*—in one sense Losey has plenty to say, Losey is the most socially conscious, *oh boy*—but that they don't have any faintest personal *feeling* about the work of art they're making, the general form of it: you see again, I get back to this classical business. I judge books, and works of art, and movies, on the basis of the *whole*, not of the part. That's where I differ from Agee, by the way, who often used to find a beautiful elbow . . .

INTERVIEWER: *Or the* auteurists, *certainly.*
MACDONALD: The *auteurists*, yes.

INTERVIEWER: *Not to connect Agee to the* auteurists.
MACDONALD: No, don't. But anyway, just to play around with techniques and be avant-garde doesn't mean anything unless you can use them to produce a general effect. My impression of Frankenheimer has always been that he overdirects his films, that he uses a tremendous amount of effects, but they never come out to anything. Didn't he do something called *All Fall Down*?

INTERVIEWER: *Yes, that was an earlier one—today it's called* The Last Picture Show.
MACDONALD: Oh really? Is it anything like—I haven't seen that one, either.

INTERVIEWER: *Timothy Bottoms is about the most interesting actor to come along since Brandon de Wilde. It's a little conventional. I would be surprised if you liked it.*
MACDONALD: I used to know Peter Bogdanovich. We saw each other quite a lot, but our friendship finally foundered on the rock of *auteurism*. He once said to me, "I can't imagine Howard Hawks making a bad movie." I said, "That

statement is absolutely impossible." I mean God himself—well, God could not make a bad movie, I agree. But anybody less than God, you can't say that.

INTERVIEWER: *If you were pushed to name the ten best films you've ever seen, or something along that line, what would you select? What films are highcult?*
MACDONALD: Please, high *culture*.

INTERVIEWER: *High culture, I'm sorry. I'm sorry.*
MACDONALD: One of the antagonistic reviewers of my book made a lot of play, saying, "He has masscult, midcult, but he's so superficial on high culture that I think we should call it—'h'-'i'—hi cult" [laughs]. So don't please . . .

INTERVIEWER: *That's an interesting observation because I've always grappled with, and sometimes my students have grappled with, what is high culture? Where can we find it in our culture? Especially in the movies.*
MACDONALD: By the way, do you know how many hard cover copies have been sold in the last six months of *Dwight Macdonald on Movies*? Exactly 34.

INTERVIEWER: *Oh no, what about the Berkley soft cover version?*
MACDONALD: It sold a lot more, of course, though so far nothing brilliant. But 34 copies! They must have lost their shirt on the hard-cover edition. Because it didn't sell very many before.

INTERVIEWER: *I didn't even get a gratis copy, so they were saving money that way.*
MACDONALD: You didn't? They didn't send you a review copy?

INTERVIEWER: *No.*
MACDONALD: I suspect that they did a bad job of promotion—almost no ads and I didn't see it in many bookstores. You didn't even get a review copy?

INTERVIEWER: *Such is life. But we're talking about high culture movies . . .*
MACDONALD: Oh well, the current modern directors that I think are high culture, they're the obvious ones: Kurosawa, Bergman, Fellini, Antonioni, Resnais, Truffaut, and some of Godard . . .

INTERVIEWER: *How does Chaplin fit in?*
MACDONALD: His movies up to and not including *Limelight*, I would think so. But I think in a diminishing scale. His best films were the least pretentious and the earlier ones. The turning point was perhaps, you know, the one about Alaska—*The Gold Rush*. Then I think after that, the other two, *City Lights* and

Modern Times—they really extended his comedy in a way. There's some very great stuff in them, but he turns out too seriously. See, it all fits in together, my point of view on things. I think Chaplin as a clown was terrific, and once he began to think he was a "little man," and get philosophical ideas—because the intellectuals way back in the early '20s were beginning to talk about him as a little man and all that stuff—then his art was corrupted. I think of Keaton, looking back on it, as the great one. I think he was much greater than Chaplin. He made half a dozen long films that are absolutely superb, and really work much better than Chaplin's long films.

INTERVIEWER: *But without any of the pretentiousness.*
MACDONALD: Yes, because he was impervious to this. He didn't have the vanity and the corrupt ego that Chaplin has. Chaplin *loved* the idea that he was being taken seriously by all kinds of dukes and rich people and intellectuals and so on. But Keaton was on such a primitive level that it washed off his back completely. Well, anyway, you asked me about—

INTERVIEWER: *Let me change it, let me say, favorite films. What are your favorites?*
MACDONALD: Well, my favorite films—I have to think about it, and I'll undoubtedly leave out things, but just right now, the ones I remember, and this is not in order, but I would say *Caligari, Birth of a Nation; La Ronde*, you know, Ophuls' film; *Citizen Kane; Magnificent Ambersons; Sherlock Jr.*, plus half a dozen other Keaton films, but that's the one I especially like, especially because of its great fantasy sequence, after he falls asleep in the projection booth. *8½, L'Avventura;* well, I saw again last year the Resnais film, *Last Year at Marienbad*, and I must say I was very much moved by it. This is about the fourth time I've seen it, and every time I see it—not that I understand it any more than I did the first time—but I'm always so impressed by the beauty of it and also I get sort of moved in a funny way; I don't know quite why, because you never know where you are in it. But anyway, I love that film. And also I like very much Cocteau's *Beauty and the Beast*, which I've seen a couple of times in the last two years; I don't like his *Blood of a Poet*, which I used to like. I like both *Potemkin* and *Ten Days That Shook the World*—things that I really like spontaneously. Also Bergman's *The Naked Night* or *Sawdust and Tinsel* it is also called.

INTERVIEWER: *Any of the French films?*
MACDONALD: Oh yes—*Children of Paradise*—how could I have forgotten it? I

like Renoir's *Grand Illusion* very much too. His *Rules of the Game* is a little overintellectualized by my standards.

INTERVIEWER: *It's extremely highly rated.*
MACDONALD: I think it's overrated. It's marvelous if you diagram it, if you parse it out, if you see exactly what the whole thing means about the relations of classes, and servants and masters, and the absurdity of life; it's all there, but somehow it doesn't work as well as it should; well, partly because I think the casting is pretty poor, including Renoir himself. I think he's very embarrassing. He's supposed to be a charming, lovable bear of a man, who's very clumsy and so on—

INTERVIEWER: *He's certainly broad.*
MACDONALD: But he seems to be just sort of a clumsy and rather amateurish actor, whereas *Grand Illusion* has Stroheim and also those three other marvelous ones, the Jewish guy and Gabin, and the aristocratic captain—really very good acting. And also it's a very moving thing, especially the last fifteen minutes or so.

INTERVIEWER: *It grows on you, doesn't it? I mean the more times you see the film, doesn't it become more beautiful?*
MACDONALD: That has what I think is very important too in films, some sort of human dimension. Well, that doesn't apply to *Caligari*, [laughs] that's true; there are always exceptions. But in general, I think you have to get some sort of relationship to the people in it. Maybe I should take that back. That's just one way that you can enjoy a film.

INTERVIEWER: *But there's a richness to it, certainly. There is that ability to return, and, as you say, be moved all over again. Perhaps more so—*
MACDONALD: And that quarrel between them at the end is one of the great scenes, in the snow, and he says, "You little Jew," and so on, and then he goes away, and then he comes back. Well, absolutely superb. And Stroheim is, as usual, great . . . I haven't seen *Greed* for a number of years, but I must say that was a very impressive experience when I did see it, but I wonder whether I wouldn't like *Foolish Wives* better, or one of those other ones, or *Blind Husbands*. But he ought to be in there somewhere, I think.

INTERVIEWER: *Did you like* The Organizer?

MACDONALD: Oh, yes, very much, yes, yes—though it's probably not as great a film as I think—and feel—it is, personally—it's one of those works that appeal so much to one's special taste it's difficult not to overrate it. I was very much moved by that film.

INTERVIEWER: *You have something of an identity of being political. Do you think film has in any way fulfilled its potentialities as a political force?*
MACDONALD: It certainly did in the silent Russian days, although I wonder what the *Mujiks*, the peasants, the Russian masses really made out of that very avant-garde school. It certainly went over with us foreign intellectuals. I'm sure many of us were really quite prejudiced in favor of those lousy Bolsheviks—I mean lousy looking back on it now—because of these movies by Pudovkin, Eisenstein, and Dovzhenko.

INTERVIEWER: *Have you seen anything in the last ten years that you felt was politically very effective,* The Battle of Algiers, *perhaps?*
MACDONALD: Oh, I saw that. I thought it was very good but no, not to me, of course. I guess I tend to look at things too much aesthetically, at least now; and I thought that was an extraordinary film, but it would never occur to me to be made enthusiastic about revolutionary action by that film, as I gather that it has been. It's used, of course, as a kind of training film, isn't it? That's a different use, which I can understand, because you would really think that that was a newsreel, all the way through, and not just because of the photography, but because of the way that the action is underplayed and the way that there are, in a sense, no real heroes and villains. In that way it's just the opposite of the great Russian silent films, where it was always clear who was the heroic character; he even had a different kind of lighting.

INTERVIEWER: *What about film criticism today? Is it evolving?*
MACDONALD: I still think that John Simon is the best film critic we have in this country.

INTERVIEWER: *Why is that?*
MACDONALD: For several reasons. First of all, he writes quite well although no better certainly and in some ways perhaps not as well as Pauline Kael. Anyway, he writes reasonably well. Secondly, he has a considerable background, not only in movies, but in other fields. I think that's an important thing. That's one reason I think that Agee brought a lot to film criticism; Agee knew a lot

about music and literature. John also seems to have a quite wide cultural background so he doesn't consider movies just as an isolated thing. Thirdly, he seems to be quite determined to apply high standards to every film and not to talk about it in relative terms of the season, but to talk about it in terms of the history of movies. And therefore, to me he seems to be the most severe of all the critics practicing now.

INTERVIEWER: *Do you think that that has become a trap for him at all—this severity? I think sometimes he makes you appear absolutely benevolent.*
MACDONALD: I think that John is certainly more unpleasant than I was. I think that's a weakness. Especially on actresses. But I'm not so sure that we had a much different percentage of films that we really liked. Although maybe my judgments were more qualified—is that what you mean?

INTERVIEWER: *I suppose so.*
MACDONALD: Like, for instance, on *Last Year at Marienbad;* that was a very, very double review that I wrote. I really thought, on the one hand, that it was a fascinating cinematic experience; on the other hand, I didn't understand it and my review even suggested it had elements of camp and preciosity. I don't exactly value Simon for his gladiatorial qualities, and yet I think that given the pretentious junk that's swallowed by audiences—and critics—in theatre and cinema today, you have to be a bit of a bruiser if you're going to maintain standards. You see, a qualified judgment again!

INTERVIEWER: *How does one prevent critical toughness from becoming atrophied, from becoming reflexive? Isn't there that danger? I read somewhere recently, maybe it was in your own book, something about how a critic had said you were unfair to the second-rate films. I'm not sure I agree.*
MACDONALD: He didn't say second-rate. Actually I think somebody said that I didn't appreciate the incompletely successful films, that I was always judging things in general terms, which I think is true, and that certain younger, more experimental directors might make a film which, true enough, wouldn't add up to a success looking at it as a whole, but which had certain indications that . . .

INTERVIEWER: *. . . were promising?*
MACDONALD: Yes, and I think there's some truth in that—I'm sure I missed certain burgeoning, budding shoots that came to something and that I simply

ignored, nipped off, and discouraged. I think that's a defect of mine. I'm not the best person to see what's going to happen in the future. As for Simon, I follow him quite regularly in *The New Leader.* Of course, he has a big thing about Bergman that maybe . . .

INTERVIEWER: *He was on the Cavett show, and he was doing just beautifully, talking about his ten best films of the year, and making a lot of sense, and Cavett asked about his ten worst, and he put everybody's favorite film on it. Everybody's favorite film was on his ten worst list. He had* The Go-Between *and he had* Death in Venice *and he had* The Last Picture Show *and he had* A Clockwork Orange—*he had them all.*
MACDONALD: He had *Death in Venice.* I thought that got rather bad reviews.

INTERVIEWER: *Yes, it did. He also had the one that you saw,* The French Connection, *on his best ten list.*
MACDONALD: I noticed that. Of course that got pretty good reviews, too—or did it?

INTERVIEWER: *It got many more favorable, because it was enjoyable and people said it did what it tried to do. What I'm really asking is, it strikes me that you and he were probably the most severe of the American film critics.*
MACDONALD: Yes, I guess we are.

INTERVIEWER: *And I'm asking, at what costs? Do you ever find yourself having to say, now wait a minute, I've got to be careful, I'm running a pattern here that's going to take over?*
MACDONALD: Yes, that's a good point. I remember in the Old Trotsky days one of these things that we were always warned about by our leaders was what they called *khvostism.* This comes from the Russian word for tail, which is *khvost.* And *khvostism* means making up your policy in reaction to your enemy. In other words, if the Nazis are one thing, then you're the other thing. Or if the Roosevelt New Deal liberals are for unemployment insurance, then you can't be for it. That sort of business. If the Nazis are against Stalinist Russia, then you must be for Stalinist Russia. This is *khvostism,* and this was rightly considered by Trotsky to be a great defect, not just morally, but tactically. In other words, obviously both the Nazis and Trotskies could be against Stalin's regime for entirely different reasons, and it would be absurd not to want unemployment relief or the Wagner Act just because these terrible New Deal liberals were for it. So I would say that the danger here would certainly be the same

idea. What it does is to give the enemy the ability to influence *your* decisions, and in the case of reviewing films, if the majority of these despised colleagues of yours come out for a film, and then if you feel you have to come out against it, then of course they've dictated your choice in a funny way.

INTERVIEWER: *This is something you were aware of, and cautious about?*
MACDONALD: I guess so—well, I don't have to be aware of it, because it never would have occurred to me to do it. The fact that Pauline Kael liked some films that I liked, and hated other films that I liked, and vice versa. I just thought that was very odd of Pauline, you know. But it would never occur to me to doubt *my* judgment because Pauline agreed with me. That's a joke; I have some respect for Pauline, of course. But that awful guy they had on the *Times*, Bosley Crowther—after *L'Avventura*, that whole business when he reviewed it badly and all the letters came in and then he had to eat crow. It's a famous episode. He said, "Well, maybe—." He looked at it again and said, "Well, maybe there's something in this" and so forth. After that, Crowther, who was as sensitive about trends as he was insensitive about reviews, kept putting down American commercial films and putting up foreign films. So I found myself agreeing with him much more than with Kael, really, in the last couple of years, on the actual evaluation. On the other hand, I never got anything from his reviews, and I got a lot from hers.

INTERVIEWER: *What are you doing today?*
MACDONALD: Three things. One is a little book on Edgar Allan Poe, who's been an interest of mine my whole life—a modern view of Poe—I think Poe is a very interesting writer intellectually—and he has a lot to tell us today about "behavior in extreme situations," in Bruno Bettelheim's phrase. Secondly, I've just finished an abridgement of *My Past and Thoughts*, the memoirs of Alexander Herzen, not Herzel the founder of Zionism—Herzen the founder of Russian socialism. Knopf put it out in four volumes several years ago in a revised translation; it didn't do much, too expensive. Herzen is my favorite nineteenth century political writer—with De Tocqueville a close second—so I suggested to Knopf that a one-volume paperback selection from his masterpiece might introduce it to a wider American public.

INTERVIEWER: *That's two things.*
MACDONALD: The third is a collection of my recent (post-1955) political stuff

called *Politics Present*, which is being published by Viking. Last year they republished an out-of-print collection of my pre-1950 political writing, originally called *Memoirs of a Revolutionist* but now retitled—by me—as *Politics Past*. So I thought of *Politics Present* as a companion volume. I've written a lot of updating footnotes and afterwords.

INTERVIEWER: *What do you think is the most important thing you have done?*
MACDONALD: Did you ask John Simon that?

INTERVIEWER: *No, because John said he's only been doing it for seven years.*
MACDONALD: Doing *what* for seven years?

INTERVIEWER: *Film criticism, and we talked about when he was in love with a local waitress, and things like that; that's the way he looks back on his life.*
MACDONALD: You mean *that* might have been the most important thing. I think that'd be a great past [laughs]. Well, I guess I can answer your question. It's what I am known for mostly and also what I think was my most important contribution—so far anyway—editing my little magazine, *Politics*, from 1944 to 1949.

INTERVIEWER: *Why?*
MACDONALD: Because it was an extremely good magazine. Also, I wrote a lot of my very best stuff there, and wrote quite a lot, too. I was very, very fertile then. It's been reissued by Greenwood Press, *Politics* in four volumes, costs $90. At the time it would have cost $8.50, something like that. And that magazine turned out to be quite significant as well as readable. It adumbrated the New Left ideology, especially a lot of what Paul Goodman and I wrote. Also, it was the one independent critical voice on the war that was published in this country. By independent I mean no party affiliations. We really gave them the works! It began in '44. I think that's my most important contribution. I'm really an editor by temperament, not a writer. And by talent, too, maybe.

INTERVIEWER: *That's interesting . . . Finally, the thing that has struck me about* On Movies *and I think it's rather remarkable, is your reconsideration of films, and the ability to go back, and not look at what you've done as* Holy Writ, *that your ideas have changed. I wonder if there's a young person, or a young critic, starting out, whether there's any way he can build that in. What can the critic do to attain that flexibility?*
MACDONALD: What you're getting at is the fact that I often change my mind

and that's been true in politics, too. This has often been made a reproach, that I'm not serious, and so on. I think that the height of seriousness is precisely to react all over again to experience, and not to get locked into some view which may have been perfectly good for you at that period of your development. But if you really are alive and developing, it's impossible to imagine that the same writers that you admired when you were eighteen or even twenty-eight would be the same ones by the time you get to be fifty or sixty. See what I mean? Because you're a different person. In politics you have another factor, which is that the world changes a lot. Works of art don't change, thank God. That's one thing left out, but in politics you have the change of the world, as well as of yourself and your development, and there there's even more reason for changing.

But in estimating movies, it seems to me that unlike the *auteur* people, what one should do is look at every movie as if you knew nothing about the guy or the movie before, even if it's the fifth time you've seen it. And I've noticed over the years—I've pointed this out in my books, of course—it's remarkable that certain things stand up and, in fact, gain. *Caligari* I didn't like so much in the '20s when I first saw it, because I was under the influence of Eisenstein and Pudovkin. But every time I have seen it in the last twenty years—and I've seen it about six times now, and taught it in class too, and it goes over very well in class, to my surprise—I've more and more liked it, and thought it was a masterpiece. On the other hand, with *Blood of a Poet* my first enthusiasm didn't last.

I think that if one doesn't change one's mind over the years, that there's something suspicious about one's attitude. I don't mean that you should change your principles, and, of course, I would say that I haven't changed my principles, but I have changed my application of them, due to experience. And *experience* should change one.

Brooks Shot Right out of Saddle by Critic's Blazing Crossfire

Jeff Simon / 1973

From *Buffalo Evening News*, 11 and 16 April 1973.
Reprinted by permission of the
Buffalo Evening News.

"I thought Woody Allen was the end but this guy Mel Brooks . . ."

Dwight Macdonald, a film critic for over 40 years and one whom many consider the best of American film critics, was in the process of denouncing the past few decades of American film comedy in the first of his lectures as Edward H. Butler professor of English at the State University of Buffalo.

Mr. Macdonald will be on the campus for 3 weeks. He discussed the comedy of Buster Keaton Monday afternoon and showed two Keaton classics—the short *Cops* and the sublimely inventive feature *Sherlock Jr.*

Macdonald continued his genial diatribe against Allen and Brooks, the two reigning Borsch-belt czars of popular screen comedy.

"So gross, so crude, so coarse, so lumpish," said Macdonald of Allen and Brooks. Brooks's *Silent Movie* is "so overdone." Brooks has no style. Brooks is a honker."

Macdonald has usually been more than pleased with his own inability to think up esthetic rules for movies. Nevertheless, he listed a few Monday afternoon.

"Comedy must be anchored in reality," said Macdonald. "Comedy is normative. One of the rules of comedy is that people in some way be sympathetic."

"Comedy must be logical. If anything goes, nothing goes," said Macdonald.

This is fairly old territory for Macdonald. As the film critic for *Esquire* magazine in the early '60s, he wrote about Richard Lester's Beatles film *Help* and compared it to the esthetic sensibility of Keaton, who knew enough to subordinate a part of a film to the whole.

One of the reasons the movies of Elia Kazan (*Splendor in the Grass, On the Waterfront*) are so "vulgar and awful" said Macdonald in an aside, is "that he won't give up anything" for the sake of composition.

Macdonald compared the films of Keaton to those of Chaplin.

Chaplin was "a much better pantomimist than Keaton" but his movies are "six or seven of his routines scotch-taped together."

Keaton's films, on the other hand, are cinematic. He cared about film-making technique. *Sherlock Jr.* whose subject is "the nature of the movies, of the art of the movies" is "an esthetically decadent and self-conscious film. But Keaton just did it because it seemed to him a good idea."

In the long run, Macdonald said he found it amazing that artists like Chaplin and Keaton grew out of the films of Mack Sennett, the "Diaghilev of slapstick."

Macdonald's career includes the editorship of *Politics,* one of America's legendary maverick magazines in the '40s, and staff writing for *Fortune* and the *New Yorker*. Among Macdonald's most famous essays are his essay "Masscult and Midcult," his "Emperor's-New-Clothes" reviews of Jimmy Gould Cozzens's *By Love Possessed* and Colin Wilson's *The Outsider* and his proposal for a new U.S. Constitution.

For almost three decades by his own count, Dwight Macdonald has been a cultural, social, and political analyst and polemicist of Menckenesque sharpness and wit.

From 1960 to 1966 in *Esquire* magazine, he was also probably the finest regularly appearing film critic this country ever had. Not encumbered by a penchant for naive rhapsody as was James Agee and far more devastatingly comic (in the Shavian way) than Pauline Kael has ever been.

Macdonald is currently spending a semester as a visiting professor of English at the State University of Buffalo. At his sufferance, he was observed, questioned, and needled for about three hours of a balmy Tuesday afternoon.

There is much to say but it's difficult in the present context because, in a lifetime of cultural journalism, Macdonald has anticipated and inveighed against all the circumstances that apply to a newspaper interview.

In an essay, "Amateur Journalism" (reprinted in "Against the American Grain") he praised the English reviewer.

"Since he is not writing for a mixed audience whose lowest common denominator he must always keep in mind, he doesn't have to go in for elaborate explanations of the obvious nor does he have to capture the reader's attention with a startling journalistic lead and try to keep it with debased rhetorical devices and constant appeals to the L.C.D."

In the same essay he talks of magazines "edited with a wary eye on an amorphous public whose tastes and interests fluctuate somewhere between lowbrow and highbrow. This means at best a compromise between quality and 'what readers will take' and, at worst, a genteel slickness that is more trying than the simple vulgarity of the lowbrow press."

Could a surgeon operate on a recognized master surgeon who is awake during the whole procedure and probably disapproving of it?

The question kept me from writing about Macdonald for a couple weeks. It should have kept me from doing it forever but it didn't. Immediately, therefore, admitting failure and genteel slickness:

Macdonald is a tall man with yellowish white hair, a neatly trimmed goatee and a good deal of well-settled heft at his mid-section. He smokes a good deal and is inclined to talk with a cigarette in the side of his mouth and his eyes crinkled up to avoid the smoke.

If his hands are full or his mind is otherwise occupied, he is also inclined to let the ash on his cigarette grow to dangerous lengths—with every millimeter it grows one is more inclined to keep silent, not out of any malice or embarrassment but rather out of some bemused and inexplicable affection.

In the length of his ash, there is something of a rakish cafe conspirator. It seems to fit in well with the career alignments and political partisanship of his past. (A few years on the staff of *Fortune* and the *New Yorker*, editor of the small magazine *Politics* from 1944 to 1949, "member of the Trotskyite party" from the fall of 1939 to the spring of 1941, an adept in the intramural contests of the American left).

There is a good deal of Manhattan in his accent. He talks forcefully like a man who's used to lengthy debate and enjoys it. He laughs often and without hesitation. Even when he is not laughing, he usually seems about to.

It is clear in the course of talking to him that he is not a man who suffers fools gladly. For reasons known only to my psychic, Freudian underparts, I twice argumentatively espoused opinions which I knew full well in advance he would find absurd: I praised the film criticism of Andrew Sarris as being ingeniously inductive like the morality of a medieval scholastic; and played devil's advocate for President Nixon's domestic cutbacks, arguing that in a way they were an attempt to decentralize executive power (an idea, in general, for which Macdonald has great sympathy).

Both times, Macdonald riveted his eyes on the wall straight ahead as if he were taking a crowded train from Cleveland to Toledo and had found himself in a compartment with an aggressive occult book salesman.

Not surprisingly though, he has a certain gentlemanly reserve in such cases.

His diabolically witty querulousness in print (he unstuffs stuffed shirts as merrily as Groucho) seems to be a manifestation of professional conscience. Personal courtesies show up in his talk that might never show up in his work.

I asked him to discuss a good many things:

"I haven't been tempted to write film criticism recently. It's harder for me to write lately. That's why I teach, of course. I think I was very lucky to begin regular reviewing in 1960. There was a lot coming up—the new wave, the Italians, Bergman. But in the last couple years of reviewing, I think things tailed off quite a bit.

"I would like to write about Ozu's *Tokyo Story* though—one of the great films."

I asked which film critics he likes and reads.

"I would think Stanley Kauffman, Pauline Kael, and John Simon are the best. I think Simon (in the *New Leader*) is the best we have because he's the most drastic. I think Kael's gotten too long-winded.

"She doesn't have to write five columns (galleys) on every movie. That tends to happen though when you write for the *New Yorker*.

"Creative criticism means either telling the artist how to do it which I think is presumptuous. Or else it means be reasonable which is what most critics are. Simon is not reasonable."

This, for me, presented only a momentary problem. Macdonald's stated explanations for his affection for Simon are clear enough. Nevertheless, there is a huge gap between the work of the two men.

Macdonald's is often breezily colloquial, contains a rich delight in the absurd and almost a comradely affection for the author of the meretriciousness he is exposing. (For instance he says of Otto Preminger "he's a sophisticated and intelligent fellow. He just doesn't care about movies. Preminger's whole interest is in promoting a movie.")

Simon's work is generally humorless and sounds like it was translated from dyspeptic German by a pedant.

In the introduction to *Macdonald on Movies*, Macdonald admits having great difficulties thinking up general standards for specific likes and dislikes. Simon frequently seems to believe in Platonic ideals of film, art, etc.

Where one's thought is supple, the other seems rigid. Where one always seems unfailingly rational, the other often seems vitriolic.

The great temptation for me was to try to fill in the seven years it's been since Macdonald stopped reviewing films—an impossibility of course but he did make some comments on the subsequent work of some men who figured so largely in the early '60s.

Ingmar Bergman?

"I saw *Persona* which I couldn't stand. It was so affected, mannered, and pretentious in an arty way. I think that what you see on the screen is all that's important. I'm very much against the kind of interpretation that goes on in Bergman. This symbol hunting, what does it mean? I think what a film means is an esthetic thing."

Fellini's films since 8½?

"I hate them. In Fellini's *Satyricon*, there was no pleasure, no sensuality. He's indulging his despair, there's something sad about those last two movies. You kind of feel that you're trapped inside this guy's libido."

Michelangelo Antonioni?

"I liked *Blow-Up* very much but, of course, I like superficial movies. I thought it was quite refreshing. I didn't even see that other thing, that—what is it?—*Zabriskie Point*—(laughs). No. I didn't see that."

Jean-luc Godard?

"*Breathless* seemed to me much less than I'd first thought when I saw it again. The only one I really like is *Weekend*. That really did get to me. I've always been quite against Godard."

Stanley Kubrick?

"I didn't like *A Clockwork Orange*—much too long, too pretentious. I thought everything was sort of hammered in. I thought even 2001 was better than that."

Asked how he would describe his current politics, he chuckled and said, "I'm not a revolutionist and I'm not a pacifist. I'm a conservative anarchist. I believe in the continuity of things and I don't want to interfere with things by abstract solutions.

"When a revolutionist comes along and says he is going to change everything, it simply interrupts the whole process of human development." That position makes for strange bedfellows. To Macdonald, "Herbert Hoover had a lot of anarchist ideas."

The standard oft-used photograph of Macdonald was taken in 1968 and displays him sporting a McCarthy button. "I think we want to get a guy who's a Hamlet in the presidency."

Earlier during his American Political Fiction class, he had said, "Whenever I had a hope or a dream, whenever I proposed anything, it never worked out. I'm almost always right when I'm negative."

The ineffectuality of political criticism as a form was held up by Macdonald to explain why he no longer writes on politics.

"Especially with Nixon, I've complained all my life about these things. It just gets worse and worse and worse. You have to have some idea something is going to be affected by writing."

For the influence and the influence alone, he did concede that "it might be interesting" to write a political column for the *New York Times*.

In Nelson Algren's *Notes from a Sea Diary: Hemingway All the Way* (for which a liberally lambasted Macdonald forms the butt of Algren's marvelous but undoubtedly unfair surrealist humanism), there is a terribly acute observation about Macdonald beneath an intended insult.

"For to one so devoid of inner sinew as Macdonald, literature is explainable only in terms of declarative sentences; his own life being invested in syntax."

While "last of a vanishing breed" and "endangered species" should both be placed on some generally accepted list of proscribed metaphors, Macdonald gives both cliches some reality when he conducts an undergraduate class in American political fiction outside on the UB campus while the new Blue Oyster Cult record chugs away at full volume over a powerful but anonymous campus speaker system.

He makes observations on the returning PWs with characteristic asperity but the comments seem to be lost judging from the faces of his students on this unusually warm day.

About his graduate Poe class, he expresses high praise and discusses his fondness for Poe.

"Poe is my favorite American author. He was a rabid intellectual, he was a critic essentially, he conquers the world by his mind. He called it ratiocination. I like that kind of classical, tight, logical style. He was a professional writer . . . like me."

Then later, I ask if he minds being considered so entertaining.

"I always like to be entertaining. I try to be funny. That goes back to this business about superficiality. I just want to be considered a clear thinker."

Taking into account some of the alternatives, that's quite a bit and even Algren couldn't gainsay him at least that.

Conservative Anarchism: An Interview with Dwight Macdonald

Paul Kurtz / 1973

From *The Humanist*, July/August 1973, 4–8.
Reprinted by permission of American
Humanist Association.

PAUL KURTZ: *What do you think is the current mood in America?*
DWIGHT MACDONALD: I think it's a mood of both apathy and selfishness. I think McGovern lost the election because he wanted to change the balance of wealth and political power in favor of the underdogs. This proved to be the thing that nobody wanted, except a few of us liberals and radicals. I'm afraid that this mood still goes on.

KURTZ: *You mean the apathy and selfishness?*
MACDONALD: I think that Nixon is getting away with murder all the time; and, unfortunately, the people in the Senate who are trying to stand up against him are having a very tough time, because the country doesn't seem to be interested in any kind of reform. We seem to be going back to the kind of mood that was prevalent in the middle twenties and the fifties.

KURTZ: *This is apathy, you say. Do you think that people are so demoralized because of McGovern's defeat?*
MACDONALD: On the contrary, I mean that people really don't have much interest in changing anything. McGovern made a lot of blunders, of course, but that's not what defeated him.

KURTZ: *He misread the country, and the country was moving more conservatively?*

MACDONALD: Yes. This is a very rich country, and we haven't had a real Depression since the thirties. The percentage of poor has been decreased since the Second World War—from roughly two-thirds to something like one-quarter. That's quite a big decrease. Two-thirds of the country was poor under Franklin D. Roosevelt. But now, the people who have made it, which is three-quarters of the population, don't really want to upset anything in order to pull the other quarter into the lifeboat.

KURTZ: *Do you think that wealth redistribution is a high priority, even in view of the prosperity of the country?*
MACDONALD: Oh, yes. I think that a nation can't exist with even one-quarter poor. By poor, I mean below the most modest kind of decent subsistence. It poisons the whole atmosphere, and also, the people who are poor are going to become dangerous.

KURTZ: *One of the great paradoxes is that Nixon, who had come out for the Moynihan negative income tax—a lot of liberals were really surprised and supported him on this—in his second term has abandoned that program.*
MACDONALD: Completely, yes. In fact, that was one of the few good ideas he had, I think. It deserved a try anyway. But the country doesn't seem to want that.

KURTZ: *You have been identified with the Left during a good part of your life—the Old Left—and also, I take it you were sympathetic to the New Left. What is the state of the New Left in this country?*
MACDONALD: Well, I'm afraid it doesn't exist. I think a couple of years ago it ceased to exist. It certainly had a recrudescence after Kent State and Cambodia, but that seems to have been the end. You see, the New Left is not to be confused with the Maoists, the Progressive Labor Party, the Communists, or the Trotskyites; those are all old-style Marxist formations. The New Left was quasi-anarchistic and centered around the SDS. One reason the SDS is no longer with us is because it was anarchistic and so it didn't have any central control. It finally split up into three parts that destroyed each other. It was at that Chicago Convention where those ghastly, nutty Weathermen materialized—only to dematerialize almost immediately. But I really don't know why the New Left disappeared so completely and so suddenly, except perhaps that young people have a very short "history span." Various things grow up in the youth culture, but before long they disappear.

KURTZ: *But was the New Left only tied to the youth culture? Do you think that this is its main base?*
MACDONALD: Its only base. Although I was quite sympathetic to the New Left—I did what I could to help in the Columbia occupations of buildings, for instance—but heavens, I could never consider myself part of it. My whole style and culture is entirely different; they weren't just political, but cultural.

KURTZ: *In other words, you think that it was fashionable and that it's difficult to understand why the fashion petered out.*
MACDONALD: I wouldn't call it just "fashionable." I would call it something that was quite a justifiable response. It began with the racial situation in this country and then the Vietnam War.

KURTZ: *Perhaps it's the end of the Vietnam War that spelled its demise.*
MACDONALD: No, because it blew up long before that.

KURTZ: *You said earlier that the country wasn't ready for wealth redistribution and that there was strong reaction against it. Do you think that the youth sensed the strong opposition from the hardhats and that this is one reason why they collapsed?*
MACDONALD: No, on the contrary, I think that the more the hardhats and Agnews keep at it, the more the youth are going to persevere.

KURTZ: *Well then, we're still without an explanation of why the youth got turned off or why they gave up.*
MACDONALD: I don't know for sure. Of course, one thing is that, after all the strikes and demonstrations, Nixon did get out of Cambodia. On the other hand, he certainly didn't wind up the war, and in fact, nothing else changed, and *he* didn't change. They might have been discouraged after so many years of fighting on this issue. But there's something much deeper than that, because it's a question of a whole lifestyle that seems to have vanished, too. The young now seem to have a very short attention span, historically speaking.

KURTZ: *You mean the counterculture?*
MACDONALD: Yes. I've been teaching at the State University of New York at Buffalo this semester, and I must say the campus is extremely quiet.

KURTZ: *The students appear reflective.*
MACDONALD: Well, it's more than that, I think. I'm giving a course in American political fiction from Hawthorne to Mailer. I gave that course two years ago

at the University of Massachusetts, and I had between 40 and 50 students. Eight students showed up for the first session of this class, and it's now up to something like 12. I really think it's because of this changed atmosphere and that the word "political," which a few years ago was very sexy, turned them off. In my other class, in Edgar Allan Poe, which was supposed to be a seminar, I now have 20 people—so many that I have to divide it into two sections.

KURTZ: *Do you think this reflects a basic shift in cultural interests?*
MACDONALD: Yes, and in political interests, too.

KURTZ: *Part of the New Left was surface phenomena—that it was fun and it was the thing to do. Do you think in digging into Poe that they are confused because they don't have the answers and they are looking for deeper kinds of explanations?*
MACDONALD: Bruno Bettelheim phrased it in his essay about his experiences in one of the Nazi concentration camps. He called it "behavior in extreme situations." That's a beautiful formulation. That's what Poe dealt with all the time.

KURTZ: *And you think he painted what people sense in the current situation?*
MACDONALD: Yes. A hundred and fifty years later it seems that Poe is not so fantastic. And I think the kids especially understand this.

KURTZ: *Is this a kind of existential despair that you think is gripping some?*
MACDONALD: Despair, and also facing of reality, and impatience. Poe is one of the few older writers that I think young people now read on their own.

KURTZ: *How do you appraise the current situation? Are you pessimistic or optimistic?*
MACDONALD: I'm very pessimistic.

KURTZ: *You are? Why?*
MACDONALD: Because the American people elected Nixon twice and because he has proved to be our most sinister and dangerous president. The Watergate affair illustrated that all too well. I think the whole morale of the country has changed from what it was 30 or 40 years ago. It seems the American people no longer worry much about justice, integrity, idealism, and other things our founding fathers worried about.

KURTZ: *Your generation was stimulated by idealism?*
MACDONALD: Yes. Well, I think youth is still idealistic enough. That's not the point. It's the mood of the country as a whole.

KURTZ: *They've given up on social reform?*
MACDONALD: They really don't care about the poor. You know, the great thing about the English is that they are a wonderfully political people because they know how to live with each other. The Englishman feels that every citizen is a part of him. He, like a good Samaritan, will pick a man up if he has a fit on the sidewalk. Well, I've always lived in New York, and I know that the only guy who is going to pick you up is a cop.

KURTZ: *If you look back at the twenties, or the thirties, or the forties, even though there was a war against Fascism, there was still great hope that we could build a better world. Do you think that that has passed?*
MACDONALD: I'm afraid so. We've had nothing but disillusionment, it seems.

KURTZ: *What kind of disillusionment?*
MACDONALD: First, there was the collapse at the end of the twenties that I lived through, the Depression. That was pretty disillusioning about American capitalist society, although we've recovered economically so that's really not the point now. The Spanish Civil War was perhaps the last time in modern history when there was a really clear-cut moral issue between the two combatants, and we know what happened there. And the Second World War was all mucked up. I was all for the defeat of Hitler but Stalin made me very uneasy as an ally.

KURTZ: *They were sad times and times of great despair, but did you not have a kind of optimism?*
MACDONALD: Sure. I had enough optimism to become a Trotskyite. I actually thought that there might be a chance after the Second World War for a revolutionary situation, such as there was after the First World War. But of course, there wasn't, because the two great imperialists, Soviet and American, sat on the whole world.

KURTZ: *Are you still sympathetic to socialism?*
MACDONALD: Good heavens, no. I resigned from the Trotskyite Party in 1942. After that, I put out my magazine *Politics* and very rapidly developed an anarchist-pacifist position.

KURTZ: *Why have you abandoned socialism?*
MACDONALD: Because the socialist thinks that if he can solve the economic

problems he has solved everything. Marx didn't speculate much about what would happen after the bourgeoisie was dispossessed. He should have, but he didn't. We see Soviet Russia as an example where things are certainly as bad as they were under the Czars in almost every way. But an anarchist believes that the problem of power is not an economic one but a political one and that the state is the enemy and not the system of production. He does not believe that things will be solved by the working class disappropriating the bourgeoisie and taking over the state and running it as their state. I think that the experience of Russia shows that Bakunin was right and Marx was wrong in their famous debate.

KURTZ: *But before you said that we need a redistribution of wealth to some extent, so you are allowing for economic factors?*
MACDONALD: Oh, yes. Man has to eat.

KURTZ: *You think the real problem is of freedom versus the state?*
MACDONALD: Yes, of course. I see anarchism as the most valuable way to approach political problems. That is to say, as a method of criticism. But the reason there is no possibility for anarchism is the same reason it is needed now more than ever. It is because there is so much concentration of power economically and politically, and that's also why it's impossible to apply anarchism in practice.

KURTZ: *Would you use the term "libertarian" to describe your position?*
MACDONALD: Yes, I would think it's a kind of synonym.

KURTZ: *What would it mean in more concrete terms?*
MACDONALD: Well, "anarchism" (or libertarianism) does not mean "chaos" as the *New York Times* and most American editorialists, think. It just means "without a leader" and it means that decisions are made from below and not from above. It's a form of cooperation.

KURTZ: *Decentralized democracy?*
MACDONALD: Yes. Decentralization is actually implicit. You couldn't have an anarchist country run from a central power.

KURTZ: *But it would involve democracy, too?*
MACDONALD: Yes. In the sense of a town meeting or a factory. For example, the Soviets in the early days of the Bolshevik revolution—that was strictly an

anarchist idea. In fact, that was exactly what the anarchists used to advocate in Spain, taking over the factories directly by the workers.

KURTZ: *But it was abandoned in the Soviet Union?*
MACDONALD: Of course. It was abandoned almost as soon as the Bolsheviks got into power, under the slogan, "All Power to the Soviets," because it conflicted with the whole Marxist idea of centralizing power in the state.

KURTZ: *Apparently the workers' syndicates have been abandoned in Yugoslavia, too. They were working toward a form of workers' self-management. Tito has been attacking what he calls the "anarcho-liberals," especially in the universities.*
MACDONALD: I think that's very disturbing.

KURTZ: *Concerning the United States, don't you think that libertarianism is now a strong movement in this country? For example, the Supreme Court has struck down abortion laws in the name of privacy and freedom.*
MACDONALD: Yes. Certainly that's true. We have libertarian traditions. People like Jefferson certainly were libertarian. Also, the one way that the American does resemble an anarchist is in his peculiar ability to form groups of citizens for certain aims completely independent of the state.

KURTZ: *Voluntary associations?*
MACDONALD: Yes, voluntary associations. The American Civil Liberties Union is one kind, but there are lots of others that have nothing to do with politics, charitable organizations, for example. This does not exist in any European state and I don't think it exists very much in England either.

KURTZ: *De Toqueville said, when Americans have a problem, they get together and form a committee.*
MACDONALD: Well, De Toqueville, of course, is always right. You can read him and think you're reading about America today. That would be in the anarchist tradition, you see, of getting together with people of like interests and working out your own destiny.

KURTZ: *Does the anarchist tradition refer both to individual freedom and cooperative social action? Do you emphasize both?*
MACDONALD: Yes. The Bill of Rights, free speech, complete freedom of the individual to express himself if he doesn't harm other people—you can't have even a bourgeois democratic society without that.

KURTZ: *I wonder if we can focus on the role of culture. You are an anarchist, a libertarian, a democrat with a small "d," but what is your view of the state of culture in our country at present?*

MACDONALD: Well, my cultural (not political) stance has been elitist since the first issue of my magazine *Politics*, which began as a revolutionary Marxist magazine in 1944 and ended in 1949 as an anarchist-pacifist magazine. I began the first issue with an essay called, "A Theory of Popular Culture." In this article, I defined two kinds of cultures: mass (or popular) culture, which only began at the end of the eighteenth century and was connected with the rise of industrialism; and the traditional kind, which I called "high" culture. This mass culture has more and more threatened the high culture and the difference is that mass culture is manufactured for a market, whereas high culture is made by hand, so to speak, for a cultural elite—I suppose you have to call it that—who are seriously interested in art. I have for a long time felt that the only hope for culture in this country is through the minority—not more than 20 or 25 percent—who really care about it.

KURTZ: *That's very high, up to one-fourth of the population?*
MACDONALD: Yes, maybe too high. Perhaps 15 percent of the population would be closer—those who are eager to read someone like James Joyce before he is "established." Of course, by now, Joyce is on the cover of *Time* and he has become massified, so to speak. It seems to me that those people, whether consumers or creators, are the only people who produce and sustain high culture.

KURTZ: *It is increasingly difficult to do so with the mass media, television, and so on?*
MACDONALD: Impossible with the mass media. But, in the traditional arts and letters, it is quite possible for a minority to produce a serious culture, because this is a very rich country. There are many ways in which you can support yourself and also produce serious work.

KURTZ: *Do you think the arts are flourishing?*
MACDONALD: Well, no, but that's for another reason, I guess. I certainly don't think our literature is flourishing, certainly not as compared to the twenties.

KURTZ: *Because of the inroads of mass culture?*
MACDONALD: It might be partly because of something I called "mid-cult" (middle-brow culture), which is a culture that pretends to be serious. You see, the

old kinds of mass culture were things like *Tarzan* and cheap Hollywood movies and comic strips. There was no pretense about that. But the new kind, this "mid-cult," is . . .

KURTZ: Time *and* Reader's Digest?
MACDONALD: Well, yes. *Reader's Digest* would be more toward the old kind. The old *Saturday Review* under Norman Cousins would really be a perfect example of what I call "mid-cult." The people who read that were mostly serious, quasi-intellectual types, teachers, small-town librarians, people like that, and they really loved books and they really thought they were getting a literary magazine, but they were getting a kind of watered-down version of the *New York Times Book Review*—the philistine old one under Brown and Markel, not the sophisticated new one under John Leonard.

KURTZ: *Would you include the* New York Review of Books *in the high culture category?*
MACDONALD: Yes, sure.

KURTZ: Commentary?
MACDONALD: Yes, although I disagree profoundly with its political line. I would also put the *New Yorker* there, although it has a large circulation and makes money.

KURTZ: *Who constitutes the cultural elite?*
MACDONALD: First of all, I don't think that the cultural elite has any direct connection with either money or class. Of course, I suppose to some extent people with enough money to go to college would tend more to be members of this 15 percent, but plenty of people with lots of money are on the same level as people without money. So, it's a game open to anybody. People always reproach me and say, "Well, what about all of these 85 percent? What are you going to do about them?" Well, I say, being an anarchist, that I don't believe in taking people by the hand and force-feeding them culture. I think they should make their own decisions. If they want to go to museums and concerts, that's fine, but they shouldn't be seduced into doing it or shamed into doing it. And the game is open to anybody who wants to play: the only requirement for admission to "the club," so to speak, is a real—that is, a personal—interest in arts and letters and other "things of the mind," as in the old term, like philosophy or history or languages or even science. This is not to be taken

for granted, you know. Most people simply aren't interested—personally. It doesn't even mean you have to have any talent, furthermore—just an odd personal interest in such odd things as art and thought.

KURTZ: *You don't think you need to have talent to be a member of this elite?*
MACDONALD: You need talent to create art, but not to enjoy it. All you need there is interest, need.

KURTZ: *Then you feel that culture is open to anyone who has an interest?*
MACDONALD: Yes, but it's quite unusual, almost eccentric to have such an interest, I think.

KURTZ: *Is it an elitist interest?*
MACDONALD: Yes, but it's not a closed corporation. Beginning with Napoleon, the bourgeois ideology was "a career open to talents," which was a democratization of the *ancien regime*'s "careers open to birth." My "elitist" rules for entry into the "we happy few" 15 percent who care about cultural matters is even more democratic: "a career open to interest—and felt need."

KURTZ: *What are your views on religion? Have you reflected much on religion in your life?*
MACDONALD: Not much. There are two subjects that seem to interest most people but have never greatly interested me. One is religion—even as an adolescent I found it boring. I didn't go through the "crisis of belief" most of my teenage contemporaries did, because, not only didn't I believe, I didn't even muster up the interest to doubt. The whole idea of God would never have occurred to me, in fact, had not so many otherwise sensible adults taken it for granted in those Sunday sermons (compulsory) at Phillips Exeter Academy. The other area I've found boring—personally—is science, with which my last real grapple was in freshman biology at Yale. Science and Religion! The two great Victorian hang-ups!

KURTZ: *Why not science?*
MACDONALD: For some reason, I've never been interested in science, intellectually or practically. I'm not curious about my bodily functions, nor about my car's, nor my telephone's, nor my solar system's. If I feel sick, I go to a doctor; if my car doesn't work, to a mechanic; if my cosmos is out of whack, to an astronomer, or possibly an astrologer; both would be about equally helpful. But why should I bother about such irrelevant details—to me—as carburetors

and pancreases and spiral nebulae and the behavior of coal under certain circumstances? I guess I'm only interested in subjects having something to do with human behavior, with people—like me. (I include animals in this category—to misquote Will Rogers, I've never met a dog I didn't like.) Subjects like history, literature, arts (including movies) and even sociology and psychology. I say "even" because the last two have been systematically dehumanized in a ludicrous and mistaken effort to "raise" (I'd say "lower") them to the level of science. There's actually a department of "Political Sciences" here at Buffalo!

KURTZ: *Doesn't religion have something to do with people?*
MACDONALD: Religion has nothing to do with people as far as I can see. By religion, I don't mean merely a code of ethics but also a belief that there is some power outside this world which is concerned with it and us in some way or other and which intervenes, therefore, into our human existence—even if only to send us off to heaven or hell after we're dead. I'd settle for that, intellectually though not morally.

KURTZ: *You find all that uninteresting even to talk about?*
MACDONALD: Yes. It's boring in the most fundamental way: I can see no evidence for a belief in such a supernatural, concerned power in our lives and fate. And if there is such an all-powerful God, then he's the Devil. For certainly this is a very wicked, painful, and evil world in which the innocent often suffer and the guilty get away. The only kind of religion that makes any sense is the old Manichean heresy, you know, the idea that down here the Devil and God are fairly equally matched and that one wins one inning and the other wins another one. This accounts for the fact that we do have wonderful things in life and some people are virtuous, and it accounts also for the opposite.

KURTZ: *Is the present situation and mood in America an expression of the Manichean strain?*
MACDONALD: It's an expression of the Devil certainly. The only other point I would like to make is that people seem to confuse an idealistic or moralistic nature like mine with a tendency toward religious belief. I don't understand why.

KURTZ: *Is your morality independent and autonomous?*
MACDONALD: It has nothing to do with a super-natural Being. I suppose I'm more like those eighteenth century Encyclopedists.

KURTZ: *Do you consider yourself to be a humanist?*
MACDONALD: Oh yes. I am a humanist. For I consider that man is the measure, and I am appalled by excesses of science as well as religion. You know, I think that men can go too far in certain directions, and I want restraints. In that sense, I am a conservative.

KURTZ: *A conservative anarchist?*
MACDONALD: In the sense that I want to conserve the past as a bridge to the future, I'm an active member of the Victorian Society, which was founded by Sir Nicholas Pesner, the architectural historian, 25 years ago in England, in order to preserve their Victorian buildings. It was founded in the United States by a group I am a sponsor of, about five years ago. We try to get people interested in the past.

KURTZ: *When you say that you are a conservative anarchist, do you mean simply that you wish to conserve the best of the past?*
MACDONALD: Yes, I want to conserve in that sense. Paul Goodman calls himself a conservative anarchist in his later years. I'm a very ardent member of the Sierra Club, and very much for ecology—that's even *called* "conservation." I'm also conservative in the sense that I have always been appalled by the excesses in anything—in reason or in politics. For instance, when I was a Trotskyite, I never like the dogmas of Marxism. I never liked the idea that we were the chosen people, that we knew what was right and everybody else was wrong. That sort of sectarianism offended me.

KURTZ: *Does this mean that there are limits to social programs of progress?*
MACDONALD: Yes. I agree with Edmund Burke about the danger of applying abstract ideas too logically to society, history and politics—which of course the youth have always had a tendency to do.

KURTZ: *Are you suggesting that we should work piecemeal with problems as they emerge?*
MACDONALD: Yes. We should adopt a kind of *ad hoc* approach and not try to push everybody into one mold, whoever he is, whether he is a Communist or Capitalist. You should have a sense of the limitations of human thought and feeling and also of the continuity of human existence and of the fact that a perfect institution would be completely dead, just as a perfect person. The only time people ever get perfect is when they die.

Post Script:

Kurtz and I talked on April 4th when Watergate was still a cloud no bigger than a ham-hand on the President's sunny horizon. Today, April 30th, comes the news that Nixon's two chief lieutenants and longtime pals—"friends" is not an easily imaginable Nixonian concept—Haldeman and Erlichman, have suddenly resigned, plus Kleindienst, successor for Mitchell (who may soon be indicted for any one of several capers, including Watergate) in what is laughingly called the Department of Justice. (Despite their names, redolent of the German General Staff, Messrs. H, E, and K haven't stood up very well under fire). As of April 30th, I'd add three points: (1) "most sinister and dangerous president" was prophetic; the Presidency itself may not survive Tricky Dick's White House wrecking crew, which includes, besides Haldeman, Erlichman and Kleindienst, a dozen or so other *Obersturmgruppbanner fuehrers* who functioned as Assistant Undersecretaries in the Department of Dirty Tricks, (2) Americans aren't quite as callous about corruption as I'd thought—at least, when the scoundrels begin to betray each other (no honor among *these* thieves) so thoroughly the good burgher can't ignore the headlines: Nixon's popularity has actually gone down in recent polls, despite his massive bombing of Cambodia and Laos, (3) "Nixon is getting away with murder," I said on April 4th—I didn't know the half of it! Now like an earlier ruler with a defective ethical sense, he is appalled to find that murder will out. If Banquo comes to Watergate with twenty mortal murders on his head, when may he expect Birnham Wood to be helicoptered to Camp David?

Interview with Dwight Macdonald

Esther Harriott / 1973

> From transcript of interviews conducted for the Cultural Affairs Program of State University of New York at Buffalo, May 1973 and September 1976. Printed by permission of Esther Harriott.

May 1973

EH: *Dwight Macdonald is, and has been for almost 40 years, one of the most distinguished literary, cultural, and political critics in the United States. He has been a staff writer on the* New Yorker *and* Fortune, *editor of the* Partisan Review, *editor and publisher of* Politics. *He was film critic from 1960 to 1966 for* Esquire *and he has published many books, among them* Parodies: An Anthology from Chaucer to Beerbohm—And After, Dwight Macdonald on Movies, *and* Politics Past. *The State University of New York at Buffalo has been lucky enough to have Mr. Macdonald here as a visiting professor in the English Department for the spring semester and to have persuaded him to return next year.*

You've been interviewed so many times and by so many different people, Mr. Macdonald, that I especially appreciate your agreeing to be subjected to the process once more.
DM: Well, I'm used to it.

EH: *My own introduction to you was in the late fifties when I had, I thought, been lucky enough to get hold of a library copy of James Gould Cozzens's much touted* By Love Possessed. *Here is the great American novel we were told. I read it and found it to be a pretentious bore and wondered what kind of Philistine I was to be so out of tune with the unanimous critical opinion. Then I found your marvelous article in* Commentary, *"By Cozzens Possessed," which cleverly pointed out how the Emperor had no clothes. And time has proved you to be the critic who was right.*

DM: May I interject on that point that you have said exactly what almost everybody says. That they read it and expected it to be a masterpiece and were told that it was by the critics. And then they thought they were some type of Philistine, you see. And then they read my review and found that their initial perceptions were correct.

EH: *But what about the critics who did praise it very highly. You mentioned in that article that Brendin Gill described it in terms that would be slightly excessive for* War and Peace. *Would someone like that come up to you and say, "Well, about Cozzens, you know. . . ."*
DM: Well one of them, Whitney Balliet (*New Yorker* jazz critic), did. But I see Gill all the time because I still have an office at the *New Yorker*, and now we sort of avoid the subject.

EH: *Are there any similarly inflated literary reputations these days?*
DM: I'm sure there are a lot. Offhand, I can't think of anything.

EH: *Well, let me ask a pleasanter question. What particular contemporary writers do you admire?*
DM: Well, I would say Norman Mailer and Nabokov are the ones I especially admire in the field of fiction. I admired Edmund Wilson . . . But I think that there is something about Mailer that is very unexpected and so versatile. He can do almost all kinds of different things. I like Philip Roth's *Portnoy's Complaint*.

EH: *Well, there's an opinion you share with Brendon Gill. There is a certain trend, at least in creative writing classes, towards experimental fiction and the notion that the traditional novel is dying. Do you agree with that?*
DM: Well, the novel has been dying ever since Jane Austen if not since *Tom Jones*. It seems to me that the novel can never die because it always pops up in another form. It's a very baggy, loose form. It can be anything. My late friend James Agee did one of the first books in a genre I would call documentary, autobiographical novels. Agee's *Let Us Now Praise Famous Men*, about the sharecroppers and the tenant farmers of the South in the late 30s, is exactly like Mailer's *Armies of the Night*. They both are in the foreground and yet it's all documentary. Now is that a novel, is it an autobiography, is it reportage? It's all three of them. So I don't think you can say the novel is dead. I don't think the so-called experimental novels, like John Barth, would be an example. I'm

not much for that kind of thing. Or Pynchon. Is that what you mean by experimental novels?

EH: *Yes, or Barthelme.*
DM: Yes, well Barthelme is a special case. I forgot Updike—I think he is a very interesting writer too. Now Vonnegut, for instance, is someone all the kids seem to be wild about, I think he's ok in a mild way, but it seems to me that he lacks the density and the form that people like Nabokov and Mailer and Bellow have.

EH: *It's odd to hear you pair Nabokov and Mailer.*
DH: Well, of course, they don't really fit together much except that I think that *Lolita*, which I think is Nabokov's great achievement, shares with Mailer a certain sense of the language. Mailer is very good at the vernacular. And *Lolita*, while it is not exactly vernacular, is a tremendous playing with words all the time. That's what I like about it.

EH: *I found* Lolita *very amusing and fun. My latest exposure to Nabokov was* Ada, *which I thought was a real bore.*
DM: I think it is essentially a bore. Part of it was as good as Tolstoy, it seems to me. But then all this business about two worlds shifting back and forth was a kind of self-indulgent fantasy.

EH: *And terribly self-conscious all through.*
DM: Very self-conscious, very arch. On the other hand, when he gets down to the actual human relations and passion, I mean there are some chapters in that which really depict sexual and erotic passion and feeling in a way that I've never seen done better.

EH: *What are you teaching here?*
DM: I'm teaching a graduate course in Edgar Allan Poe. I've talked to a lot of undergraduates about Poe, and I think they really "dig him," as they might say. I think it's because Poe is the poet of what [Bruno] Bettelheim, would call behavior in extreme situations. Like the Nazi concentration camps. Poe's horror stories have now come true, you know. The atomic bomb of Hiroshima, what Hitler and Stalin did to people, that sort of thing. I think that's one reason why the kids are interested in him. Another reason, of course, is that there is something very hallucinatory about his prose and his approach, not

that he was so much of a drug person himself. It would go very well in a drug-filled culture. My other course is called American Political Fiction. I begin with Hawthorne's "The Black Tale of Romance" and end up with Mailer's *Armies of the Night*.

EH: *You no longer write political criticism or movie criticism, do you?*
DM: No, I've written very little in the past couple of years.

EH: *Is there a special reason for that?*
DM: I've written so much [laugh], I'm a bit tired of writing. That's why I am teaching, to be quite frank about it. I mean I enjoy teaching very much.

EH: *It isn't that you have given up on political criticism and film criticism as unimportant?*
DM: My word, no. Given up on it. Not when you have this Watergate thing. Someday I will have to do something on that. That's the most extraordinary episode in American history at least in my time. I've never seen anything like it, the way it keeps mushrooming and building up every day. Today the *Times*, for about the fifth time in two weeks, had complete banner headlines all across the paper. That's very rare, the *Times* doesn't do that.

EH: *I read in an article about you that you felt that political criticism was essentially ineffectual.*
DM: No, I never said that: I may have said that as a radical, a revolutionary, which I was in the days of my publishing *Politics*, that I really wanted to have a completely different system of government here, you see. Socialism is not just reforming, it calls for a total transformation of the basis of society, which I felt was unlikely to happen. I may have said that, that's true. But muckraking, digging into facts, and so on is a very effective way of changing things, and I have done some of that in the past.

EH: *If you were a revolutionary during that period, how would you describe yourself now, politically?*
DM: Well, I call myself a conservative anarchist. The anarchist part means that I profoundly mistrust and detest the state and power from above and I think people should cooperate with each other at the grass-roots level and build up from there. This is just a theory, because there is no anarchist movement. But it's a healthy skepticism, which is amply justified by Watergate when you see what these SOBs have been doing with their position of power.

The conservative part is that I also have a sort of contradictory belief in the principles of Edmund Burke that there is a certain kind of continuity in human history and human affairs and that you can't, you shouldn't break it too drastically. In other words, the French Revolution and the Bolshevik Revolution, these two great revolutions, I now see as much too violent and drastic, and terrible things happened as a result. I like the Constitution too; that's one reason why I am so appalled by Watergate. Nixon and all these other people are the most subversive people because they do everything outside the law. Nixon has no more interest in the Constitution than the late Senator Joe McCarthy had. He's another one of these right-wing radicals, I call them.

EH: *I heard on the news this morning that Congress didn't vote the money that was requested for the continued bombing of Cambodia. But I was disappointed when it was reported that the Pentagon had other ways of getting the money anyhow.*
DM: That's exactly what I mean. This is completely unconstitutional. Nixon is an absolute rascal, a scoundrel, and he's still up to these tricks. He hasn't got a straight bone in his body.

EH: *I have been signaled that we have one more minute. In that minute can you talk about any project you're currently engaged in?*
DM: Yes, in fact in about a month Knopf is bringing out an abridged edition of Alexander Herzen's great book of memoirs, *My Past Thoughts*, and I've reduced it from four volumes to one large volume. I edited it, and added footnotes and a preface. It's just an abridgement job, but it's a great work of nineteenth-century political literature. Herzen was the first Russian socialist, you know.

EH: *Yes, I read about him in [E. H. Carr's]* The Romantic Exiles.
DM: That's a very good review of him.

EH: *Thank you very much for coming and being with us this evening.*
DM: Well, I enjoyed it.

September 1976

EH: *You have written on so many subjects: politics, society and culture, film and so on. Do you have a favorite?*
DM: Well, I would have answered a few years ago that movies have always

been my special favorite. But now that movies are so disappointing, I guess I'd rather write about books. And politics I certainly don't want to write about now. I've always had a special feeling about movies.

EH: *And you think movies have declined in the past few years?*
DM: Yes, in the past 10 or 15 years. Even the old masters haven't produced very much. Bergman is the only one who has maintained some kind of level, and I don't see much in his new ones either. So I think that movies are in a decline. Well, every art does that, you know. Nothing goes all the way up forever.

EH: *What was the heyday?*
DM: I think the movies have had two aesthetic peaks. One of them was the great silent period of Russian, German, and American cinema roughly between the first world war and the introduction of sound in 1930. And I think that the second peak began with most of the work of Bergman in the 50s. Then you had Kurosawa in Japan and Ray in India.

EH: *You didn't mention Ozu. I thought he was your favorite.*
DM: I only heard about Ozu about four years ago. Yes, I'm glad you mentioned that. *Tokyo Story* was one of the great movies. Then you had Fellini and Antonioni in Italy, and the French New Wave—Truffaut, Resnais, Goddard. I think this second period reached its peak somewhere in the 1960s. Now there is another slump.

EH: *And you say that you wouldn't want to write about politics now. Is that because it is depressing or uninteresting?*
DM: Well, I don't know—I mean, I'm for Carter but it's all baby talk now, it seems to me, compared with the New Deal period when things were really happening and when you had certain hopes of some radical solutions. And then with the Vietnam war, and the Nixon era, in a horrible way you had something very bad and sinister.

EH: *But you had something to write about.*
DM: Yeah, something to write about, something to protest about. Now we have to get rid of Ford just like we had to get rid of Hoover, but I don't see anything interesting to write about politics. There is no radical politics anymore, is there?

EH: *No, I wonder though if the idea of Carter's born-again image appealed to you in a literary way if not in a political way.*
DM: Born again, that's just the Baptist way.

EH: *No, I mean if there's some kind of feeling going through the U.S. that's a sociological phenomenon?*
DM: It's a religious thing, isn't it, born again?

EH: *Yeah, that's what it comes from.*
DM: I'm not interested in that. It doesn't interest me much. Carter seems to be a very decent and serious fellow, but a rather vague one, and so far I don't quite know where he's coming from. Except that he seems more humane than Ford.

EH: *But that's not enough.*
DM: Well, it's enough I guess to vote for him, but not enough to write about it.

EH: *Of the various magazines that you worked on, did you have a favorite?*
DM: Well, my own magazine *Politics*, from '44 to '49—the last part of the war and postwar period, a monthly magazine of political and social commentary remains my favorite. I did a great deal of writing in it, too, some of my best writing I think. I suppose I favor it because I am, by nature, an editor even more than a writer. I love to edit and there I was the only editor.

EH: *If you say that you are an editor by nature, then how is it that you've done more writing than editing?*
DM: Well, because except when I was paying my own money to publish it, nobody has ever asked me to edit a magazine all by myself. I've been on editorial boards with other people but I don't know that I'm recognized as an editor. But I'm really much better at that, I think. The first couple of drafts of my own writing are absolutely nothing. It's only after I get it down on paper and edit it that it takes shape. I'm really very good at taking a terrible first two drafts and making something pretty good by the fourth draft.

EH: *So you serve as a self-editor.*
DM: Yeah, right, and that's the part I enjoy, too. I hate the creative part of beginning to put something down on paper.

EH: *Brendan Gill in* Here at the New Yorker, *talked a lot about William Shawn and Harold Ross. Was that a fairly accurate reflection of the ambiance of the* New Yorker?
DM: Well, I wasn't there in Ross's day. I arrived just after Ross died. But I assume Brendan knew Shawn very well and I think he's pretty good on him. I think the trouble with the book is that it has a curious maliciousness about it. It's a little too strong. Almost unconsciously, because I think he thinks he's just been genial and amusing.

EH: *Sort of malicious fun. Perhaps there is a lot of revenge in it.*
DM: Perhaps. I think one of Shawn's contributions is the number of serious people he got to write for the magazine. Hannah Arendt became a regular contributor. Now he's getting Bruno Bettelheim, and he has a lot of serious people on the staff, too. Those are the people who write the nonfiction, you know, the idea things. But Gill doesn't seem to be interested in that aspect.

EH: *Getting back to that difference between being an editor and a writer. Do they really demand an entirely different set of qualities?*
DM: Well, they couldn't. Otherwise I couldn't be both. There is, I suppose, a spontaneous, natural writer who really enjoys the beginning, enjoys the idea of shaping something from the start—likes starting off.

EH: *Except a lot of writers talk about how depressing it is to sit down at that page.*
DM: Well, it's depressing to write in general. I mean, it's a hard job whether you like it or not. You see I'm a critic, too. That's another thing. I've always been a critic, even when I was in college. I wrote a few poems and stories then, but I had no idea of ever writing more poetry and fiction. I never did. I knew that I wanted to be a critic. So, if you are a critic, that's like being an editor. A critic is always reacting to somebody else's work or some art.

EH: *There is no question that you are one of the great critics.*
DM: There may be some question in some people's minds.

EH: *Well, in my mind there isn't.*
DM: Well, thank you.

EH: *But what I was going to say was that I don't remember reading—and I've read a number of your critical pieces—I don't remember reading favorable criticisms. Is that because you deliberately go after things that could use puncturing?*
DM: Well, I must say that the longest review I have ever written was a review

in *Esquire* of Fellini's 8½ and that was completely *favorable*. But one swallow doesn't make a summer. I can think of a few other examples. I have written about some good books. Agee's letters and *Let Us Now Praise Famous Men*. But it is true, in general, that my other kind of journalism, my social and cultural journalism, has been mostly critical such as my reviews of the third edition of *Webster's New International Dictionary* and the *Revised Standard Version of the Bible* [RSV]. In these instances I felt some terrible crimes against standards were being committed. In that sense I was kind of a muckraker.

EH: *The term "popular culture" is used a lot these days. Did you coin the words "mass-cult" and "mid-cult"?*
DM: I coined those words and even "popular culture," I think. I used it in my initial essay on popular culture in the first issue of *Politics*. Well, actually, [Marshall] McLuhan was using the term around the same time. We were writing about it quite early back in the 40s.

EH: *What's the difference between mass culture and popular culture and, for that matter, mid-cult?*
DM: "Mid" means middlebrow culture and mass-cult means mass culture, lowbrow so to speak. There really isn't any difference between "popular culture" and "mass culture." I first used the term "popular culture," but then I thought "mass culture" was more descriptive, because mass culture implies the essence of the thing, which is that it is exploitative. It's not like folk art. Folk art is a real expression of the common people. You know it's the expression of a peasantry. Whereas mass culture is something that entrepreneurs turn out, who are not of the people—tin pan alley, movie producers, cheap book publishers, and so on. They provide the bulk of this stuff, which is written to make money and is imposed from the top. You do see the difference don't you?

EH: *It's imposed from the top and doesn't answer any needs.*
DM: Well, it answers the need for entertainment, it answers the lowest common denominator. But it doesn't answer, it can't answer, it's not its function to answer any real spiritual, moral, or psychic needs that art answers. You know, the art experience is not just entertainment. That's part of it, but it also changes you and that's what even folk art does too.

EH: *Where does mid-cult fit in? That's the most objectionable, right?*
DM: It has the potential to be the serious stuff. My contention is that classic

mid-cult writers have been people like Thornton Wilder. Wilder was a perfect example, and especially *Our Town*. *Our Town* is probably the greatest mid-cult, middlebrow play. People think that it is quite serious, that it is a real play, I mean highbrow, about actual people, and they are moved by it. And it is very skillfully done. But, actually if you examine it, it's like those *Saturday Evening Post* covers by Norman Rockwell. In fact, they're all Norman Rockwell scenes, really—the soda fountain, the young couple's wedding, and the funeral. And it all has a surface of experimental staging—you know, the stage manager and no scenery and so on. Wilder has borrowed all of the tricks and the feathers and plumes of serious modernist writing and stagecraft in order to put on what is essentially a series of Norman Rockwell scenes. It's sentimental at heart, and false. That's what the mid-cult thing is. It gives the impression of being serious but it isn't really at all. It is done according to formula.

EH: *And what's the formula?*
DM: Different formulas. My point is that anything that is real in art is an expression of one person talking to one person. The artist isn't talking to a million people or 100 million people, he's talking to an ideal reader or an ideal viewer who is sort of like him. That is what an artist does and he expresses only himself. But what they do in the mass-culture and in the middlebrow culture is to fabricate models, they fabricate things by their brains, not by their unconscious or their hearts or their minds, just by their will.

EH: *And you think that unless the unconscious comes into it, it's not art?*
DM: The whole personality has to come into it. You can't be just a craftsman to be an artist or a writer or even a critic. You have to engage yourself and you have to engage other people at a conscious level and not just entertainment.

EH: *What critics writing these days do you respect?*
DM: Well, of course two of them have just recently died: Wilson and Trilling. I think Mary McCarthy is very good. I think Updike is sometimes very good, sometimes not so great. There must be others [laughs]. Movies: John Simon without question is the best I think. We don't always agree but he has somewhat the same approach that I have.

EH: *I don't think so, he's always so sour.*
DM: Well, I'm sour, too, except that I make jokes. But really it's amazing. I've

known John for at least 15 years now, I guess. I wrote the introduction to his first collection of critical essays many years ago. And I know everybody says he's awful and he has bad manners in print. But he really knows his stuff. He has a broad cultural background, not just movies but books and languages, and he knows something about art, about all kinds of things. Of course he's been doing theater reviewers as long as he's been doing movie reviews, with equal success, I think. And he has very good standards. What they really don't like about him, and a lot of people didn't like that about me either, is that he refuses to compromise. He keeps saying this movie or that play is really tripe even though every other critic says it's absolutely great. And he tells why, too. He's very good at explaining why he doesn't like them or why he does. Of course, he's gone overboard about Bergman. I mean, he's been good about Bergman, therefore, he's not just negative. But, anyway, he is with no doubt the one guy in the movie end.

EH: *What about Pauline Kael?*
DM: Well, I don't know. She always disappoints me. She writes very well. I think she is very good when it is a question of common sense and social penetration. She's very good with everything around movies. She can tell you what a movie means in social and cultural terms and what the audience is like, and so on. I don't think she's interested in, or she doesn't have any feeling for the actual movie itself, the art itself. Do you think some of that is true?

EH: *I agree with the first part of what you said completely. I often find that I'm amazed at certain movies that she likes. An example is* Shampoo, *which she thought was a great American movie.*
DM: She thought *Mash* was a great thing. Oh and many, many other ones. She has a great weakness for well-made Hollywood tripe, I think. She tends to be a little too contemptuous of what she calls these pretentious foreign films. She's got a very good brain you know, but she certainly goes overboard about a lot of things. I thought *Last Tango in Paris* was not only a big disappointment as pornography—as a dirty movie, it was a great disappointment on that level—but also I was bored by it. It was so pretentious, so mannered, I thought. Brando was never heavier and more self-indulgent.

EH: *Do you tend to prefer the English style of criticism to the American? The kind of gifted amateur in the best sense.*

DM: Yeah, I do think that is a great thing in England. When I was over there some years ago, I noticed that you ran across stockbrokers who knew all about Proust and not only had read it all, but had done a lot of research on it. You'd find members of Parliament who knew a great deal about Chinese porcelains or something.

EH: *Why?*
DM: Because the English have a much more integrated culture. You see, they have a class culture and there are certain advantages to that. Over here everybody knows something, everybody goes to college, there isn't any upper class or lower class in a way. But in England there is a very distinct upper class, a cultural upper class. And somehow it seems natural for Englishmen of this class, no matter what their occupation is, to take interest in these kinds of things, and they do. It is really extraordinary the way some very important discoveries have been made by these so-called amateurs there.

EH: *Would that be true in other European countries?*
DM: I don't think so, not as much, no. There's something about the English. The English are a bunch of amateurs anyway, you know.

EH: *What do you mean?*
DM: Well, I mean that when they ran their empire, there was a lot of improvisation, a lot of schoolboy heroics, and amateur kind of stuff. I mean the American tends to be very much of a big corporation. And we tend to be heavy handed. But the British never get entirely serious about something. I like that very much. We have fields over here, and big shot scholars and professors rarely go outside of their so-called fields. In England some of these Oxford or Cambridge dons surprise you with what they know, what they write about.

EH: *What happened to* Encounter *magazine? That was a British/American co-venture.*
DM: That still goes on, doesn't it?

EH: *Does it?*
DM: Of course, I was one of the editors for one year. This was before the horrible news about the CIA financing it. That was one of the biggest scandals in 1968, when it all broke. Don't you remember, the article in *Ramparts* magazine?

EH: Ramparts *magazine broke a story about CIA financing of* Encounter?
DM: Well, not just *Encounter* but all kinds of cultural projects and institutions.

EH: *Yes, but I didn't know that* Encounter *was among* . . .
DM: Yes, yes, absolutely yes. And I was on it before that, about 8 years before that. . . . But it seemed to survive all that, at least Lasky is still there, as far as I know, and it still comes out. I haven't seen it for a long time.

EH: *I noticed in your book* Discriminations *that you criticized Buckminster Fuller, and I thought that was almost like criticizing motherhood; I thought he was in the Pantheon.*
DM: I grant him a lot in certain scientific fields, but have you ever heard him talk? He talks for five hours. It takes him three to get warmed up and then he goes on for another two hours and he absolutely is like a kitten chasing its tale. He's completely disorganized, chaotic, associative, very pretentious, and he says a lot of nonsense. He sounds like a primitive revivalist except that he happens to be talking about scientific things. Why do you think he is so revered?

EH: *I am not in any position to judge him, I just thought he was beyond criticism.*
DM: Why aren't you in a position to judge him?

EH: *Because I am not familiar enough with his accomplishments.*
DM: Granted that he is a scientist, God knows I'm not either, I'm not criticizing him about that.

EH: *You're talking about his style.*
DM: Not just his style, but what he says, I mean, in those columns that he writes. You don't have to know anything about science, you just have to have a little common sense. He's talking about the future here, and he doesn't have any charts and stuff—that's not what he's doing. He's making all kinds of ridiculous euphoric predictions. I think people like him because he is optimistic. He makes everything fine. He's like McLuhan. Why did McLuhan get such a big ride after being so obscure in that third book, *Understanding Media?* Because it was positive, because it said that television was the global village and everything was fine.

EH: *Do you think that it was the positive aspect of it, or the fact that it was timed very well for discussion about the medium?*
DM: It wasn't timed well for the discussion of television. There couldn't be

any such time because television was bad then, it's bad now. No, I think people need to be reassured. You see, we are stuck with television, we're stuck with scientific progress, we're stuck with all this environmental stuff—you know, we're rats in a human trap. Then people like McLuhan and Buckminster Fuller come along with tremendous intellectual and pretentious jargon. McLuhan has a whole vocabulary, you know. You read a McLuhan thing and you think you're in *Alice in Wonderland*. The inside is the outside, the medium is the message.

EH: *Hot and cool.*
DM: Yes, hot and cool, and boy does it take a volume to discuss that? But anyway so does Fuller, too. Fuller's got a whole launch of gimmicky tricks and they sound scientific and people need reassurance. They are really witch doctors, you know, except they do it in a scientific way.

EH: *We've only got one minute left and I wanted to ask you if you liked teaching as well as writing.*
DM: I enjoy teaching very much. It's much easier than writing.

EH: *It is easier than writing?*
DM: Well, of course, anything is easier than writing. But teaching is easier, too, because you're just sort of talking about things you know and love and tell people that don't know nearly as much as you, so you have quite a lot of freedom.

EH: *Yes, but then you have to deal with the response of the students.*
DM: Right, I enjoy that too. If they are impudent, I like that, and if they listen, I like that. If they are impudent, I like to argue with them, and if they listen, that's even better. So I like it. And I like this university especially.

EH: *The university especially likes you.*
DM: I feel right at home in academia, I really do.

EH: *I hope that you come back. Thank you very much, Dwight.*

Notes from Interview with Dwight Macdonald

Alan Wald / 1973

> Notes from an interview conducted at State University of New York at Buffalo. The Dwight Macdonald Papers, Manuscripts and Archives, Yale University Library. Printed by permission of Alan Wald and Yale University Library.

I. Macdonald and the Trotskyists

I was a member of Trotskyist political parties for two years, between 1939 and 1941. I joined in the fall of 1939, and I left the movement with the conclusion that although the Trotskyist political line was better than the Communist Party's, their organizational methods were not much different and their intellectual level was deplorable.

The way I came to Trotskyism was that I attacked an article that Malcolm Cowley had written on the Moscow Trials in the *New Republic*. I then received a letter asking me to join the Trotsky Defense Committee. Next, James Burnham—whom I had known long before, and for whose magazine, the *Symposium*, I had written—encouraged me to write some articles for the Trotskyist publication, *New International*. This magazine, incidently, was on a fairly high level.

Then, in the fall of 1939, after the invasion of Poland, I felt that I should join the Trotskyist party at the outbreak of war. I felt it was my responsibility. I went to James Cannon to have a talk. But already the divisions inside the Trotskyist movement were beginning to develop around the question of democracy and other issues, and Cannon suspected where I would probably stand. He tried to persuade me not to join the organization. This only made me want to join more—although I also felt it was my duty. Cannon, who was a hard-as-nails type guy, said that I just wasn't the type—and he was later shown to be correct. He said that I could be more valuable on the outside.

To my knowledge there were only about 800 members of the Trotskyist party at the time; when the split between Cannon and Shachtman took place, there were 400 in each faction. Shachtman won half the party. Also, I would say that about 400 of the total membership were in the New York area, and another 400 in the mid-West and San Francisco areas. There may have been as many as 10,000 fellow travellers of the Trotskyist movement in the broadest sense.

The split that took place between Cannon and Shachtman in 1940 was very educational. An unbelievable amount of writing took place. I myself collected a pile of bulletins two feet high, containing arguments of both sides. And much of the dispute was on a high level.

Both Shachtman and Cannon were great speakers, although totally different. Shachtman spoke with New York Jewish slang and Yiddish references. He was witty and inexhaustable. A three-hour talk was nothing to Shachtman. Cannon spoke in the old Wobbly style. He sounded patriarchal, Lincolnesque, and honest. He talked as if he believed that everything he did was for the good of the movement. He was slower, but probably more impressive.

Then there was C. L. R. James, whom we called "Mellow." I knew him well. Personally, I think he was a bit nuts. He read Hegel and it changed his entire life. I once told him that I couldn't understand Hegel. C. L. R. told me that if you don't understand Hegel you'll never be a genuine revolutionary. Hegel, he said, is our kindergarten. James was the greatest speaker of all. He used the entire range of vocal qualities. But his content had no coherence—he was like a madman.

I remember the last party meeting before the split. Shachtman spoke for three hours and Cannon for four. Each tried to blame the split on the other faction, but both sides really desired it. It was sort of like a divorce. Finally, at the end of the discussion everyone got up and sang the International together with raised fists. Everyone, that is, except for myself—I couldn't see how we could do it together after all the viciousness of the debate.

I actually didn't speak during the entire discussion, and I played only a small role in the dispute. I wrote three contributions to the discussion bulletin, but they only allowed one to be published. They said they decided this because I was too new.

The controversy over dialectical materialism was a side-issue. The real issue was the Red Army and organizational matters. And both factions were mostly petit bourgeois in composition. Cannon, however, did have the few genuine proletarians that existed in the party on his side. These were Dobbs and others in Minneapolis. But having proletarian supporters constitutes no virtue in itself. That claim was part of a mysticism that Cannon built up.

The reason I eventually left the Shachtman organization, the Workers Party, was because they wouldn't publish my unorthodox economic ideas. There seems to be a pattern here: I left *Fortune* because they bowdlerized my articles, and then the Socialist Workers Party wouldn't print my stuff either. Finally, the Shachtman group did the same thing.

I see that Fred Dupee mentioned Leon Trotsky's guard to you—Leon Frank. That was perhaps his party name. He was a Czech and he had no money. So when he came to the United States he stayed with myself and Nancy, my first wife. At that time I was just in the process of getting out of Shachtman's Workers Party. In fact, I was about to attend my last meeting. As I said, Shachtman wasn't going to print all of an article I wrote on Nazi economics—he said that they'd publish only 7,000 out of 30,000 words, because the article expressed heterodox views. Frank happened to be present at this final meeting where the argument occurred, but he never said a word. Afterwards I asked Frank why he wouldn't say anything against this refusal to print a perfectly good article. Frank replied that he thought the article was badly written! The next morning he left.

I naturally became disillusioned with Trotsky when he backed up the wrong side in the dispute between Cannon and Shachtman. It's now my opinion that an important factor in the Russian coup d'etat was a large quantity of German gold—as much as $50 million—which enabled the Bolsheviks to start five daily papers. An enormous press like that is a big factor.

I no longer have the personal feeling for Trotsky that I once did. Trotsky was once a hero to me; he seems more tragic now. I see his weaknesses more than his mastery.

II. Trotsky and the Intellectuals

There were three levels of Trotskyist intellectuals in the 1930s. First, there were those who were members of the Trotskyist movement. Then there were fellow travellers of the movement. And finally there were types like Edmund Wilson and Mary McCarthy, only peripherally involved. Mary McCarthy's short story, "Portrait of an Intellectual as a Yale Man," is based on John Chamberlain and myself, and I consider it a good account of the polemics between Stalinists, Trotskyists, and sympathizers. The story makes it clear that the main character is not a Trotskyist and not really committed, which reflects McCarthy's own outlook at that time. The person joins the Trotsky Defense Committee because of simple indignation. So this third layer—of types like Wilson and McCarthy—was not really a component of the Trotskyist intellectuals, but more accurately an anti-Stalinist current.

Edmund Wilson had originally been a Stalinist-oriented intellectual. When *To the Finland Station* was published I personally thought it was a poor book. I thought that Wilson wrote like a patronizing outsider. I think that the best part of the book is the straight textbook exposition and the character portraits. But I don't consider it as giving a serious rendering of life.

The Moscow Trials were undoubtedly the watershed for most of the intellectuals. The more active-minded intellectuals were the ones that came toward anti-Stalinism.

I don't think that it's really accurate to portray Trotsky as the central leader of the rebellion of artists and writers against Stalinist policy. Our inspiration was much broader than just Trotsky's ideas regarding the theory and freedom of art. We didn't need Trotsky to tell us that literature and politics were not the same thing—that they were not weapons. I'm sure of this, at least, in regard to Fred Dupee and myself; Rahv's case might have been different. Anyway, in my opinion Trotsky actually straddled that question. Sometimes he seems to be saying both things; for example, he made fun of Russian literary tendencies as being "petit bourgeois," as if that proclamation really meant something. But compared to Stalin, Trotsky was certainly tolerant.

I remember especially one incident while Fred was literary editor of the *New Masses*. I was then working for *Fortune* and Fred invited me to come on down for lunch with the editors of the *New Masses* in the spring of 1936.

Actually, this was just before I left *Fortune*. Back in 1934–35 I had been friendly with the Communist Party. I was a mild fellow traveller who used to go to their activities around the sharecroppers issue. Once I went as an observer to a down-town Communist Party branch meeting with Nancy. It reminded me of a Boy Scouts meeting: pious, humorless, the people seemed to have blinders on. Well, I felt exactly the same way at the *New Masses* luncheon. Probably Fred's experience with the Waterfront Unit allowed him to enjoy his stay with the Communist Party more. The people on the waterfront were rough and tumble fellows, on the firing line. Like all bourgeois intellectuals, we enjoyed getting into real contact with actual primitive working people.

The 1937 American Writers Congress was an important event in the evolution of the Trotskyist intellectuals. Myself, Rahv, Phillips, Fred, and Mary, all got admission cards and decided to attend the Critics session. The chairman was Granville Hicks. I sat right next to F. O. Mathiesson. He was one of the few fellow travellers of the Communist Party who would speak to us and write for *Partisan Review*, which took courage. I knew F. O. from Yale. Phil, Mary, and myself all got up and made diversionary remarks. Hicks went both red and pale. But the Stalinists couldn't do anything about us because we were legitimately there with credentials.

When we spoke we made points about the separation of literature and politics. This was about six months before our launching *Partisan Review* and it was actually sort of a trial run for our views. Rahv made an eloquent speech about the history of freedom and human thought. I made a speech about Trotsky's prose style—how excellent it was and even though that didn't make Trotsky right, at least he was a writer to be appreciated. The Stalinists went wild about that! The session was effectively disrupted. I knew that F. O. was sympathetic to us and I asked him to say something, but he wouldn't speak. F. O. remained a Stalinist fellow traveller until his death.

James Burnham was a completely abstract guy. That's why he had such sudden shifts and did a real turnabout in one year. But life just isn't that abstract.

It's funny that in your interview with Fred he tended to remember George Novack better than Max Shachtman. In my recollection Novack was mild and pale while Shachtman was vivid and alive. Furthermore, I find Fred's comments about Novack to be way off base. I recall him as an absolute scoundrel with no ability. He never smiled and was a complete hack. In fact, many of the so-called party intellectuals, like Novack and Morrow, were bores. Shachtman was closer to being a genuine intellectual. Most of the intellectuals sided with him and formed the Workers Party—Shachtman, myself, Carter, Burnham, Howe. Howe was young then, but he was always bright.

Herbert Solow, at the time of the existence of the Trotsky Defense Committee, played a marvelous role. He did a good organizing job. Although he was by that time cynical about all political organizations, he thought justice should be done.

Harvey Swados may have attended the mid-west conference we organized for the Shachtman group. His widow in Amherst would probably know the details of his political involvements. Swados' roots were in the working class; he really came out of the class and he continued working for a number of years.

Harry Roskolenko was sort of a Bohemian Trotskyist. I remember him as a swashbuckling fellow and a big lover.

Bernard Wolfe became a literary pornographer and a Hollywood screenwriter. I thought his novel about Trotsky, *The Great Prince Died*, was terrible. He is a mass cult hack.

John Wheelwright, however, was a good poet. He was a fantastic Boston aristocrat and appeared at party meetings in full evening dress, and with a fur collar. He never made any political concessions. He was strange, wild, very sincere. And he gave out leaflets and did Jimmy Higgins work along with the rest of us. He was killed in a cab accident. But Wheelwright was a very committed fellow.

Sherry Mangan became *Time* magazine's fellow in Paris. He was basically a frustrated intellectual. He knew an awful lot. He was a big drinker and had personality problems. I knew his wife also. Mangan was important in the *Time* magazine organization.

In France, Trotsky found sympathy among some of the surrealists. André Breton split from the other founders of the movement who had become Stalinists. He came out for Trotsky in the mid-1930s.

The Committee for Cultural Freedom and Socialism was not set up by the Trotskyists, although they participated in it. It was set up by *Partisan Review* magazine. One of the things we did was to support the rights of John Gioni, who was a rightwing French novelist being harassed by the authorities. I have folders on the work of the Committee, which was mainly civil liberties. Yale, in fact, is interested in my archives and when I go through my papers in January, I'll see if there's anything that might be of use to you. André Breton was our "French Connection," so to speak, for the Committee—he was then living over here.

In competition with us, Sidney Hook set up the Cultural Freedom Committee—he left out the socialism part. He claimed that he set his up first. Hook's eventually became a bit operation; it became involved with the CIA, the Congress for Cultural Freedom, etc.

III. Partisan Review

When *Partisan Review* was reorganized in 1937, all we had were basically two things: the mailing list that Phillips and Rahv had retained from the first version, plus the financial backing of George Morris.

I can't say that I agree completely with Fred Dupee's recollection about Trotsky's attitute toward *Partisan Review*—that Trotsky never really expected the group to join up with the Fourth International. I have two letters from Trotsky, and my impression is that even though Trotsky may not have wanted *Partisan Review* to actually join the American Trotskyist organization, he did think that the magazine should definitely come out for Trotskyism.

IV. Farrell and the Trotskyist Intellectuals

James T. Farrell was admired mainly for moral reasons among the Trotskyist and anti-Stalinist intellectuals. Farrell was generous, courageous, and decent. And he was no dope. He played a good role in that milieu. But it was wrong to think that Farrell was the leader. *Partisan Review* magazine was much more in the center. Farrell was more of a follower; he really didn't have that many ideas of his own.

In fact, Farrell was not really an authentic intellectual. There was no actual depth or range to his thinking. He was not interested in all kinds of things, the way an intellectual should be. Max Eastman was quite different: he was a poet, he wrote on the theory of laughter (not that his achievement there was so great), he was a man of wit and cultivation, a talented and skillful writer. Farrell was essentially a Chicago provincial. Saul Bellow started out that way but became cosmopolitan and would not let himself be limited. Farrell was not at all wide-ranging. However, Farrell was definitely ideologically a Trotskyist and lasted much longer than the others.

Jim was a voluminous letter writer, as Fred and others have commented. His letters would never be less than three pages. But in my opinion this reflected the fact that he just didn't know how to write. It took him three times as much space as it should have to communicate anything. Even at the end of the 1930s, with several novels under his belt, Farrell never knew anything about writing. His sentences wandered around.

My opinion is that Farrell's books don't even read any more. Recently I tried to use *Judgment Day* in a course and I found it to be as out-of-date as Dos Passos's *USA*. I don't think the *Studs Lonigan* books will ever be revived. Farrell's work just lacks intensity and complexity. It's superficial.

The attitude that *Partisan Review* took toward Farrell's column was representative of our feelings about and our relations with him. Farrell was a quite prominent figure in those days, and we didn't have too many famous persons writing for us at that time. The column in *Partisan Review* was Farrell's idea. And we couldn't see any way of getting out of it. Frankly, we all thought his column was flat and banal. But we felt a moral sense about retaining it and we didn't want to hurt Farrell. Finally we invented an excuse to get rid of it.

I also believe that after the split in the American Trotskyist movement between Cannon and Shachtman, Farrell was exploited by the Cannonites. The two issues in the political split centered around the question of whether the Soviet Union remained a workers' state, and also the issue of internal party democracy. Farrell tended to go along with the Cannon group. And during the 1940s he was simply used by them.

Farrell wasn't really a deep-thinking intellectual who saw all the issues; and also, he may have genuinely believed that the theory of bureaucratic collectivism was a basic challenge to Marxism. Burnham had sold that bureaucratic collectivist idea to Shachtman, who embraced it, although a bit nervously.

When *Partisan Review* got rid of Farrell's column, it was an example of our acting on principle. But the Cannonites just used Farrell. And then they dumped him the minute he raised an objection to their morals and maneuvers.

V. Politics

Probably the most important thing about *Politics* was its opposition to World War II; and opposition to the war was also important in my friendship with C. Wright Mills. After Pearl Harbor most of my former friends—and especially Phillips and Rahv—became critical supporters of the war. I was attracted to the old-fashioned Luxemburg-Lenin opposition to both sides.

Nancy Macdonald started the Packages for Europe campaign. She was very efficient, energetic, and an activist. Packages for Europe was an attempt to forge links with the independent anti-Stalinist radical left in Europe. Out of this grew Spanish Refugees Aid, which Nancy started. We sent packages to anti-Stalinist radicals.

Interview with Dwight Macdonald

Paul Avrich / 1974

> From notes of interview conducted by Paul
> Avrich, New York City, 22 March 1974.
> Printed by permission of Paul Avrich.

Holley Cantine, Jr., was a haunter of our offices at *Politics*, a Dostoevskian character with long hair and beard. He would sit there for hours and say nothing. Nancy got awfully upset. A sort of catatonic. He actually had more than that to him. He later wrote a very interesting scientific spoof of Indians taking over America. He printed it himself. It was a kind of futuristic fantasy, ironical and quite good. He used to set type for *Retort* himself, by hand, so he couldn't go for too much bullshit; that kind of cut down on the rhetoric.

Robert Bek-Gran was a familiar character. Nancy and I knew him when he lived on 10th Street. He lived across the street from us. A fascinating fellow, always reading with a quip. He seemed an authoritarian personality, though maybe an anarchist in the intellectual sense. He was open to ideas. Yet his manner was often extremely abrupt and sharp. He would put down fools and sometimes not fools. He was not a bad painter, either.

Peacemakers was an offshoot of the War Resisters League. I broke with them and with pacifism right after the Berlin airlift. I didn't want Britain and France to withdraw from Berlin and see the Russians take over. That was the period between 1948 and 1960, when everyone was worried by the prospect of nuclear annihilation. Now it seems to me that conventional war, like the Vietnam War, is utterly wrong. I can't imagine any war that we would be involved in that I would be in favor of, except perhaps a war to prevent Israel from being annihilated.

Paul Goodman? I never knew him very well. In fact, I would say that nobody knew him well. He was a poor writer but had many valuable ideas, which were often aborted because he didn't write well. He told me he doesn't revise. He writes it all out in first draft. But a craftsman must rewrite. He couldn't have close relations with his intellectual equals. He saw himself as a messiah, a guru, which he was! He functioned personally with younger people who were his admirers, disciples, or potential disciples. I used to meet him every year at his brother Percival's place. He would say "Hello, Dwight," but always looking off to the side or down. He just wasn't there. He had no interest in talking to me at all. He evaporated! It was a credit to him, a sign of his genius, that he could make such an impact without taking pains with his writing.

Abbie Hoffman is an anarchist. [Jerry] Rubin is a dope and a sidekick. Abbie opposes respect for institutions and paying homage to leadership at the top. Who is that Veysey who wrote on communes? I looked at his picture and didn't recognize it. If I ever met him it was very briefly and in a group. Yet he wanted to put me down. In that footnote he says I never heard of Voltairine de Cleyre. An obscure figure. Yet in fact her name does ring a bell, if vaguely. His book isn't very good, rather disjointed. The Stelton chapter is best and much of the rest is boring.

I am not an anarchist in the way that Kropotkin was, but I am in the sense that I believe in the decentralization of authority and the ability of people to decide their own destinies. If politics begins at the bottom, people can decide much better for themselves than well-intentioned liberal bureaucrats or badly-intentioned Nixonian bureaucrats. I believe in local groups and individuals deciding their own affairs. I see, though, that there are dangers to anarchism, if you think of it as just busting up things. I was appalled by the view of some student rebels that libraries were not sacred and that they could fuck up the file cards.

Interviewing Dwight Macdonald

Diana Trilling / 1979

> Excerpted from two interviews done in the spring of 1979 on a grant from the National Endowment for the Humanities as part of a series on the advanced literary, intellectual culture of New York. A shorter version of this interview appeared as "An Interview with Dwight Macdonald" in *Partisan Review* 51.4 (1984), 799–819. Published and reprinted by permission of *Partisan Review* and the Yale University Library.

TRILLING: *Will you tell us a little about your background, Dwight: where you were born, what your parents did, where you went to school, the jobs you have held.*

MACDONALD: Well, I was born on March 24th in 1906 in New York City, and I've always lived there. My father was a lawyer. My mother was from a rather rich family and there was great objection on her family's part to her marrying my father—he went to Exeter and Yale, but he was penniless. At that time, he ran a tutoring school and was getting his law degree. But she did marry him, and in general it was an extremely happy marriage. I was very fond of my father, but I didn't take to my mother so much. She was very fond of *me*. I was never disciplined because I was a very good boy. I was fond of my father because he was interested in me. In fact, he should have been the woman and she should have been the man because he wasn't a very successful lawyer and left nothing at his death, and she had all the qualities that a businesswoman should have. That's one of the reasons I liked my father better.

TRILLING: *You went to Exeter?*

MACDONALD: First to Barnard School, a private school at 122nd Street. Then to Exeter for four years; Yale for my B.A. I didn't like Yale at all but Exeter was a great place in those days. I got a very good education, especially in Greek and English. At Yale I just felt I was churning water. Even though I was the editor, you know, of everything: the head of the *Yale Record*, managing editor of the *Lit*, a columnist on the Yale *News*.

TRILLING: *Was Fred Dupee at Yale with you?*
MACDONALD: Yes, he was.

TRILLING: *Were you friends?*
MACDONALD: Very close friends the last two years he was there. He was a couple of years ahead of me. I graduated in 1928.

TRILLING: *And after that?*
MACDONALD: Well, first I was on *Fortune* magazine, working for Henry Luce from 1929 through 1936. Then I resigned because I felt I'd gotten enough out of it. Which I had—I should have resigned a couple of years earlier. I was making ten thousand bucks a year, which was quite a lot for then. My mother thought I was crazy. Then I immediately became involved in trying to write a history of the steel industry in the United States, which I spent at least half a year on; it never came to anything. Then the Moscow Trials came along and I joined the Trotsky Defense Committee. Then I got involved in *Partisan Review*.

TRILLING: *What year was that? 1937?*
MACDONALD: The end of 1937, when Dupee and Morris, both of whom were Yale friends of mine, joined with Rahv and Phillips to take it away from the Communists. It had really been suspended for a year. Rahv and Phillips had a mailing list which, after all, is all that matters in such a magazine. So we stole it from the Communists. Morris financed the magazine. I left in 1943 because I was the only one of the editors who was so against the war.

TRILLING: *And you went on to found* Politics *in '44? And you stayed with that until 1949?*
MACDONALD: Yes. That was a one-man thing.

TRILLING: *Then what?*
MACDONALD: I became a staff writer for the *New Yorker*, although in the first issue of *Partisan Review* I had an article satirizing and analyzing the first articles

in the *New Yorker*, called "Laugh and Lie Down." Precisely for that reason, I discovered later, Shawn was delighted to offer me a job as staff writer. My period of real productivity there was from '50 to '60. I wrote an awful lot of stuff. I wanted to be the movie critic but for some reason they wouldn't let me do it. So I became the movie critic at *Esquire*.

TRILLING: *What year was that?*
MACDONALD: '60 to '66. Then I did the political column: that lasted about a year and a half. After that, since I couldn't write—

TRILLING: *You had a writing block for a while?*
MACDONALD: I had a writing block then and turned to teaching. I did a great deal of teaching: Buffalo, Texas, California, Santa Cruz, and New York.

TRILLING: *Did you teach English literature or literature and politics?*
MACDONALD: I had three courses that I managed well. I taught a sort of general course in Masterpieces of the Film. And I invented two courses: one was called American Political Novels, from Hawthorne to Mailer; the other was a course in Edgar Allan Poe. He's always been my favorite American writer. I think he's much underestimated.

TRILLING: *Now I'm at once led to a big question: looking back over your career, Dwight, and asked to characterize your professional life, would you think of yourself as primarily a political person, or someone commenting on society and culture, or a literary person?*
MACDONALD: Actually, I would consider myself all three, at different times. For instance, when I was at Yale, I had absolutely no interest in politics at all. I considered myself a literary person; a literary critic, by the way. I wrote a few poems and stories for the *Lit* but that's something that everybody else did. But I had no illusions; I had no interest in anything except criticism. The job on *Fortune* taught me a great deal about journalism: how to organize and research. I was still not at all interested in politics then. My political period began with the Moscow trials.

TRILLING: *The Depression didn't hit you?*
MACDONALD: Well, you know, *Fortune* radicalized me, so to speak. I saw what idiots and coarse and stupid people these big captains of industry were and how scared they were and how Roosevelt had saved their bacon and yet they were always grumbling about him. They were inferior people. I saw that, and

so I turned naturally to the only party I'd heard of—I hadn't heard of anarchism and Trotskyism in those days—and I became a mild fellow-traveller.

TRILLING: *You're talking about the early or mid-thirties?*
MACDONALD: The mid-thirties: about 1932 to 1936.

TRILLING: *Let me stop you for a moment with a question. Or perhaps it's a remark of mine to which we'll want to return. If I look back on your career, I'm struck by the contradiction—this is of course in my subjective view of you—between your work as a literary critic or journalist—*
MACDONALD: Yes, I always thought of myself as what Edmund Wilson called himself, a literary journalist.

TRILLING: *—and your work, or perhaps only your positions, as a political writer and thinker. In literary criticism I was almost always wholly in accord with you, but as political writers, while we shared some general grounds of agreement, we have almost always been battling each other throughout our acquaintance. I don't mean that these were major battles in your life or even in mine, but whenever we came up against each other it was in controversy. I think of you as having had the best literary judgment of any of the people around* Partisan Review. *But perhaps I'm prejudiced because you were the one who recognized that Lionel's "Of This Time, Of That Place" was a very fine story. The others didn't think it was so wonderful.*
MACDONALD: They didn't? I've re-read that story about six times. I think it's a little masterpiece.

TRILLING: *So do I, but you were the one who saw that, the others didn't.*
MACDONALD: I must say, I also saw the quality in James Agee's *Let Us Now Praise Famous Men* at a time when it got about two good reviews.

TRILLING: *Lionel's and yours. Or in later years I remember how right you were about the new dictionary. Or Eugene O'Neill's* Long Day's Journey into Night.
MACDONALD: Did we agree on that?

TRILLING: *Did we not! We'd neither of us ever thought much of O'Neill, but here suddenly he'd produced the best play ever written by an American.*
MACDONALD: I still think that's true.

TRILLING: *It's always seemed to me that you were best in your literary journalism: your wonderful incisive style, so swift and precise, in addition to your sound judgment. Yet this same intelligence, when it operated in the field of politics, raised large questions in my mind.*

MACDONALD: I don't know. If you read my first book, Politics Past—

TRILLING: That's one of the things I'm talking about. I wrote about it in the New Leader: "Dwight Macdonald's Reminiscences of Radical Politics before the War." That was in April of 1957. In the March issue of Encounter you'd run the first installment of a two-part memoir of your experience of radical politics in the thirties and forties. You called it "Reminiscence of Politics Past" and gave it the rather arch subtitle, "A Backward Glance at Roads Once Travelled More Than Now." I remarked that archness was not what I expected of Dwight Macdonald. I also didn't expect this kind of frivolousness about his past from a serious man.

MACDONALD: I remember that review. If I might say so, I thought it showed a certain lack of humor on your part.

TRILLING: A certain lack of humor, indeed.

MACDONALD: I mean, I think you failed to understand that it's possible to be very frivolous and humorous about my political past and yet be quite serious. I was making fun of myself all the way through because, you know—it was called Memoirs of a Revolutionist, the book was—and I was constantly making fun of the pretenses of these little groups, including the Trotskyists. Yet I had been part of it. But that didn't mean I didn't learn a lot and that I wasn't perfectly serious.

TRILLING: Well, it was followed by a long letter from you and then a rebuttal by me. I said you seemed embarrassed by your recollection of yourself as a Marxist and could treat that period of your life only with irony or humor. It was to that view of your past that I addressed myself in accusing you of frivolity.

MACDONALD: But I wasn't embarrassed at all. On the contrary, I learned a great deal in those years as a Trotskyist. That was my second big intellectual weapon. The first was Exeter and the other school was the Marxist school, and I wasn't at all embarrassed about it. Why should I be embarrassed?

TRILLING: You yourself said I should go on and read the second part of your memoir, that that was when life became serious.

MACDONALD: Oh, you mean when I founded Politics.

TRILLING: You said that it wasn't until the forties that politics actually became serious—that's the chief point I want to raise here. We all did many things in the radical movement that were hilariously funny when we look back on them. In its way, the whole movement was crazy. But it was a very serious time, the period of the Depression. And we came to our Marxism in the Depression.

MACDONALD: It wasn't the Depression.

TRILLING: *I'm talking aboaut the thirties.*

MACDONALD: But I wasn't at all involved until 1936. I had no interest in politics at all when I was on *Fortune* from '29 to '36. I said I became *radicalized*—

TRILLING: *Isn't that what we're talking about?*

MACDONALD: Well yes, I suppose I did become a *mild* fellow traveler. But it didn't amount to anything. In fact, I remember, they [the Communists] tried to recruit me and they let me into a branch meeting, which was a big honor in a very secret time, and when I left I said to myself, my God, these people, they're just simply wobbits. They don't have any brains, and they're scared to death of each other and they have no sense of humor, no *life!* How could anybody live in this airless atmosphere? Of course, I had no intention of joining them. What I did was the usual kind of liberal things like—they gave a pay party for Angelo Herndon and for the silicosis business—you know, that kind of stuff. Which you can hardly call political, really.

TRILLING: *The fact is, though, that it was in that period in the thirties that you got your grounding in Marxism, wasn't it?*

MACDONALD: No, not until '37.

TRILLING: *You mean that you sprang full-blown into the Trotskyite movement?*

MACDONALD: Yes. I first read Marx on a summer vacation abroad in 1935. I never even had read Marx before, or Trotsky, or heard of them. Well, I'd heard of them, of course. But I remember distinctly first reading Marx and thinking that it was quite boring. Not my style at all.

TRILLING: *In the mid-thirties?*

MACDONALD: Yes, just about a year before I left *Fortune*. When I left *Fortune*, I left because I simply had learned enough of my trade. It was the Moscow trials that awakened the old moralist in me. My attitude, by the way, towards politics has always been extremely moralistic. I'm a very moralistic guy. So I was appalled by what I soon learned about Trotsky and the Moscow trials. Now, that was in—the first trial was in '36, wasn't it?

TRILLING: *So as soon as you were really learning about the Soviet Union, you were learning it in the spirit of dissent from it?*

MACDONALD: Yes, sure.

TRILLING: *Well, okay. It was of course not the common experience. The common experience was that one became a fellow traveler, one went along with it, and then became disillusioned.*
MACDONALD: Well, you can read an article I wrote about the Communist Party in *Fortune* around 1934—I think it was—with illustrations by Walker Evans. We went up to camp—it was a camp for the families of Communists. Don't-give-a-care Camp.

TRILLING: *It was called Camp* Nicht gedaiget. *Camp Not-to-Worry. (Laughter).*
MACDONALD: Anyway, Walker Evans took the photographs with a marvelous camera he had in which he had a little lens on the side and a fake lens in front.

TRILLING: *He could take pictures of people without looking at them. He was always doing that in subways too.*
MACDONALD: Well anyway, this article on the Communist Party and the faction parties: the Trotskyists and the Gitlowites and the Weisbordites. Some of those. And my attitude towards all of them was certainly not respectful. I mean, it's not Communist-baiting—I wasn't even interested enough to be against it. If anything, I suppose I thought, well, they must have something if they have all that country and so on. Well, read it. It certainly wasn't enthusiastic, it was ironical. And that was '34. And one more thing about Marxism. I first read Marx, as I said, in '35 and didn't like him at all, but respected him and still do as a great thinker. The second time I read Marx was when I was trying to decide whether to join the Trotskyist party in the fall of 1939. I spent the whole summer reading Marx and Engels, and finally I decided that I *really*, on the whole, was not a Marxist. I didn't like their rather arrogant, know-it-all tone. I hated the whole scientific pretensions of the thing. I recognized Marx's genius when he was being polemical and when he was writing *The 18th Brumaire* and the first volume of *Capital* and so on. But I wasn't a Marxist, on the whole. It didn't appeal to me. One more thing. I joined the Party, typically, characteristically, after the pact and when war had broken out. The British had declared war.

TRILLING: *And then you joined the Communist party?*
MACDONALD: The *Trotskyist* Party. I joined the Party for purely moral reasons. This is typical of me. Because I said, if I really do have this view of the world,

which I do, my place is there, too. You know, I have to suffer with them. Of course, I didn't suffer anything.

TRILLING: *But didn't Trotsky follow the Soviet line about war? If the Soviet Union was involved in a war, then one had to be on the side of the Soviet Union.*
MACDONALD: Right. I joined the Trotskyist Party just when this split was beginning. I knew that and so did Jim Cannon, the leader. Cannon slyly tried very hard to persuade me not to become a member. He said, oh, Dwight, you wouldn't be happy all tied up with us, and second and more important, you'd be much more valuable to us if you weren't a Party member. But I saw, of course, what he was getting at. He knew perfectly well that I would immediately join the Burnham-Schactman faction, and a faction fight did break out over exactly that point, the invasion of Finland. And of course I was on the side against Trotsky. It was about Finland. Trotsky said it was a revolutionary army that was invading Finland and we said, it's not a revolutionary army that invaded a country; it's an imperialist army invading a country and even the cats and dogs don't stay to be liberated. Oh, it drove Trotsky wild.

TRILLING: *What was the year of the Trotsky Defense Committee and the Mexican hearings?*
MACDONALD: That was '37, wasn't it?

TRILLING: *It was before the split in the Trotskyists. You went down to Mexico, didn't you?*
MACDONALD: No, I didn't go down. As usual; I never do anything. I miss everything.

TRILLING: *But you were a member of the Trotsky Defense Committee.*
MACDONALD: Oh, sure, I joined the Committee.

TRILLING: *When did you first meet Trotsky?*
MACDONALD: I never met him. I always miss everything.

TRILLING: *I hope you won't mind a question I want to ask you, Dwight. You came very substantially from the middle class—*
MACDONALD: My mother was upper middle. My father, too.

TRILLING: *By birth you were firmly fixed in the middle or upper-middle class. And as far back as what—Exeter? Yale?—you began to feel some kind of separation from the class in which you were bred—*

MACDONALD: No, not with the class. Just as an intellectual. But that's natural, of course.

TRILLING: *Was this a separation from the bourgeois ethic?*
MACDONALD: No, not at all. If anything, I daresay I was rather a priggish conservative. Certainly at Exeter and Yale, I despised my classmates. I felt a distance from them.

TRILLING: *You felt they were stupid?*
MACDONALD: Not stupid but they were just ordinary guys and I was quite a bright fellow. I just had the biggest contempt for them.

TRILLING: *You looked down on people with less intellectual gifts than yourself. That's of course a natural feeling.*
MACDONALD: Yes, but it's sort of priggish.

TRILLING: *You still didn't make any separation from your bourgeois background?*
MACDONALD: No.

TRILLING: *And certainly when you went to* Fortune *you couldn't have had a very active principle of opposition to the bourgeois world or you wouldn't have been able to take that job?*
MACDONALD: Well, first of all, this wouldn't be possible. I got the job in 1929, at the depth of the Depression. I would have taken any job. I had no money and I had to support my mother.

TRILLING: *Well, at what point did you become conscious of the middle-class world not representing your moral position in society?*
MACDONALD: I told you, when I met all those big captains of industry. I did all of those industry stories: U.S. Steel and Republic Steel and the great A & P. All that stuff.

TRILLING: *What I'm trying to find out is, were you always a rebel or did you become—*
MACDONALD: Yes, I was always a rebel.

TRILLING: *How did it show itself before?*
MACDONALD: It showed itself—Okay. At Exeter Academy it showed itself by the fact that we founded a club of three members called The Hedonists and we used to go out walking with canes and we wore batik neckties.

TRILLING: *You were aesthetic rebels—*
MACDONALD: Well, you didn't go out with canes and so on. And it was called the Genius Club, of course, by the hoi polloi. Well, that was at Exeter. And at Yale, my God, the silly things I did to show I was a rebel. There was a tradition you had to wear hats on the campus until you got to be a senior. I mean, outdoors. So I actually spent a lot of time, and got Morris roped into it, trudging up and down all these hallways and dormitories hoping to get signatures from something like two-thirds of our class, saying that they'd take their hats off on a given day. But we just didn't get two-thirds so nothing happened. Also I got in trouble over a parody issue of *Film Fun*. Remember that magazine? We had a lot of postcards of ancient statues and Renaissance paintings of the Loves of Jove and stuff like that. You know, nudes. Art work. It was a parody issue of *Film Fun*. I was the editor of the *Record* then and I almost got fired for that. But I really finally got fired when I wrote an editorial calling on William Lyon Phelps not to teach Shakespeare on the grounds that if he really thought it over, he wasn't competent to do it. I was very reasonable about it. I said, you know, you really just don't show much competence. He was the god of all these athletes and so on. The Dean called me in and said, "Did you write this?" I said, "You certainly aren't going to supress that, are you? It's free speech," and so on and he said, "Of course I'm not going to suppress it but if you print it, you leave Yale."

TRILLING: *What happened?*
MACDONALD: You know what happened.

TRILLING: *You graduated.*
MACDONALD: As usual I made the compromise sensible decision.

TRILLING: *Do you feel that your life has been a series of compromises, Dwight?*
MACDONALD: Everybody thinks I'm a wild man, but I'm always in the middle.

TRILLING: *That's the way you see it?*
MACDONALD: That's the way I see myself.

TRILLING: *No doubt that's the most valuable thing you'll say in this whole interview. You don't see yourself as being absolutely, finally, the sturdiest, most principled, unimpeachable character going?*
MACDONALD: No. This was a compromise, a practical one. But I'm not of the

stuff of martyrs. It would never have occurred to *me* to go to Spain in 1939, the way it occurred to Orwell and all those others. It's true, I had a wife and dependents. No, but what I mean is that I always find myself—I'm absolutely squarely in the middle. The Arab-Israeli issue, for instance. My one son is a violent Zionist, the other son is a violent Arabist. But I'm always in this middle position, it seems to me.

TRILLING: *When you say you're in the middle on the Israel issue, I suppose what you mean is—*
MACDONALD: It should have been a biracial state. And also they should have let back the refugees. They shouldn't have stolen their vineyards and so on. I was called an anti-Semite by my old pals William Phillips and Clement Greenberg and Philip Rahv and so on, because I said, "Why the hell don't you Jews do something about this? You shouldn't give all your money to Jewish relief. Give some to these Arabs."

TRILLING: *One can take that position, can't one, and still be opposed to the violence and terrorism of the PLO?*
MACDONALD: Good God, I'm opposed to violence and terrorism on any front.

TRILLING: *You say you became a Trotskyite after the war began. You had stayed on at Partisan Review for another few years after the beginning of the war. What in general was the attitude toward the war of the New York advanced literary intellectuals? So far as I can remember, Philip Rahv, for example, wasn't opposed to the war on principle at all.*
MACDONALD: He was in the beginning.

TRILLING: *He didn't want to be in it, that I recall. He asked Lionel to write a letter saying he was neurotic.*
MACDONALD: You're talking about actually serving? Oh, yes, Rahv was up to everything to get out of it.

TRILLING: *But what was his principle about it? You must remember this better than I do.*
MACDONALD: Yes, I knew him very well. Rahv and Phillips had exactly the same position that I had. It was the official position of the magazine, which was that it was an imperialist war, et cetera. But it changed the day of Pearl Harbor when the United States got into it.

TRILLING: *As soon as the United States was involved they were in favor of it?*
MACDONALD: Sure.

TRILLING: *And what about somebody like Will Barrett? What was his position?*
MACDONALD: Barrett is such a *schnook*. I have no idea.

TRILLING: *Delmore Schwartz?*
MACDONALD: Delmore had no position.

TRILLING: *He had no position about things?*
MACDONALD: No, none whatsoever.

TRILLING: *What about Clem Greenberg?*
MACDONALD: Well, Greenberg and I wrote that ridiculous ten propositions on the war, don't you remember? And Rahv came back with ten propositions and eight errors.

TRILLING: *Look, this tape recorder has no memory. Would you mind telling it about these propositions and errors?*
MACDONALD: Oh, I'm sorry. Well, Greenberg and I—I got Greenberg on the magazine. In fact, I invented Clem Greenberg.

TRILLING: *That in itself is interesting: let's take a diversionary route and go to Clem Greenberg and how you invented him, and then come back to the war.*
MACDONALD: I'm in the position of Frankenstein, you know, because I have no regard for Greenberg at all. I invented him as follows. He was a clerk in the Customs House in New York City and apparently had no contact with literary circles and I wrote an article in *Partisan Review*, a three-part series on the Soviet cinema. In the last part I made the daring speculation that the Soviet cinema was very popular with the peasants of Russia. I don't know where I ever got such a wierd idea; maybe because they showed their movies all over the place. The reason was because either an extremely sophisticated person can appreciate Eisenstein's movies or an extremely naive person, since he has no preconceptions about *kitsch* in his mind. And then I said, look at what wonderful things the Africans do. Well, Greenberg wrote an absolutely brilliant letter to the editor refuting this whole position, called "Avant Garde and Kitsch".

TRILLING: *His most famous piece.*
MACDONALD: But it began as a letter to the editor and he was absolutely right. He pointed out that the first thing that these marvelous native tribesmen in Africa and Australia, who do such wonderful abstract work, demand of the

explorer is not the works of Picasso but picture postcards and things like that, gaudy, horrible Manchester prints with illustrations on them. So I said, listen, you're right, this is too good for a letter to the editor. I suggest you expand this into an article. Which he did and we published it and that's how it all began. It was immediately recognized as an extremely important article and has been reprinted in anthologies. I still think it's much the best thing he ever did. Now, as for his suddenly bursting into *The Nation* as its art critic. You know, Clem has many of the aspects of the old-fashioned con man. I never knew that he knew anything about art and I'm not so sure that he did know anything about art. But he had something that was very important: a moralistic approach to everything. He made people feel guilty if they didn't like Jackson Pollock, that's what it amounts to. And that's very powerful medicine, you know, with all this worried, jumped-in, wartime-educated public.

TRILLING: *In other words, in the forties, when he was art critic for* The Nation, *you were finding his work spurious?*
MACDONALD: Oh, I thought he was a great boy. I mean, I personally didn't like Jackson Pollock, I didn't like the whole abstract movement. I can see something in it now that I didn't then so I guess he was right in that sense. But the way he made you feel guilty! With all his right-thinking people and everything's so obvious. And so on and so on.

TRILLING: *Yes, but you said that you yourself always had a moral base for all your thinking. Wasn't this a moral base that Clem took?*
MACDONALD: No, of course not. He uses morality as a way to make people feel guilty. I don't want to make people feel guilty. I'm serious. (Laughter) I'm moral.

TRILLING: *Let's just go on free-associating, Dwight. How about your feelings about the other editors you worked with after 1937? Between 1937 and 1943, you got to know William Phillips and Philip Rahv. And there was George Morris. What about them? You understand, of course, that anything you want to put under closure, you can.*
MACDONALD: Rahv is dead and anyway—Well, what I'll talk about briefly is, first of all, that magazine in that period was entirely dominated by me and Rahv. We were the two strong people. Morris really didn't care about anything except abstract art. He had no interest in politics and no interest in most of what was published. He just went along.

TRILLING: *And he gave money? He supported it?*
MACDONALD: He met the entire deficit until '43, yes. And actually, Fred Dupee wasn't on the magazine so very long. A couple of years.

TRILLING: *Fred came later than the rest of you, didn't he?*
MACDONALD: No, he didn't. He was the link between Rahv and Phillips and me and Morris. He was a member of the Communist Party, as you know, after a while, and he therefore knew Rahv and Phillips. Fred was my best friend, of course, practically all of our lives. We had terrible rows and long periods, sometimes lasting years, in which we practically didn't speak to each other. Yet even then we had some sort of communication. The rows were really temperamental. It's hard to explain really. I'm not sure what it was but I thought he was too prissy, not tough enough. A little sort of pompous sometime. And I'm sure he thought I was a bully and crude. And I guess I was. But anyway, we always came back together.

TRILLING: *He was a very lovable person. And always appropriate to himself. He never violated his own style.*
MACDONALD: No. He was completely honest and also extremely intelligent. One of the few people I've known in my life that I really considered absolutely my—I could talk to him about anything and he would get it, you know. I remember one of the spells when he was down in Mexico and we'd sworn that we'd never see each other again for life. Eisenstein was making *Que Viva Mexico*, this must have been sometime around 1930. I was writing an article on Eisenstein and I must have asked Fred for information, and he came through with a long, long report.

TRILLING: *I remember when I was about to make my first speech in public and I told Fred how nervous I was. He asked me if I had my speech written, and when I said I had, he told me to come and read it to him aloud. That was in this very apartment: the Dupees lived here before we did. He rehearsed me for more than an hour, made me stand up straight, speak slowly.*
MACDONALD: Did it help?

TRILLING: *A great deal. And it was such a nice thing to do.*
MACDONALD: He was a sweetie. Anyway, my impression is that for some reason or other he wasn't on [*Partisan Review*] terribly long. When he was on, he

was always the swing man, so to speak. Phillips was just a shadow of Rahv. And Morris, out of indifference and affection, generally sided with me.

TRILLING: *As the years went on, the magazine became just Rahv and Phillips and a rather fierce tug of war developed between them.*
MACDONALD: Oh boy, I'll say. I made a good crack about that period when they were together on *Partisan Review* and yet fighting like hell. I said, they're staying together for the sake of the child, which was actually true. Rahv was a big bear, you know, and a pretty brutal guy in many ways. For some reason or other, women loved him. My wife thought he was adorable. He was quite a womanizer but also very avuncular with women. But boy, with his equals and with men, he could be pretty damn tough. And he had a power complex, too. He thought power was a big thing. He was very paranoiac, very suspicious, as power people are. Boy, we had some terrible fights, he and I, about how to run the magazine because I thought he was very cowardly. They didn't want to print André Gide's *Return from the USSR* because they didn't want to go that far in criticizing the—they thought it was a reactionary article. With the help of Fred and Morris, I prevailed.

TRILLING: *What about Mary McCarthy? At what point did she come into the picture?*
MACDONALD: Mary came in pretty much at the beginning, I think. She used to do drama for us.

TRILLING: *She did her first big piece elsewhere, as I recall, with Margaret Marshall in* The Nation. *A five-part piece on the critics. It was Peggy Marshall's idea, I was told, but Mary's energy got it done. Peggy Marshall had a great deal of difficulty getting things done. That was in 1935 and Mary's initiation as a figure in the literary community. She must have begun to write for* Partisan Review *not long after that.*
MACDONALD: Yes. She wrote those stories.

TRILLING: "*The Man in the Brooks Brothers Shirt*" *and all those things. They were later published in book form, like a novel.*
MACDONALD: *The Company She Keeps.* I guess they weren't all published in the magazine. She wasn't on the magazine very long for the simple reason that she ran off with Edmund Wilson.

TRILLING: *What year was that?*
MACDONALD: It was quite soon. She and Rahv were living together in a little

love nest, right around the corner from where Nancy and I were living on the East Side, and we used to visit back and forth. And one day Rahv came home whistling merrily and there was a note on the bureau saying that she was utterly ashamed, but she was in Greenwich with Edmund Wilson and they were going to get married. Well, it was a crushing blow to Rahv—

TRILLING: *Before that, had Mary and Rahv been living together for some time?*
MACDONALD: It wasn't some time. Six months or so.

TRILLING: *That's some time.*
MACDONALD: I remember Rahv saying, my God, why did I ever introduce her to that guy? Of course Wilson was a very eminent guy, and so on. And she didn't find him unattractive sexually. Apparently he was not, oddly enough. Also I think she might have had an instinct that she needed him as a kind of, you know, a guide.

TRILLING: *She was doing a Colette to his Willy? At least as a writer of novels?*
MACDONALD: Yes. Right, yes. Nancy and I wouldn't even see Mary for a while.

TRILLING: *You were so indignant about her having walked out that way on Rahv?*
MACDONALD: We were shocked, yes. Then we finally went to visit them; they were living with Margaret de Silver then in Stamford and I remember that visit because it was exactly as though Mary was the third visitor. It was the most peculiar thing, you know. I mean, that was his house and Edmund treated her exactly the way he treated us—there was no sense of any equality or anything going on between them as man and wife at all. Well, she's really in a sense my oldest surviving friend. I knew her right after she got out of Vassar. I knew her when I was on *Fortune*. We were good friends.

TRILLING: *Tell me about the other people you knew around* Partisan Review. *Isaac Rosenfeld?*
MACDONALD: He wasn't on it. But yes, I knew him.

TRILLING: *I consider him to have been among the most talented of the writers for the magazine.*
MACDONALD: Yes, he was.

TRILLING: *His* Passage from Home, *or* To Home, *whichever it was, was really one of the most talented first novels of the period. It was a real loss that he lived so short a time after that. He was very crazy and very gifted.*

MACDONALD: Very crazy, yes. The one thing I remember distinctly about him is the phase when he was an orgone box guy.

TRILLING: *Did you ever get into an orgone box?*
MACDONALD: Oh sure. I sat there for an hour and when I came out he said, how do you feel? And I said, just the same, I feel sort of hot. After all, it's hot sitting in a telephone booth. And his face fell and he said, why I thought you looked as if your whole vitality was revived.

TRILLING: *Who else believed in the orgone box? Did Saul Bellow? Wasn't Saul more rationalistic than that?*
MACDONALD: Yes. But there were a lot of Reichians around.

TRILLING: *Mailer? He was interested in Reich, wasn't he?*
MACDONALD: He very well might have been. Of course, Reich was a lot more than the orgone box. He was a brilliant—

TRILLING: *Brilliant and crazy.*
MACDONALD: He wasn't crazy in his earlier books. He became crazy when he got to this country but his analysis of repressed sex and fascism was an extremely interesting book.

TRILLING: *Did you know Saul Bellow?*
MACDONALD: I knew him slightly. We published his first stuff, you know. "The Mexican General," I think, was one of his first published things. Of course, the most outstanding thing about Saul Bellow is his absolute—his sensitivity to criticism. I remember a time at some party; I'd been reading *Augie March* and I made some criticism. I knew he was sensitive so I pretended to like it more than I did. But I said, some of that early stuff on Chicago, it seems to be a little bit heavyhanded in style. Something like that, but *surrounding* it with garlands of praise. He said, well, so that's what you think of me, that's the gratitude I get for publishing in your magazine! I'll bet that even with the Nobel Prize under his belt, he's still the same. There's no way to satisfy him. It's like a man with a thirst that can't ever be quenched. I don't understand it. He became very, very well known, you know. I mean, one of the outstanding young American writers, along with Mailer, and most people thought he was more solid. I guess he is more solid in some ways than Mailer, although not as brilliant. He made more practical use of his talent whereas Mailer had enor-

mous possibilities. I saw him the other night—Mailer, I mean—and for the first time in several years he's become Senatorial. He's got a new wife now and a baby. You know what he does every summer? He's a very original guy. He's bought a farm in Maine on which he lives for one month every year in the summer and he has all of his children, from twenty-three to the baby, come up and spend that month only with him. He does everything. He does all the cooking.

TRILLING: *I thought he did that just as a gimmick for* The Prisoner of Sex.
MACDONALD: No, no. Every year he takes all the children up to Maine and nobody is there but him and them.

TRILLING: *What about Bernard Malamud? Was he somebody you knew then, too?*
MACDONALD: No. He never wrote for *P.R.*, did he?

TRILLING: *He published "The Magic Barrel" in* Partisan Review. *That's a remarkable story.*
MACDONALD: It must have been after I left.

TRILLING: *You say you left because you didn't share their views about the war. America was now in the war and they all became prowar?*
MACDONALD: Just Rahv—

TRILLING: *And you had a Trotskyite antiwar position at that time?*
MACDONALD: Yes.

TRILLING: *What about the beginning of* Politics? *Did you edit that as a Trotskyite?*
MACDONALD: I'd left the Trotskyites by then. I was only in the Party from '39 to '41.

TRILLING: *I was looking at 1944, your first issues of* Politics, *and certainly your politics were Trotskyite.*
MACDONALD: I wouldn't say so. I was completely disillusioned with the Trotskyites. I left them because I discovered that they had absolutely the same internal rigidity that I'd objected to in the Stalinists. And also for a very typical writer's reason and a typical Macdonald reason too: I left them primarily because they would not publish in their press *in toto* a long—God, when I think of my energy!—thirty-thousand word critique of the Nazi economy, trying to show the Burnham thesis, that it was neither capitalism nor socialism.

It was something that Marx had not anticipated, just as Russia is not, but that Burnham called bureaucratic collectivism.

TRILLING: *You had quite a bit in the earliest issues of* Politics *about this new third form of state power which is not socialism but also not democracy.*
MACDONALD: Bureaucratic collectivism. Well, I had a long piece in *Partisan Review* about it which came from that material I did for the Trotskyists. But anyway, the Trotskyists would only publish a quarter of it, and they said it was really so dull and I didn't know my stuff and so on, and I said, "I'm the only professional writer you've ever had, and I couldn't possibly write an article as dull as everybody else on this goddam magazine. And you tell me I don't know my stuff about economics—I spent six years on *Fortune.*" Well anyway, it was just an excuse.

TRILLING: *And that was the break?*
MACDONALD: Yes. You see, that little thing showed something very serious, that they were not willing, as I thought they were, to go all the way in breaking with the Old Man and with Marxism. It showed that Schactman was not willing to carry out the logic of the thing at all: he didn't want to publish an article that repudiated Marxism.

TRILLING: *Did you used to write for the* Militant *in those days?*
MACDONALD: Yes. Sure. I had a column called "Sparks in the News," from *Iskra—The Spark.* That was every week. And I did a monthly column and some more articles in *The New International.* I wrote a great deal for the Trotskyist press. Before I joined them.

TRILLING: *Where did you get the money for* Politics?
MACDONALD: Partly from the remnants of my savings from my *Fortune* job. Partly, perhaps mostly, from a small income, a trust fund, that Nancy had. Of course, in those days, it didn't cost much. Actually, our deficit in some years was under a thousand dollars.

TRILLING: *But you and Nancy did all the work.*
MACDONALD: Yes, of course, and we didn't have any salaries. But we paid—five dollars a page. Not very much. Sure, yes, we did all the work, of course. One of the reasons I gave it up, outside of being tired of it and realizing that no magazine can go on forever—you know, they have lives just like people

do—is that I was just fagged out. Also, I didn't believe in the revolution any more; I knew it wasn't going to happen, after the war.

TRILLING: *Until what point did you really have any confidence that there was going to be a social revolution in this country?*
MACDONALD: No, not in *this* country. I never thought there would be one in this country for the simple reason that it's much too prosperous. We'd won both wars and so forth. But I did think there would be social upheavals abroad. You know, as a result of the war. And I did not foresee that Stalin—that Russia and America, the two great imperialisms, would control the entire postwar world. At that point I decided there was no use in putting out a revolutionary magazine because I'm not a lost-cause guy.

TRILLING: *What did you feel about Yalta?*
MACDONALD: I felt disgusted. When was Yalta?

TRILLING: *While Roosevelt was still alive. February 1945. It gave the Soviet Union all of Middle Europe.*
MACDONALD: Well, of course, that was a sell-out. We just delivered it over—they didn't have to do it, you know. Stalin was leading from weakness. He just bluffed them, that's all. We didn't have to stop at the Elbe and all that kind of stuff, and Berlin didn't have to be divided.

TRILLING: *Yet there was very little objection to Yalta in America. You were very much ostracized, looked down upon, if you were opposed to Yalta.*
MACDONALD: Yes, I know. Because the Russians were our allies and so on. In fact, that whole Soviet myth was revived again in the most peculiar way during the war. Of course, it soon disappeared with the Cold War, but during the war everybody began again to love Stalin.

TRILLING: *Do you really believe that the Soviet Union and America, when they have detente, have something that has significance? Don't you always have it in mind that it's simply a momentary strategy and tomorrow it can change?*
MACDONALD: Well, sure, of course, but I don't think it's a one-sided thing. I don't think it's a plot on the part of the Soviets against this country or vice versa. I think that detente is useful just as I thought it was useful for that bastard Nixon to go to China, and bring it back into the community of nations, recognize the fact that there is such a thing as China. And I'm

delighted by what's happening in China now because, as you know, it's completely counter-revolutionary. I discover, every time I hear the word revolution, that everything revolutionary is lousy.

TRILLING: *Don't you want a revolution?*
MACDONALD: Of course not. I mean, yes, I want a revolution, but an anarchist revolution, which will never happen in this country, but anyway—No, what I mean is, this rift between Mao and Russia took place after Stalin died and Khruschev began to humanize the place a bit. It's a much better place than it was. But the rift began because Mao always thought, quite rightly, that Khruschev was bourgeoisifying the country, and that's, to me, a very good thing. And the present China is a great thing too, because it's counter-revolutionary. It's against Mao.

TRILLING: *But look, in the symposium that was run in* Commentary, *"Liberal Anti-Communist Revisited," in your reply to the question, are you still an anti-Communist, you say, yes, maybe, no. Then you break it down and say what you mean by each of these words. And you say that the reason you say "maybe" is because although the basic forms of the totalitarian state still exist, there's a great deal more freedom than in the worst Stalin days. I find that an invalid argument because when the totalitarian form exists, the practice can be switched from one day to the next.*
MACDONALD: Well, it hasn't been.

TRILLING: *But it could be.*
MACDONALD: Well, so what?

TRILLING: *Isn't it the difference between living within a democratic structure or a non-democratic structure?*
MACDONALD: Well, of course, I'm in favor of having a democratic structure, that's not the point. But you just admitted yourself that it's much more humane in Russia today than it was.

TRILLING: *Dwight, you wrote about the 1949 Waldorf Conference . . .*
MACDONALD: You mean the conference of the Stalinists? I wrote about it in *Politics.*

TRILLING: *Yes, I know that but I want to talk about it more personally. Who was the moving spirit in the plan to break it up? Who got the idea—was it Sidney Hook?*
MACDONALD: No, no, not at all. On the contrary. First of all, it wasn't a plan

to break up the conference. There was one section of the conference that three or four of us, and some others we didn't expect, Mary McCarthy and myself and Cal Lowell, decided to attend—we applied for tickets together. That was the critical section, the only one we were interested in. And then we found out that Jean Malaquais, I think it was, and George Counts were also there to make trouble. Malaquais was a French novelist, a friend of Norman Mailer. Hook, on the other hand, the Hookworm, the Hookites, or whatever you want to call them, did everything possible to discourage us. They said that this was not a good idea at all; we would make fools of ourselves. We would also give the Stalinists a talking point: it was rude to go to their functions and so on. And they, of course, held their own separate thing at Freedom House. But we thought that this was just the thing to do, and that we were not humiliating or insulting Shostakovich, but showing our solidarity with him. The poor guy—you know, he was there and you could see that he was doing his best to be a good boy.

TRILLING: *Shostakovich was the star of that panel?*
MACDONALD: The Russian star, yes. Norman Mailer was the big American star. Of course, the sensational thing that happened was that—We didn't even know this was going to happen. We didn't address any questions to Norman. We'd known him before but we assumed that he still was what he was before. You know, a loyal Wallaceite. But we did ask a lot of questions about what had happened to people like Mandelstam and I forget who.

TRILLING: *Do you mean that in 1949 you were aware of Mandelstam? I was not.*
MACDONALD: Well, maybe it wasn't Mandelstam.

TRILLING: *It would more likely have been the guy who wrote* Red Cavalry: Babel.
MACDONALD: Well, I'm not sure. Anyway, we asked about several such people because that was our aim, to ask embarrassing questions, and we did. And we asked other questions about the way that things were being run, and at one point I remember that the chairman, Louis Untermeyer, made some crack about Hook being a four-letter word, and either I or Mary got up and said, "We object, Mr. Chairman, to such language from the chair. You're not supposed to use such language." But of course the sensation was Mailer's speech. He was the most highly applauded when he got up because he was the darling of the session. But when he sat down there was hardly any applause, and when

he was talking there were audible rustlings of discontent among the mob because that's where he announced that there were two imperialisms, America and Russia. That was the first time anybody heard that. And then we were invited to a party by Howard Fast, given by the Stalinists. And what struck me was that they weren't so different from the Trotskyites and the other radicals I'd known.

TRILLING: *In what sense?*
MACDONALD: It was just that there was a river of blood between us. But otherwise they were just the same type, you know. They were perfectly nice, amiable people and idealistic and so on, but they just happened to be—They didn't behave like totalitarians: that's what I'm getting at. That was true of most Stalinists. These weren't the party leaders, V. J. Jerome and so on. These were the rank and file.

TRILLING: *Were they people like Lillian Hellman?*
MACDONALD: Oh, no, no, no. I know she was there but—

TRILLING: *Garry Wills makes her the heroine of the occasion.*
MACDONALD: I know, but she wasn't in this session at all and I never saw her there. She was in the big public session which we also attended but didn't say anything because we didn't have that much nerve. You know, they had a big dinner and so on, something like that. She wasn't at the critic's session.

TRILLING: *At what session did she make the remark attributed to her by Garry Wills in the introduction to* Scoundrel Time, *that you don't insult your host at the table?*
MACDONALD: That was directed at us, of course.

TRILLING: *But she was referring to what had happened at another session. At which she hadn't been present? I'd never got that straight. I thought you were all in the same room.*
MACDONALD: No, as far as I can remember. I would have remembered her because she's a big shot. No, she wasn't at the critic's session.

TRILLING: *And she wasn't at Howard Fast's party?*
MACDONALD: Not that I remember, no. I just remember talking to the rank and file there. And believe me, Diana, they were not totalitarians. I mean, that is to say, they were and they weren't. You know what I mean. Their philosophy was but they were part of the ordinary—

TRILLING: *Like Howard Fast?*
MACDONALD: Well, Fast was the guy that invited us, of course. Which was all right. He's sort of a muttonheaded guy. Why did he invite us? That was strange too, come to think of it.

TRILLING: *Where did you get the idea that totalitarians weren't human beings?*
MACDONALD: Yes, well, I didn't get that idea. I never had it but—

TRILLING: *Yet you were surprised that these people were human?*
MACDONALD: I was surprised that they were just like the radicals that I'd been associated with.

TRILLING: *Did you expect them to have horns or fangs or something?*
MACDONALD: Yes, something like that, or at least to be antagonistic. Of course, we were very careful to avoid the deadly subject of Stalin.

TRILLING: *I take it, Dwight, that you've just re-read Lillian Hellman's* Scoundrel Time?
MACDONALD: Yes, for a certain purpose I have.

TRILLING: *Would you like to comment on it while you have it freshly in mind?*
MACDONALD: I thought it was an absolutely disgusting book. And as a matter of fact, I've been quite friendly with Lillian for a long time, especially after she signed the protest I got up about Sinyevsky and Daniel in 1969, which I think was a turning point politically for her, because in three distinct places in this book you'll see, if you read it carefully, she's given up on Stalinism. She says in so many words, I was wrong about it. But she then goes on to say that the people who really were wrong and vicious and bad for America were *us*, you know. That's why I think it's a silly book and also a very dishonest book. The reason I think it's a dishonest book primarily is that she gives us this self-dramatizing impression that she was isolated, that the liberals didn't help her, that nobody helped her. The book itself makes clear that this isn't true, that even Arthur Krock wrote her a letter saying, I admire your stand but not your politics, et cetera, et cetera. There are thousands of cases. The head of the Passport Department gives her a visa because she's a New England lady of conscience. I mean, if you read the book you'll see all through it that everybody is on her side. Not politically, but for civil liberties. But she has the gall to say, and the dishonesty to say, that she didn't get any support. What she means is that nobody was on her side as a Stalinist. It's true, by that time the

Stalinists had no currency in this country. And why the hell should we be? She was then still a Stalinist. Hammett of course made no bones about being a Communist. She supported the whole Wallace business, she apologized for the rape of Czechoslovakia, and all that kind of stuff. That's why this book is so really disgusting. I don't understand why she writes this all up now and pretends that she's the Joan of Arc and so on—

TRILLING: *Because a new generation only knows that there was a phenomenon called McCarthyism in this country and that it was dangerous to civil liberties. They take her to be a symbol of the forces that withstood McCarthy and McCarthyism because she tells them she was.*

MACDONALD: Well, that's true to some extent, of course. And it's probably true that she was damaged and harassed. Not by McCarthy, by the HUAC. But it certainly is not true that she didn't get plenty of support.

TRILLING: *She went into the House hearings with a public relations gimmick that had been devised for her by that very clever man, Joe Rauh.*

MACDONALD: It's called the diminished fifth, yes, in which you tell all about yourself but you don't say anything about your friends. You don't give any names.

TRILLING: *I'm talking about the statement she made. But then she went on to take the Fifth Amendment like everybody else. That's in her book, of course, too, but most readers skip right over it and don't believe it if you tell it to them.*

MACDONALD: It's a very disgusting book, I think. I don't understand at this late date why she has to try to pretend these kinds of things.

TRILLING: *It works, doesn't it? She's put it over and become the culture heroine of our generation.*

MACDONALD: I know. When she was given an ovation at the Oscar Awards—I don't know if you saw that television thing—she got up there and, my God, all these people who had been blacklisting Commies like mad—she was a scapegoat for their guilt, you see. By applauding her, all these big executives who had been doing the worst thing possible to Commies all the way, blacklist and so on, were getting off the hook.

TRILLING: *What about Hannah Arendt: you haven't spoken about her yet. Did you know her well?*

MACDONALD: I can't remember when I first met her. I know I published in my magazine, *Politics*, before *The Origins of Totalitarianism* came out, a couple of things about the behavior of the guards in the death camps and so on, which I thought was very significant. In my *Responsibility of Peoples* in 1945, I remember that's when I was first aware of Hannah. And then I reviewed *The Origins* at great length for *The New Leader*. I guess that at that time I must have met her. We soon became very, very fast friends. In fact, she was one of my real—I mean, best friends. I certainly had more pleasure with her. I used to go to dinner there, drinks and so on. And her husband, who was an anarchist like me, Heinrich Blücher, I liked him very, very much too. I think he had a very good effect on Hannah, by the way. I think Hannah's one trouble was that she had this Germanic, scholastic training: people like Jaspers. Her great fault, I think, was that she tended too often, as she did in some of her later books, to become extremely Germanic. Extremely vague, extremely abstract, and *general*. And I thought the great thing about that first book of hers was that it was extremely complete. You know, it was historical, not philosophical. And I think that Heinrich's pressure was always in that direction. Well naturally, since an anarchist's view of things would be exactly the opposite of the Hegelian, German, Jaspers kind of view. She was my literary executor until her death.

TRILLING: *And you were a great admirer of* The Origins of Totalitarianism.
MACDONALD: A great admirer also of *Eichmann in Jerusalem*.

TRILLING: *I wanted to come to that—*
MACDONALD: That's all in the record. What's the use of going over it? I wrote an article about *Eichmann in Jerusalem* in *Partisan Review*. Wasn't it in *Partisan Review*? Yes, it was in *Partisan Review*. People can read, can't they?

TRILLING: *I thought Lionel Abel wrote the review in* Partisan Review.
MACDONALD: Yes, right. He published a very vicious attack.

TRILLING: *And then William Phillips wrote an editorial exception to it. And then you did a piece.*
MACDONALD: Well, Mary did a piece and then I did a piece. Mary's piece, I guess, was directed entirely at Lionel Abel's piece. My piece came after Mary's and I took up the broader question, including some nasty remarks about Lionel Abel she hadn't made. He wrote two of the most vicious articles against Han-

nah Arendt I've ever read. This was the second one. The first one was in some Jewish magazine. He wrote it with—oh, God. He and some woman collaborated on this. See, he can't stand intellectual women like Hannah, apparently. I don't know why he had such a down on Hannah, but he did. He was very personal and very insulting and, you know, saying she was a joke as a philosopher. All this kind of stuff. Really very bad. What interested me was that practically all of the people, the Jewish intellectuals, that I grew up with—you know, around *Partisan* and the Trotskyist movement and Irving Howe and so on—all tended to line up against Hannah. They tended to think she was attacking in some way or other the Jewish people and saying that they were cowards, they should have risen up. Of course, she said nothing of the kind. She was talking of their leadership and not the people. And, of course, within a year or two her book was serialized in the chief Zionist paper in Jerusalem. I mean, these Jewish friends of mine were rather premature in their opinion that this showed anti-Semitic thinking on her part.

TRILLING: *Do you have any recollection of how Hannah Arendt personally responded to the attack? Was she surprised by it or had she foretold that there would be this kind of uproar over the book?*
MACDONALD: If she didn't foresee it, she certainly was much dumber than I think she was. I think anybody could foresee that. Jews have a—the New York Jews that I've spent my life among—in general, when their ox is gored, Jesus Christ.

TRILLING: *Were you ever involved in any of the public debates on the Eichmann book?*
MACDONALD: No. I don't know why not. I never even went to them. Maybe I wasn't in town or something. Irving Howe was the chairman of one of them, I remember.

TRILLING: *Do you remember what his position was?*
MACDONALD: Oh, very much against the book. Daniel Bell was the only one who behaved with any common sense at all. As usual, Bell was in the middle, which perhaps isn't the most heroic position but it was perfectly intelligent.

TRILLING: *Sometimes it's a very heroic position.*
MACDONALD: Yes, well, I mean it was an intelligent position; he wasn't frothing at the mouth and so on and so forth. What was always strange to me was that all these people that were leftists and Marxists together with me suddenly

turned out to be, you know, Jewish nationalists. We wouldn't have spit on that position when we were Marxists.

TRILLING: *What did you feel in 1969 or '70, whenever it was, when there were big banners slung across the Theological Seminary up here, asking for reparations for the blacks?*
MACDONALD: A lot of nonsense. What do you mean, reparations?

TRILLING: *They were trying to collect five million dollars at the Riverside Church for our past mistreatment of blacks. We were to pay it back because of our collective guilt.*
MACDONALD: First of all, you can't make it up in money. Secondly, these present blacks have no right to the five million dollars. The blacks that were slaves have the right to it. 1970 was when the blacks were riding high and when all these white liberals were so scared of saying a word against the blacks. I wasn't. I used to get into lots of trouble by saying the blacks are no better than we are. Of course, now it's all changed and these same white liberals are hardly even conscious of the existence of blacks. It's really disgusting what's happened to them.

TRILLING: *I want to get to your film criticism, Dwight. You said earlier that, as far back as your connection with the* New Yorker, *you wanted to do film criticism.*
MACDONALD: Oh, long before then.

TRILLING: *But you spoke of the* New Yorker *not letting you do it for them.*
MACDONALD: Yes, but that was about fifteen years later. That was in the fifties.

TRILLING: *When did you want to do film criticism?*
MACDONALD: I *did* start in the very early thirties. I wrote several long articles on D. W. Griffith and on the Soviet cinema, very long articles. And before that, in the magazine we had called *The Miscellany.*

TRILLING: *Well, for a long time you were best known, I think, for the distinction you had made between mass cult and mid-cult. In that period did you specifically have in mind the film as the medium that reached the widest audience, as opposed to the novel?*
MACDONALD: Well, TV would be the—

TRILLING: *But TV didn't yet exist really.*
MACDONALD: No, film didn't enter into it in any specific way because I was never interested in the movies sociologically. My interest was entirely aesthetic, as an art form.

TRILLING: *You didn't think of the movies as social and historical documentation.*
MACDONALD: Of course, obviously they are. But that didn't interest me.

TRILLING: *Are you still more interested in them as an art form than as social document?*
MACDONALD: Not more than. But it wouldn't be the way that I would approach them. Only a tiny, tiny minority of films have some pretensions to be an art. My friend Jim Agee, we were both—

TRILLING: *You and Jim Agee both had this same view, as opposed to somebody like Robert Warshow who saw the film as a cultural commentary.*
MACDONALD: Oh, sure. Warshow's approach was very brilliant and very interesting. That was a classic little book he wrote on some of the things in the movies, the Western and so on. But that's entirely different from our approach because Agee and I thought—We were almost contemporaries, we were four years apart. I used to visit him at Harvard when I was on *Fortune*. We were absolutely convinced that movies were the most exciting and interesting art form of this century. We were much more interested in movies than in books. We wanted to make movies and we were bored with writing and finally Agee did that. He never directed a movie but he wrote some scripts for movies. If he'd lived even another five years, he would have undoubtedly made movies. His luck was bad: he died just before it became possible to make a movie on practically nothing. In the 1960s everybody made movies. College students and so on. And ultimately he would have made movies in Hollywood, too, because Hollywood was becoming civilized just when he died. We had this feeling about the movies in the 1930s. We were very excited, especially about the Russian movies and about Griffith, Stroheim, and the great comedians, the silent comedians.

TRILLING: *I'd like for you to talk about Agee. Not about his work so much as about him as a person.*
MACDONALD: I expressed myself at great length about him in two books. In my film book, I have a long thing on Agee and the movies, with a lot of correspondence and stuff. I have a letter that he wrote me when he was seventeen years old, and this letter gives a view of the movies and of what he wants to do with the movies, if he ever could make a movie, which is incredibly mature. I found it in my files years and years after he died and I put it in my movie book. The other place is in that book called *Against the American Grain*. I

have a long memoir on Agee with a lot of letters and so on. Yes, I was very fond of Agee and I think he was fond of me, too. We liked each other very much and we respected each other, which is perhaps equally important, you know. He was pretty much of a bum in many ways. He didn't wash very much, his clothes were filthy, and he was very bad sexually, to say the least—you know, a loose liver. And he drank too much and he had a lot of faults. But I must say, he's one of the few people that I've met that I would consider, without any question, a genius. Like Auden, Eliot, people like that, without any question.

TRILLING: *I wrote alongside of him in* The Nation *all through the forties. I thought those film reviews were fantastic.*
MACDONALD: I didn't think so.

TRILLING: *You didn't?*
MACDONALD: Well, compared to other film reviewers he was very good, yes.

TRILLING: *Tell me why you didn't think those were—*
MACDONALD: Because I don't think he's a critic, first of all. Well, he was very unfortunate: he did films just at the time when there was nothing to talk about. But for one thing, he wildly exaggerated the merits of some of the movies that he did write about, including Chaplin's—that *Monsieur Verdoux*. I wrote a long thing about that. I think he tended to be a creator and to see values in movies that only a guy that wanted to make a movie himself would see. He was consistently overrating movies. He didn't have a critical mind. After all, why should he? He wasn't a critic, he was a creator. Anything he wrote was bound to be gracefully expressed. He had a great cultural background and on the level of movie criticism, I think he's good, one of the best. But I don't consider that to have been his main achievement at all. His main achievement was only one book, really: *Let Us Now Praise Famous Men*. You mentioned that Lionel was one of the few people who really saw what a very great book that was. It got very bad reviews.

TRILLING: *Yes, it sold 600 copies when it came out. How well did you know Walker Evans?*
MACDONALD: I knew him quite well too, yes.

TRILLING: *Were you an admirer of his work, as I was?*
MACDONALD: Tremendous. I think Walker—well, not his later work. When he

got on *Fortune* it seemed to me he became rather bland. But I think everything he did for the Farm Security Administration, all those early things—He was one of the very few photographers that I would call really artists. I've seen many exhibitions of photographs and almost always you see that they're just clicks, because the artist has so little control. The machine gets in the way so much. Where with Walker Evans, he had such a pure aesthetic and srong and original aesthetic view. Almost a childlike view. In spite of the camera, it came across.

TRILLING: *It was an extraordinary combination on that book, Evans and Agee. The work of either one of them, without that of the other, would have lost some dimension. The photographs had a kind of fierce directness and then there was this extraordinary sensibility of Agee's, this almost exacerbated sensibility. It was a world-beating combination.*
MACDONALD: In fact, that's what Agee himself thought because, if you'll notice, it's signed by both James Agee and Walker Evans. It doesn't say, "Photographs by." And I remember when I reviewed it in the *New Yorker*, I spoke of James Agee's *Let Us Now Praise Famous Men*, and Agee said to me, you know, it's me *and* Walker. They were of course much closer friends of each other than I was of either of them. They were friends all their lives. What interested me was that they were completely different. You couldn't imagine two people—

TRILLING: *Evans was so fastidious.*
MACDONALD: And quiet and very, very sly. Not sly in a bad sense, but subtle and underplayed and cautious and muted and so forth. And the other one a wild, Whitmanesque, crazy man. They couldn't have been more different and yet they apparently got on—I guess that was the reason why. But Evans had an absolutely first-rate mind. He wasn't just an artist.

TRILLING: *I was coming to that. Do you remember the film* Mission to Moscow?
MACDONALD: We picketed it.

TRILLING: *Jim Agee rather praised that film.*
MACDONALD: He did? Good God? As a film?

TRILLING: *I'm talking about its content rather than its aesthetic. Several people I knew tried to tell him what was going on in it politically, what time of day it was, but he refused to listen.*
MACDONALD: I think what's amazing isn't the politics—He wasn't political.

But it was such a lousy film. I mean, if you look at it as a movie. I wonder if he was being perverse or something.

TRILLING: *He may have been perverse in the sense of resisting all the people who were trying to talk him into a different political view of it than he'd brought to it.*
MACDONALD: You mean he really praised it as a picture of what was going on in Russia?

TRILLING: *Oh yes. But you know, Walker reviewed that film, too.*
MACDONALD: I didn't know he reviewed anything.

TRILLING: *He seldom did but he did review that film. He loved to write. He wished that he had been a writer.*
MACDONALD: He was a very good writer. His introduction to the paperback, do you know that? In four pages, he tells you more about Agee than anybody else could in forty. Where did he review *Mission to Moscow* though?

TRILLING: *That's what I was going to ask you. Could it possibly have been for* Fortune?
MACDONALD: I can't imagine. And he took a different view?

TRILLING: *So I remember. Totally. But he'd gone around asking everybody questions about it beforehand. He was humble before the politics—he thought there were other people who had had more experience in that department than he had had and that he had to educate himself. He asked questions and he read and he talked to people whose knowledge he respected—it was in very marked contrast to Agee. He was annoyed with Agee: that was one time that I saw Walker rather contemptuous of him.*
MACDONALD: Of course, Agee had a wildly romantic and sentimental idea of Franklin D. Roosevelt. I once published a long excerpt from a panegyric after Roosevelt's death. He practically had an orgasm about that sly politician. So he did have a big streak of a kind of sentimentality in him. Agee did. Politically. Maybe that was it.

TRILLING: *He was born before his time. He should have been a sixties character.*
MACDONALD: Yes, I agree with you entirely, especially about movies, as I said.

TRILLING: *But Walker Evans was absolutely suited to his own time.*
MACDONALD: Right.

TRILLING: *He could be a pioneer in the kind of photography that he did so brilliantly.*

MACDONALD: He needed the Depression and he needed those people, the Dust Bowl people, and so on.

TRILLING: *But to return to your own film criticism: it didn't ever really have a relation to your political life, did it?*
MACDONALD: No, not really. Except I was of course enthusiastic about the Russian Revolution, not knowing anything about it but just being a rebel. So I liked Eisenstein's films.

TRILLING: *You would have liked them anyway, for their photography.*
MACDONALD: I now think they're a complete lie. Not *Potemkin* but the other one [*Ten Days That Shook the World*]. That's another lie—like *The Birth of a Nation*, in fact—about the Bolshevik Revolution. But I still think it's a great film.

TRILLING: *Dwight, you've said of yourself that you have a cultural conservatism existing side by side with a political radicalism and anarchism.*
MACDONALD: Yes. Well, I belong to various societies for keeping things as they are. The Victorian Society and the Sierra Club, things like that. And every time they do anything new in New York, I'm against it. Pull down things and put up other things. Also I've discovered that culturally I'm a snob. I'm an intellectual snob. But politically I've always been very radical and for the people and so on. And this does present all kinds of problems. One of them, which I know you're going to bring up, about the sit-in at Columbia—

TRILLING: *That's our next subject, in fact.*
MACDONALD: Right. But let me just go on about this. Almost my only big idea I've had in my life, that I exploited far too much perhaps, is this mass culture business—I was really the originator even of the phrase—I myself called it popular culture to begin with, but then Meyer Schapiro said it should be called mass culture. Anyway I wondered why it was that I was there taking a completely undemocratic position. For instance, I'm in favor of public libraries and in favor of public art museums but I'm against trying to get people to use public libraries or to use art museums. I'm against the whole technique of the Museum of Modern Art, the Metropolitan, and so on, of trying to get people to come and see their pictures. My idea of a good museum is a warehouse. The Louvre or something like that. A place where everything is made as difficult as possible and the only people that go there are people that want to see the pictures. And the masses don't go there because the masses don't give a

damn about art. My theory is that any culture, including a High Renaissance, even with your aristocracy, not more than twenty or twenty-five percent, at the most, give a goddam about culture. That's my theory anyway, based partly on my experiences from my class at Yale, and also other well-to-do, upper-class people I know. This whole business is a kind of a cultural—a peculiar kind of democratic snobbism. It's everybody's right to be cultured but it's not everybody's *duty* to be cultured. What I want is a Carnegie Library: if you want to go there you can go there and find the books but you're not encouraged to and the library isn't the center of talks and movies and community actions and so on, and the museum doesn't try to get you to come by having the *Mona Lisa* and stuff like that. This King Tut exhibition is everything that I'm opposed to in the museum world today. People lining up. Applying for tickets. By the millions. And the Tut is bad Egyptian art. It's much too late to be any good at all. It's just interesting because it's very valuable material but it's not even good—and they have much better art from Egypt there, which nobody pays any attention to, in the Middle East Department. But anyway, that always bothered me, and I solved it as follows. I think that politics is in itself a democratic operation, that everybody can be and should be a politician because politics is something in which your own neck is involved, in case of a war; in any case, when your own interests are involved. In case of a new highway—

TRILLING: *Or a nuclear reactor—*
MACDONALD: Yes, of course, and many less dramatic things. So therefore everybody is an expert in politics. You have a right to have an opinion and to be respected for your opinion—not to be respected for it, but you see what I mean. It's a democratic thing. Whereas art is, to me, a completely snobbish thing. You have no right to crowd the museums if you don't know anything about art and if you just go because you think it's your democratic right. You have no right to do it because you make it hard for me to go and see the pictures, for one thing.

TRILLING: *All right then, how do you feel about universities?*
MACDONALD: All for them. Of course. One of the things that bothered me about the SDS, which I was all for too, because they were very anarchistic, you know, and I love anarchism—they weren't Marxists at all—was that they were ignoramuses. They had no respect for the past, no interest in the past.

The Old Left considered that culture was the heritage of the working class and should therefore be preserved and paid respect to; the only trouble was that the working class was excluded from it. You see what I mean? You know, Marx was himself a cultured person. But when I read of the New Left attacking the libraries it was as if I was religious and they were profaning a cathedral.

TRILLING: *Then you're not anarchist?*
MACDONALD: I *am* anarchist. Kropotkin was an anarchist. Emma Goldman was anarchist. But they were very cultivated people. It would never have occurred to them to be anti-cultural.

TRILLING: *Their political act transcended their commitment to education.*
MACDONALD: Whose political act?

TRILLING: *The SDS.*
MACDONALD: I'm talking now about the old nineteenth century.

TRILLING: *I know you are. But I'm talking about what happened at the universities in the sixties.*
MACDONALD: That's what I say: the SDS politically was anarchist and that was very good, because they didn't have any leadership and they got rid of all this Marxist junk and they really behaved towards each other much better than we Trotskyites ever did. They were very, very kind, supportive towards each other. That was a very good thing about them really. And I was entirely for their contempt for bourgeois society and their thumbing their nose at it and so on. All that's fine. But I was not in favor of their anti-cultural stance.

TRILLING: *How did you feel about such things as their urinating on the President's carpets and defecating in the wastepaper baskets? You, with your fastidious feelings about these things?*
MACDONALD: Are you kidding? I'm opposed—especially those acts, especially the defecating. I have a special horror of anything like that.

TRILLING: *Well, there you are—*
MACDONALD: What do you mean?

TRILLING: *Those were the very things they were doing in the name of their freedom to do anything they wanted.*
MACDONALD: That's not anarchism. That's just hoodlumism.

TRILLING: *You make a nice distinction.*
MACDONALD: I do not make a nice distinction. That's not anarchism, that's just animalism. Anarchism is a very idealistic philosophy and the great anarchists have been people—Emma Goldman was one of the most cultivated women of her day. She used to lecture on Ibsen and Strindberg. I mean, that's anarchism. I think anybody that would pee on anything or shit on anything is an animal and should be severely humiliated.

TRILLING: *But you did know that this was going on over here at Columbia under the aegis of the SDS, didn't you?*
MACDONALD: Yes. Well, I heard—

TRILLING: *How did you feel about it?*
MACDONALD: I didn't know about the excreting but I knew about the peeing, yes.

TRILLING: *They were peeing out of the windows of the library. Didn't you know that was going on?*
MACDONALD: No. I don't know whether I did or not. I guess I did. But if I did, I was against it. I don't see what this has to do with it.

TRILLING: *You believed that they could occupy the buildings: that was all right?*
MACDONALD: I was all for that, yes. Because they didn't do any damage. And there were no bombs.

TRILLING: *But on what ground is it all right to stop another person from pursuing his democratic right to have his education by blocking a building and making it inaccessible to him?*
MACDONALD: Well, there were only four buildings involved.

TRILLING: *Yes, but those four—*
MACDONALD: They had the majority of the students with them, didn't they?

TRILLING: *That was after the bust, not before. All you have to do is invite a police bust and then you'll get the masses of people. There's nothing like cracked heads to mobilize sympathy for a sit-in.*
MACDONALD: Nobody took a poll. Nobody knows what the support was. I visited the campus a number of times and crawled into two of the buildings and I thought the atmosphere in both of those buildings was extremely

healthy, including the one in Mathematics. That's where one of my least favorite radicals, Tom Hayden, was. I attacked his One Columbia, Two Columbia thing in a speech in public at the Commencement. Remember that mock Commencement?

TRILLING: *I didn't go to hear you. I looked for you to say hello. I wanted to make peace with you. You had thought I was absurd because I wouldn't contribute to the SDS.*
MACDONALD: I had nothing against having the regular Commencement either. And one of the conditions that we had that Commencement, me and Harold Taylor and that marvelous Erlich, he was the best—

TRILLING: *I couldn't agree less with everything you're saying, Dwight. But that's all right: it's your tape, help yourself.*
MACDONALD: —was that there should be no mixing up with the police, no violence. We should get permission from the college authorities and so on. We were not in favor of any kind of making it a Roman holiday for Tom Hayden. I attacked him by name in my speech and was roundly booed by a section of the audience. I said, "I do not agree with the idea of closing down universities or locking them up but I do agree with this particular thing." Because I think Columbia had become absolutely fossilized. And Grayson Kirk, if anybody's windows can be peed out of, it's his windows. He was a big stuffed shirt and of course they got rid of him, thank God. I think the main trouble was that the students had lost contact with their teachers. They'd become just a kind of harvest machine. And also the Vietnam thing played a big part, too: those war contracts should have been given up. The gym, I think, was a fake issue. But anyway, regardless of the issues, I thought that the campus was just seething with discussions, and I saw jocks arguing with longhairs and I saw everybody giving out pamphlets like mad and little mimeographed things, and there were dozens of things going on, and I thought this was absolutely marvelous. This is what a university should be. It should be something alive and something, you know, anarchistic in a sense.

TRILLING: *Anarchism without violence. That's your slogan?*
MACDONALD: Yes. Well—

TRILLING: *That'll be the day.*
MACDONALD: There wasn't any violence there. They did put aside gently a

couple of aged guards that tried to say you can't go in there, but they didn't beat them up.

TRILLING: *They just paralyzed a policeman.*
MACDONALD: Oh, that was a mistake. It's true, somebody jumped out of a window—

TRILLING: *And landed on him and he's permanently paralyzed.*
MACDONALD: I know, I agree with you. But you cannot say that they meant to do that. That's absurd. It's like the fact that somebody burned up the research papers of that guy. He made a big thing out of that. I agree that's absolutely horrible. This is all in that thing in the *New York Review of Books*: the controversy between me and Ivan, the late Ivan Morris.

TRILLING: *Dwight, I just want to say one little thing here. I'm not going to answer and I'm not going to argue with you because I've put all my point of view on this on paper and here I'm just inviting your remarks; it's your tape. I only intervene—*
MACDONALD: As long as you don't have any right to reply, that's the perfect position.

TRILLING: *I would end the tape at once if I were really to reply to you. But I want you to know that I'm not agreeing with you even if I'm not arguing with you. Now go on.*
MACDONALD: Well, the fact that the guy jumped on a policeman is of course very sad but I don't see what it has to do with the question—unless you think he did it on purpose.

TRILLING: *And what about the fact that some of the students picked up a tub in which a tree was planted—it was on that bridge across Amsterdam Avenue; it's decorated with huge tubs that have trees in them—and dumped it over the railing onto a police car? Thank God, the car was empty; if anybody had been in it, he would have been killed.*
MACDONALD: Well, not by a tub—

TRILLING: *I'm talking about a tub with a tree in it. It took a group of very healthy young men to lift it.*
MACDONALD: Well, to play with such a chance I think is absolutely disgusting.

TRILLING: *Maybe they meant to kill the people in the car.*
MACDONALD: Well, I don't know whether they did or not. I don't think they did mean to kill them. If they did, then I think they're pathological people

and I can't help it. What the hell am I supposed to do? Any movement at all, probably among them the Jesus Christ followers—I can't help that. And the guy that burned up the ten years' research of that unpopular professor—that little business I thought was absolutely disgusting and horrible, of course. But I don't see what that has to do with—

TRILLING: *What do you consider to be the results of the uprisings?*
MACDONALD: Well, getting rid of Kirk, for one thing. And also getting a kind of a [new] spirit into the university. It put the faculty on notice that they can't just go on. In fact, many of the faculty, like Fred Dupee, wanted to be more involved with the students. At least, not to be so cut off from them. And also I think it did liberalize and democratize—it gave the students more of a say in what goes on, didn't it?

TRILLING: *There's been a Senate formed. That was all that was ever accomplished in terms of student rule.*
MACDONALD: Well, has that been of any interest?

TRILLING: *It may have been. I wouldn't be prepared to say, but I have no reason to doubt that it's been useful.*
MACDONALD: But anyway, for a couple of weeks, at least, things were sort of buzzing around here.

TRILLING: *Anything for a good buzz, right?*
MACDONALD: No, no. No, Fred Dupee and I had just the same view about the whole thing. He said, come up here, this is a revolution.

TRILLING: *I have no doubt he went over there with an old revolutionary's receptivity to something that was spontaneously happening in the student body. But after two or three days he began not to like what he was seeing—he saw some of the acts of violence that the students were indulging in and was very disgusted by them. Of all people he might have called, he called me and said he couldn't stand any more; he was leaving for the country and I should phone him if anything happened that I thought required his return. I did call him very soon, in a day or two, for a sudden meeting of the faculty, an official faculty meeting, and after he came back he indeed supported the uprising. But there had been at least this brief interim of distaste—he called me to talk about it, after all: I wasn't his friendly neighborhood revolutionary. He'd seen the students spit at an old physics professor—I don't remember his name— and what Fred said to me was that this campus didn't need another breakdown of a middle-*

aged professor, himself. But he forgot all this after his return from the country. It was different with you: you came and stayed sympathetic—

MACDONALD: I came *un*sympathetic, actually. In fact, I remember that, the night before, I was talking upstate somewhere and I had just read the papers and I said, these students, they have no right to occupy the buildings and interfere with the course of education and so on. I actually said this. So when I came down here, Gloria [Macdonald] said—Gloria is a little like Andy [Dupee] politically—you're wrong, you're wrong, you should go up there, don't be such an old curmudgeon, and so on. I said no, no, I'm against all that. And then Fred called up and said, come up, it's a revolution. I said, "Gloria said I should come up there and I really think it's a very bad idea." And he said, "Dwight, you're wrong, you're wrong. It's a revolution. Come up."

TRILLING: *He was in favor of it?*
MACDONALD: Of course.

TRILLING: *Can you remember how long it had been going on when you got that call?*
MACDONALD: Oh, I don't think very long—maybe a couple of days. And I got into two of the buildings and I thought everything was conducted with the utmost democracy and spirit. The SDS was never my first choice for the leadership, and especially this awful guy that founded the Weathermen—I thought he was a real demogogue. A guy named Lewis Cole was my candidate. He was the second in command.

TRILLING: *You're talking about Mark Rudd?*
MACDONALD: Yes, I disliked him even more than I did Tom Hayden. But there was a group that developed in Fayerweather Hall that was a centrist group, and if that had been at the beginning, that's the group I would have been in. They weren't for spitting on people. They were for much more of an attempt to work out a sensible compromise.

TRILLING: *Dwight, tell me, in the period you were up here, did you hear speeches against the Vietnam War?*
MACDONALD: I suppose so. I don't know.

TRILLING: *I think I was on the campus every day and I never heard an anti-Vietnam remark. That's another of the fallacies about the uprising, that it was a protest of the war. After all, similar university uprisings were taking place in Mexico City, in Japan, in Berlin, all over the lot. Not to mention the Sorbonne.*

MACDONALD: That was a month later.

TRILLING: *None of those countries were at war with Vietnam.*
MACDONALD: No, but they got the idea from Columbia.

TRILLING: *There had to have been a common denominator for all those student uprisings to take place at that time. You said in America it was because of the Vietnam War—*
MACDONALD: I didn't say that at all. I said, the main thing *I* felt was that they were revolting against a machine of learning, in which the faculty was way up there and they were down there. I mean, there was just a heartless, stuffy machine of learning. And I liked the idea of its being broken up.

TRILLING: *It wasn't any heartless machine of learning. But I'm not supposed to argue with you.*
MACDONALD: No, you're not supposed to. (Laughter) One of the risks, of course, is inconsistency when you have this conservative position and so on. And I won't deny that there was a certain contradiction in my position there as shown by the fact that my original view was quite opposed to it. And I can't deny, if you want to insist on it, that a minority did coerce a passive majority. But I do think the passive majority got something out of the whole episode.

TRILLING: *I think the university as a whole—*
MACDONALD: Now, no arguments.

TRILLING: *No, not an argument, just a little statement. (Laughter) I think the university hasn't recovered from it and may never recover from it. Now Dwight, I think we have about two minutes more and from my notes I think I've asked you everything I meant to. But perhaps there's something you want to say?*
MACDONALD: Well, I want to make one confession—in a way, it's a confession. Two things that shocked me very much: one of them is the way that the whole student movement, not just the SDS, but the whole anti-Vietnam War radical student movement disappeared overnight, the minute they stopped conscripting college students and had a volunteer army. I remember sort of thinking in the Black Panther weekend at Yale they were breathing fire. That was when the Cambodian invasion took place. But then by the fall, everything had changed, and they didn't even turn out to help, if they got time off to do it, to elect a liberal Congressman.

TRILLING: *They were given time off to help McGovern.*

MACDONALD: Yes, that's what I mean. At Buffalo, they had practically burned down a building, bombs and everything, but by the time I taught there, they were all off on some goddamn religious kick and there was no interest in politics at all.

TRILLING: *That's the difference from being a Marxist—a Marxist view of society produces a certain sense of responsibility because your judgements relate to a set of fixed premises. You don't just put your politics on and off like a hat.*
MACDONALD: What are you talking about now?

TRILLING: *Just what you're talking about. The students didn't have any responsibility to a position they'd held because they hadn't held a position; they had held an attitude.*
MACDONALD: Yes, exactly. That's what I liked about them, their primitive instinct.

TRILLING: *That's what was so wrong.*
MACDONALD: No. Yes. Out of order. What I liked about them was their primitive instinct that there was something very constricting and very wrong about Marxism. I think Marxism has done more damage to the world. I'm sure you're not going to disagree with me about *that* certainly. And Karl Marx was a hideous person personally too. A genius and a great analyst of society and so on but I think his ideas have done more harm than good.

TRILLING: *I won't say that awful crimes haven't been committed in his name but I think he added a permanent new way of viewing society to our vocabulary of understanding.*
MACDONALD: I just said that. I said that I thought he was absolutely superb as a sociologist and historian. He introduced a new way of looking at the world which is still of great value. But I'm talking about him as a practical political instrument for revolution. And I think he's been very bad. Anyway, that's one thing: the way many student activists became nutty religious people. The second thing is even more disturbing, and that is the large numbers of refugees from South Vietnam. Now, when you think of the chances they take in those boats, it certainly shows that this regime is very unpopular.

TRILLING: *This worries you?*
MACDONALD: Well, sure, of course. Very much. And also, something I read, I think it was printed in the *Times*, by some young Vietnamese ardent leftist against both Diem and Thieu. He was a leader of the radical opposition to

both of these American-supported dictators—And he said he still thinks that everything would have been much better if the Americans hadn't come because they probably made the North Vietnamese into much worse people than they would have been without them, but still he had to admit that his expectations of liberation had proved to be—well, they'd exchanged one horrible situation for another.

TRILLING: *But look, Dwight, with your knowledge of Communism, how could you foresee anything else? What was the nature of my debate with Mary McCarthy on Vietnam except that I was trying to say (I'm afraid I didn't do it very well) that of course the Americans had to get out of Vietnam but it was a tragedy because of what was going to be left behind them. Mary made it out to be of no consequence: the Communists would take over and everybody would live happily ever after.*

MACDONALD: Yes, but you said we must get out in some particular way. With honor or something like that.

TRILLING: *I did not. I never said with honor, I couldn't have cared less about that. I wasn't talking about us; I was addressing the consequences of our withdrawal and wrote about the future that awaited the South Vietnamese. Yes, we had to get out but our departure would leave tragedy behind us. I wanted Mary to write of our withdrawal in a way that was appropriate to tragedy. I didn't yet know about boat people but I was foreseeing just such a devastation as has taken place.*

MACDONALD: Well, that's just a matter of words and so on.

TRILLING: *It's far more than words. It has to do with hard facts and deep emotions. Listen, you're the person who was referring only to his emotions in assessing what was going on at Columbia. You loved that spontaneity. Maybe what I'm saying is that I'm able to face up to tragedy but I can't bear irresponsibility, the unwillingness to recognize the consequences of one's decisions.*

MACDONALD: I have good intellectual reasons for liking this kind of nose-thumbing at certain kinds of authority, represented especially by that pompous ass, Grayson Kirk.

TRILLING: *It's terribly difficult not to fight with you, Dwight—*
MACDONALD: Let me just finish. Then I'll go and we'll close this delightful—

TRILLING: *It's been marvelous.*
MACDONALD: Yes, it's been wonderful for me too. On the whole. Except for

everything *you* said. (Laughter) But no; the thing is that we had no business in Vietnam in the first place. That's my point. We had no business in that civil war over there, if there was going to be a civil war, and, in fact, by intervening we probably made the North Vietnamese worse than they would be normally. I'll conclude with this, what Cal Lowell once said to me. He said this about the tactics of certain of the more enthusiastic demonstrators at the Pentagon, jeering—I'm not certain if they were spitting—but certainly jeering and taunting the military policemen who were confronting us with their clubs, not using the clubs, you understand, but they were—

TRILLING: *Standing there holding them.*
MACDONALD: They were just standing there and they were really young—

TRILLING: *There's a marvelous portrait of that in Mailer's* Armies of the Night.
MACDONALD: Yes, yes, right. Yes, we were with Mailer then. Anyway, Cal said about these taunts and so on, you know they're making these policemen worse than they ordinarily would be. And this is actually a profound statement and it may be true of some of the things that were said to the police at Columbia.

TRILLING: *Oh, I have no question of that.*
MACDONALD: So on that harmonious note—

Dwight Macdonald Interview

Shirley Broughton / 1980

From an unpublished transcript of an interview conducted in fall 1980, East Hampton, New York. Printed by permission of Shirley Broughton.

SB: *About two weeks ago when we were talking about World War II you said that at the time of Pearl Harbor, you were opposed to the United States entering the war against Hitler. The only other people I have known who were opposed to America's entry were pacifists: I assume you were not a pacifist. What were you?*
DM: Well, I was [a pacifist], God help me, and I was a Luxemburg Leninist. I thought it would be a replay of the First World War and that the main enemies were at home, and that this was an imperialist war—I was wrong. I keep looking back on it.

SB: *Be more specific about what you mean by an "imperialist war."*
DM: Well, I mean that if the cadres of the working class did not go into the armies and the ideologues didn't support the war, that there would be a situation after the war in which one of the contenders would collapse and there would be a chance for some sort of revolutionary outcome—in the debris of the collapsed side. Now, of course, Hitler did not collapse, but what I should have foreseen but didn't was that the two great empires at that time, the United States and the Soviet Union, came in and then there was no possibility of a revolutionary outcome.

SB: *In other words, the country you were thinking might collapse was Germany, not the United States?*

DM: Oh yes, that seemed quite obvious to me, to everybody in fact except James Burnham, my late comrade in the Trotskyist movement, whom I remember saying it was not going to happen.

SB: *Tell me more about Mr. Burnham.*
DM: Well, Mr. Burnham, because he has this position, he still has it, he wants to start this third world war. He thought Hitler's Germany was more organized for war, more than the so-called democracies, the United States and England, and therefore the Germans could and would win the war. Of course, he turned out to be quite wrong. It was clear to me, once America got into the war, that there was no question that Hitler could win, especially when he was attacking Russia too—you can't pick on both.

SB: *Let's go back specifically to Pearl Harbor. If at that moment you were against America entering the war, didn't it occur to you that Germany might win and therefore it was absolutely necessary for our survival to go into the war?*
DM: No, no, I don't think it was anyway. No, it didn't occur to me. I think Germany, once we got in the war, was done for. America outproduced Germany and I was certain the allies would win. That our side would win.

SB: *I am a little confused because you say you were against us going into the war at the time of Pearl Harbor, correct? Now if America had not gone into the war, everyone says in retrospect that Germany would have won. Do you agree with this?*
DM: Well, I think—I am not so sure if Hitler ever could have invaded England, but let us assume he could have . . . I can't see this as being a final solution. I think that Hitler would have been much too occupied with—heavens, if he was going to conquer both Russia and England. Now I don't see how he could have. I think he would have collapsed finally, but, of course, it would have been a terrible thing—it would have been horrible, suffering, torture, and misery—so I wouldn't be in favor of it. I might have been in favor if I thought he was going to win. But I didn't ever think that.

SB: *So you really disagree with the majority opinion, that it was necessary for American to get into the war.*
DM: Well, I still don't think it was necessary. I now think it was desirable because it shortened the sufferings of millions of people. If Hitler had won, even temporarily, it would have been a horrible thing. So, I should have been in favor of the allied democracy side of the war.

SB: *But at the time you were not? At the time—when did you change.*

DM: Well, when did I change? I guess I changed after the war didn't produce any revolutions, or rather all the revolutions were short circuited by—possibly because America and Russia were there and by the end of the war I had become both an anarchist and a pacifist.

SB: *By what time?*

DM: By the end of the war, by 1945 or '46. I began the war as a revolutionary Marxist Leninist, but after the war when the revolution didn't take place, I felt that all wars were bad, so I became a pacifist. Then I shed pacifism, in the, let's see, it is the last issue of *Politics* which must have been in 1948 or so—well, when was the Berlin airlift? I was for the continued occupation of the city of Berlin by the French, American, and British forces. . . . The reason I was for the airlift was because I realized that if these two million people that were in Berlin and had suffered all through the war and had made a strong stand against the Communists, you know, I mean, I was opposed to selling them out and turning them over to the Communists—and so I said we should keep those military forces there. But as a pacifist, you couldn't be in favor of military force anywhere. So I shed pacifism and my brief period of membership in the War Registers League ended. What bothered me was that the pacifists had this idea that if a totalitarian government such as Stalin and Hitler actually took over your country you could reason with them—do what Gandhi did in India. Of course, the point is that Gandhi was dealing with a very imperialistic, hypocritical government, and a government with a free public press and so on, which was in favor of what Gandhi wanted. Anyway the British government was not willing to go to extremes. Gandhi wouldn't have lasted ten minutes in a Stalinist or Hitler regime. They would have executed him immediately as well as thousands of other people connected with him. So that never impressed me as an argument. But I guess one did sort of think there would be some chance, because we always thought, and correctly, that the common people, the common soldier of say Russia, assuming they came to this country, which is impossible to imagine, they would have needed a supply line of three to six thousand miles. In any event it was believed that one would be able to talk to them. Pacifists believed that we would be morally stultified by killing other people.

SB: *Pacifism in the face of the Nazis sounds like a ridiculous position.*

DM: It is a ridiculous position in your opinion, but in my opinion it is not ridiculous. It is too profound a part of my soul to pursue this issue.

SB: *When you were thinking at the beginning of the war that there might be revolutions in some countries, what countries were you thinking of specifically?*
DM: I was certainly thinking first of all of France, the great revolutionary country of the nineteenth century, and also the country that had so much widespread and violent resistance. To some extent Italy—it was never really wholeheartedly behind Mussolini. And in fact as it turned out, the partisans in Italy did a great job, as you can see from such movies as *Open City*. Of course, Greece also. I have in my magazine an article about EAM with its military arm ELAS [*Politics* January 1945], the pretty much communist-infiltrated but very heroic resistance against the Nazis and against the king. Those were the countries I was thinking of, but it turned out that since America and Russia controlled everything—the Russians controlled the French resistance, so obviously there was not a peep out of them after the war. So again I was wrong.

SB: *What is your opinion now in 1980 of revolution as a means to political ends?*
DM: Well as I wrote in *Politics* in 1944, revolutionary tactics and the ideology of Marxism were not viable. In fact, now I would do almost anything to avoid revolution. Even if it is successful, it seems to me that the cost you pay for the revolution in our time, with the possible exception of Cromwell's revolution, which was a typical English kind of revolution, a rather limited revolution, but anyway, I think that an exception. As to the French and Russian revolutions I wish that neither had happened. The values in both revolutions were corrupted. But now I believe that it all began with Lenin and Trotsky in 1917. It wasn't that Stalin betrayed the revolution, according to Trotsky, but that the revolution was always a totalitarian, bloodthirsty, horrible revolution.

SB: *Does this come down to the old saw that the tragic flaw was the idea that the ends justify the means?*
DM: My position is, of course, that the end doesn't justify the means. Yes, that was a big part of the article because the point about the ends and means business came up quite clearly when I was a Trotskyist because there was a famous discussion between Burnham and Trotsky, and Trotsky's position was that the end justifies the means. Burnham's position was that not only does

the end not justify the means, but much more important—that the end becomes completely lost in the means. When you see what happens, after Lenin, and now I think even during Lenin, then after Stalin got into power, that his means became the ends. The whole idea was that Lenin and even Stalin were communists, and their idea was that once the working class was in power, the State would wither away. But, of course, on the contrary, the exact opposite happened.

SB: *Whose idea was it that the State would wither away?*
DM: It was Marx's idea. Of course, Marx didn't live in any time of any working class taking power. Now, of course, it didn't wither away, and even though the working class didn't take power, another class took power, the bureaucratic class, as Burnham called it—the managers, so therefore the means became the ends. There was no end to that. There is no question now—no one thinks that the Soviet Union is going to become a working class state. The bureaucracy is there and will always be there.

SB: *Do you think it would have made any difference if instead of the bureaucrats taking over, the working class had taken over? Do you think that would have made a difference?*
DM: An enormous difference. In fact, the working class did take over in the first period of the Revolution. Remember the slogan on which the revolution was made, when the palace was seized: "All power to the Soviets" and the Soviets were actually anarchistic formations based on factories, schools, communities, farming communities, and so forth, which was a very anarchist idea in which power would be, according to these segments of society, and all a part of the Soviet. When the Soviet Congress took place, about four months later, Lenin and Trotsky and the Bolsheviks broke up the Constituent Assembly when it looked as though the Mensheviks might gain power. The Bolsheviks sent in the troops and squashed [the Assembly] with bayonets and rifles and simply closed the Assembly down. That was the end of the Soviets.

SB: *Is there any country today where you feel the working class is in power?*
DM: No, No! I think if there is going to be any revolutionary class, and I don't think there is right now, it would certainly be the bourgeoisie—the people that made the revolution in Russia for that matter. Lenin and company. I mean Lenin and Trotsky, the Bolsheviks were petty bourgeois. The working class very rarely rises above the level of trade union consciousness. They are

great on wages and strikes and that kind of stuff, but they don't have a strong influence on government. So I think if there is going to be any working class, it would be the students, and the blacks, for that matter. But, really, I don't think there is going to be any revolution anyway.

SB: *Why did you switch from being a Communist fellow traveler to a Trotskyist?*
DM: Well, I was interested in communism and the communist movement in the United States for a while because I thought there was something going on that was important. I actually read Marx for the first time in 1935. I was much impressed. I was astonished. Then after about a year and a half, the first of the Moscow Trials took place and I began to have terrible doubts about the Soviet Union. Then they published the complete reports of the second Moscow Trials in 1938, I think. They sold them for seventy-five cents in the Workers Bookstore in New York—500 pages of testimony. They wanted to show that they were on the level. Well, it turned out just the opposite. I saw they were not on the level, there was something wrong with this thing and then I got in touch with the Trotskyists. I wrote a letter expressing my doubts [it was published in the *New Republic* in response to a defense of the trials by Malcolm Cowley]. The Trotsky Defense Committee got in touch with me and I became a Trotskyist.

SB: *If you no longer believe that revolution is a good means of change, what is?*
DM: Well, I don't know really. I think you have to cultivate your own garden. I think anarchism is the only possibility. Anarchism doesn't just mean bombs, for Christ sake. It doesn't mean bombs, that's only one form of anarchism—dynamite and that kind of stuff. Anarchism means to me the encouraging of any form of community involvement, associations in community that involve your own life and interests. For instance de Tocqueville points out in his *Democracy in America* that important change in America occurred through the efforts of small voluntary associations. They are still very powerful in this country, organizations like the Civil Liberties Union for example, and there are a lot of other ones. The League of Women Voters—they can be found in every field you can think of. These societies are organs facilitating change. Ralph Nader and his workers are a good example of this. This is what I mean by anarchistic association. There is no answer in organized politics. You have a situation such as Carter vs. Reagan. How can one possibly choose. There is no answer there.

SB: *I agree that your idea of anarchism and of people banding together offers the possibility of a positive force in this country. What then is the role of the government in this kind of society?*
DM: The ideal role is as Milton Friedman is saying in his marvelous talks that he is giving every week. He articulately delivers his lamentably reactionary ideas. Which I must say I agree with to a large extent, because, you know, I also had a lot of sympathy for Herbert Hoover too—ha. But he was so lousy on the working class that I was against him. But there are anarchists who do believe there is a role for government as Friedman insists, and I agree with him. Keep out of the market but maintain a police force and a system of courts that would preserve contracts and so on, preserve law and order and that is all. We should not have any HEW and all these other huge bureaucracies.

SB: *I should think that if you are for minimal government, and that is what I understand you to think anarchism stands for, why should you not be for Reagan because Reagan wants minimal government?*
DM: I know, well I voted against Hoover for that matter. I voted for Franklin D. Roosevelt. I voted for Al Smith. I guess I am as much for Reagan as for any of them. I will not vote for Carter that is true. In that sense I would vote for Reagan, and if you give me one good reason, I might be a little bit less sad if he gets elected.

SB: *Now Paul Goodman was also an anarchist. Do you know of differences or similarities in your point of view as compared with the views of Goodman?*
DM: I am glad you mentioned Paul because I would say that I owe a great debt to him. He wrote frequently for my magazine and he was able to articulate a lot of those ideas about anarchism and apply them to the current situation in this country, both on cultural and economic issues, in a way I think nobody else has done. For instance he and his brother Percy, who by the way is out here [in East Hampton], in their book *Comunitas* offer a whole theory on the application of anarchist ideas to industrial society. The most interesting thing from one point of view is that they point out that you don't have to be against technology and the machine. You can have a decentralization with big plants because of electric power. That is one of the main points of the book, which is a new way of looking at the problem. They argue that industrialization and decentralization is logically possible.

SB: *Now was Paul actually for minimal government. What was his position on the role of government?*
DM: It was to preserve contracts and have police to preserve law and order and that is all. That is all.

SB: *What do you think the United States should do about the invasion of Afghanistan?*
DM: Afghanistan? Nothing, nothing. I think it is a big mistake to get involved. Carter is doing just the wrong thing. I am all for helping the Afghanistan rebels, of course. Who wouldn't be. I think the idea of his stand on the Olympics is just absolutely wrong. As if we didn't have teams in the Olympics during the Vietnam war and so on. Nobody said we should be kicked out. I think we have no right to be so moralistic about this whole business. When we were in Vietnam, we were in the Olympics and we hosted the Olympics, and so on. I don't think we are such a great country from that point of view either. I think the less we do about Afghanistan the better, the better for the Afghanistan rebels and for world peace.

SB: *Well, I certainly agree with you that the United States is in a very difficult position to take a moral stand, especially considering our position on Chile and so forth. But maybe one has to do that. Maybe you have to take a moral stand and hope that the next time there won't be a Chile from the American point of view.*
DM: Well, on this whole question of intervention, particularly in the Iranian business, you know, hostages and so on, it seems to me what we are doing in every way is to make it possible for the Iranian Ayatollah Khomeini and the militants to view the United States as their great enemy, their oppressor, and the Soviet Union as their deliverer. This is absurd. Russia is a violently anti-religious state and right on their border, and we are situated 10,000 miles away and we are no threat at all. We have freedom of religion and so on, no threat in any way. It seems to me that what we should do in the hostage situation is nothing. Just not reply. Just not make any efforts to promote a boycott. Just forget about it and they will soon run out of gas. We will not be doing anything. Now we are making it possible for them to portray us as the big oppressor and enemy and not to see Russia as their real enemy. I think the same thing can be said with respect to Afghanistan.

SB: *Let's separate Iran and Afghanistan and go back to Afghanistan. George Kennan, an ambassador to Russia at one time, said that when the Soviets moved into Afghanistan, we*

should have blockaded Cuba—which incidentally Reagan said as well. Kennan's position was that, when you have two great powers and one power moves, the other power has to check the move in another part of the world. It is very convenient because Cuba is so close.
DM: I am completely against it, and where did Kennan say this? I read something in the Times a few months ago in which he was talking about the terrible atmosphere in Washington. Where did Kennan say this?

SB: I heard it on the McNeill Lehrer Report.
DM: That sounds very strange to me.

SB: As a matter of fact, he smilingly said: "I don't have a high regard for Reagan's political position necessarily, but I do agree with him on this one point to check the Afghanistan situation we should have blockaded Cuba."
DM: I can't understand that at all because he was taking the opposite line a couple of months ago about the whole situation. He was very appalled by the warlike atmosphere in Washington. It seemed to me he was just saying we should be . . . you know, try to cool it. That's just the opposite. Furthermore, I don't see any possible gain by blockading Cuba. What sort of business is that? What has Cuba got to do with it? It seems childish to me. I don't see how this would produce any results at all. I think on the contrary we should keep on being friendly with Cuba now that Castro has let all those people out and we have taken them all in. You know, we are making Castro into a symbol of revolution and liberation as against the rest of those oppressive military regimes in South America. We do that by antagonizing Cuba. I don't understand it. I think Castro, as civilized monsters go, is a rather civilized monster. Being friendly to Castro would pull the rug out from under him, it would neutralize him to some extent as a revolutionary force. And also if we were friendly with Castro it would be for his benefit as well as ours. He would be less dependent on Russia. That is another thing, too, you know. All these Cuban troops, all over the place in Africa and so on. The way to wean them away from Russia is to give them some market for their sugar in the United States, which all governments since Eisenhower have cut off.

SB: Now, Dwight, just for a second, let's go back to the Soviet Union. Would you agree that the present conflict in the world is between the Soviet Union and the United States and its Western allies?
DB: Yes, I would agree with that.

SB: *So that is the major world conflict. Is the Soviet Union an aggressive force?*
DB: Yes, it is, as much as it can be. But I think we are pretty aggressive, too.

SB: *For instance, I assume you would cite the Soviet invasion of Afghanistan as an aggressive international act. What would you cite as an aggressive act on the part of the United States?*
DB: Well, we would begin with Vietnam, obviously, under several administrations. I think that the encouragement of the CIA to the anti-Allende forces in Cuba is another immediate example. That has led to the victory of the dictator—what's his name, you know, the head in Chile now? [General Augusto Pinochet] Also, I think we got too much involved in Angola, really we didn't have to. Angola, right? Where all that fighting has been going on.

SB: *So what you are saying—I don't want to put words in your mouth, but that what we have are two aggressive regimes. The Soviets are aggressive and the United States is aggressive. Is that what you would say?*
DB: Yes, because I think that since the Second World War, since the Soviets took over Eastern Europe—all those countries, Estonia, Latvia and so on down to Bulgaria, Rumania—once they had taken over they became nonaggressive. They were satiated so to speak. We have been more aggressive.

SB: *What do you think the American position should have been at the time of the uprisings in Czechoslovakia and Hungary?*
DB: Well, I think we certainly should have been sympathetic to the rebels, but I certainly don't think we should have used any armed force for two reasons. The obvious one being that it might have resulted in a clash which could have resulted in World War III. The other reason is that it wouldn't have been welcomed by the rebels because it would have been bad publicity for them. It would have made them dependents of an imperialistic regime, the United States!

SB: *What about the technique of sanctions—curtailing trade? I mean you are against boycotting the Olympics, but what of these other various techniques which are not direct confrontations but are another form of pressure? Do you think we should have tried those pressure techniques during the time of Hungary and Czechoslovakia?*
DB: Yes, I'm in favor of those in general as a much better alternative to military threats and so on. I have no objection to that kind of technique. My big objection in the case of the Olympics and in the case of Iran was that in these

cases our intervention results in the opposite of what we presumably want. It simply strengthens the anti-American elements and helps the Soviet Union.

SB: *Why do you put Iran and the Olympics together? Let's just stick with the Olympics. I don't understand how us boycotting the Olympics will work against us. This I am not clear about.*

DB: Well, you might have a point Shirley. The fact is I did read recently that it would be a good idea because the dissidents in Russia would like us to boycott the Games. So perhaps I am wrong about that.

SB: *On responding to Soviet aggressive action. In the Cuban Missile Crisis, Kennedy stood up to that and we were all terrified. But he did, and insisted they take the missiles out of Cuba.*

DB: I remember the Missile Crisis. I was not only terribly frightened, I was appalled and shocked, and I thought he was absolutely wrong about it. It turned out all right because Khrushchev was a very bold and marvelous guy. He was the one bright spot, you know, since Stalin, and those Khrushchev years were great. Khrushchev didn't retaliate as he might have. He didn't press the issue, so Kennedy got away with it. I remember sending Kennedy a telegram at the time in the White House saying: "I implore you to withdraw from this and to think of Bismarck, Metternicht and (ha ha) some other— Machiavelli."[1] I wanted him to think of those people who make policy not for moral reasons, not for swashbuckling reasons, but to gain something for our country. Because I thought we might all be killed. In fact, a lot of us thought that at the time, didn't we? Norman Mailer wrote a column in *Esquire* which expressed exactly that feeling. For the first time in my life I thought I might be obliterated in a nuclear holocaust.

SB: *When you say Khrushchev was the first bright light since Stalin, did you consider Stalin a bright light?*

DB: I never said that! I meant that Khrushchev was the single bright spot— period.

SB: *(Laugh) Well, I was shocked. Do you feel that the Cuban Missile Crisis and the fact of*

---

[1] Macdonald's actual telegram read: "APPALLED BY REJECTION OF UNEXPECTEDLY GENEROUS COMPROMISE PROPOSED BY KHRUSHCHEV STOP HE IS ACTING IN REALISTIC TRADITION OF BISMARCK GLADSTONE AND METTERNICH STOP YOU ARE BEHAVING AS I WOULD HAVE EXPECTED HIM TO STOP IMPLORE YOU TO RECONSIDER. See Michael Wreszin, *A Rebel in Defense of Tradition: The Life and "Politics" of Dwight Macdonald*, New York 1994, p. 380.

the stand made by Kennedy—which was a tough stand—did have the effect of slowing up Russian expansion?
DB: Well, no. Was there so much Russian expansion under Khrushchev? I don't think there was. No, because I think Khrushchev was a rather reformed and liberal character.

SB: *Well, let me return to my question. If, as we have agreed, there are two aggressive forces, the Soviet Union and the United States, and if we do nothing as you seem to suggest, what is to keep them from eventually dominating much of the world, and even of our oil supplies?*
DB: I am not in favor of doing nothing—not in favor of being passive about the whole thing. Passive resistance does not mean just passive. It means more than that. It means to react and I said we should react appropriately in every way—in all kinds of economic or non-economic ways, in logical ways. For instance, it is a fantastic example, but I thought it was a good anarchist's idea to try to win away Soviet citizens during the Second World War, from their love of Stalin by dropping enormous numbers of pages from the Sears Roebuck catalogue. This was thought up by somebody, and I thought it was a great idea, you know. At the time I would be in favor of it and also in favor of other economic boycotts. Boycotts are good anarchist ideas.

SB: *Let's move on to something else. Something I have always wanted to know and others have wanted to know. Were you one of the founders of the* Partisan Review?
DB: No. The *Partisan Review* was originally published as an organ of the John Reed Club between 1934 and 1936, with editors which included Philip Rahv and William Phillips, who became the most important editors. In 1936 that was a communistic club. It was an open Communist front. In those days the Communists didn't make any pretense at all. Everybody was very glad to be called a Communist, and I myself, at the time, helped organize the *Fortune* unit of the Newspaper Guild in my department, and the chief organizer was a devout member of the party. I forgot his name, Kaufman, I think it was, but anyway, nobody thought anything about it. In 1936 the Communists had the so-called French Turn. They turned toward populism, toward a popular front, and they lost interest in the magazine. They stopped their subsidy and the magazine ceased. And then Rahv and Phillips, who had become as horrified by the Moscow Trials as myself, along with Fred Dupee, who had been an editor of the *New Masses*, joined forces with George L. K. Morris. He was a classmate of Dupee and myself and a great friend. He was an abstract

painter—intellectual, had no interest in politics, but was a friend and had a lot of money. The idea was to restart the *Partisan Review* and to try again, on a Marxist revolutionary basis.

It was not to be Trotskyist. We didn't want to be Trotskyist, quite rightly, but we did want to be a Marxist Leninist revolutionary magazine. It was to follow Karl Liebnecht and Luxemburg—a more liberal idea. We published our first issue in December of 1937—the new *Partisan Review*.

SB: *You said you didn't want to be Trotskyist. Why were you so against Trotsky?*
DB: We weren't against him at all. In fact, I myself was a Trotskyist and the other people were very much for Trotsky. No, it wasn't that we were against Trotsky, but we wanted to be independent and I think that is quite right, you know. Trotsky tried to get us to be his organ, but we wouldn't do it, and we published several articles of Trotsky in the first two issues.

SB: *Did you personally have conversations with Trotsky at that time?*
DB: No, no. I never went to Mexico, so I never met Trotsky. Our contact was all done through the mail. [Macdonald had an exchange of letters with Trotsky concerning the direction of the magazine.]

SB: *You broke with the* Partisan Review *in 1943. Why did you break with them?*
DB: Well, you see I had this opposition to the Second World War and the Lenin/Luxemburg line [which looked for an independent revolutionary movement], and the *PR* editors, after Pearl Harbor, were opposed to that. So our positions became more and more antagonistic. I mean I kept writing these antiwar things and they didn't write anything. They wanted to avoid the whole issue of the war. They looked for financing from someone else, other than George K. Morris, and I left to put out my own magazine.

SB: *When you started* Politics *did you have a particular political position that you wanted to establish?*
DB: Yes, I started *Politics* with a Marxist Leninist position. Revolutionary defeatism so to speak.

SB: *What is Revolutionary Defeatism?*
DB: It means the main enemy is at home and therefore you are in favor of officers revolting against the officers and so on—mutiny in the ranks, that is what it means—fighting a mutiny and also opposition on the home front.

Well, anyway, that was my position in the beginning. But as the war went on, and especially after the peace, I realized this was inadequate, so I then became an anarcho-pacifist. I realized the only solution was in small actions. From 1945 the magazine became more and more anarcho-pacifist.

SB: *When did* Politics *cease publication?*
DB: In 1949, when I really ran out of energy because I was not only the publisher—my first wife and I were able to keep on with a little deficit—I was also the only editor and the main contributor So we ran out of money and also out of steam and interest. I saw there was not going to be any revolutionary movement in the near future, near future and far future I think, and since the magazine was a radical magazine, which I really meant by that, to change the American system, I decided to give it up. I did give it up and turned to writing for the *New Yorker*—mostly on cultural, literary subjects.

SB: *When you decided to give up the magazine, had you decided that the radical position that you had been advocating was an impossible position at the time?*
DB: Yes, yes, sure—yeah, and I still think that's the truth. There is no revolutionary possibility anywhere that I can see.

SB: *Now, would you mind telling us where your politics were prior to your* Partisan Review *years? You have been a Leninist, a pacifist, an anarchist. What were you in those early years?*
DB: My politics didn't really exist until I was finished at *Fortune*, in the middle, late 1930s. When I was at Yale as an undergraduate, I had absolutely no interest in politics at all. The only thing on the campus was what was called a Social Club and I had absolutely no interest in that at all. I wasn't even a member of the Communist Party at that time. I was only a critic and wrote imitative stories influenced by Anderson and Aikin and things like that. I was a literary guy entirely at Yale.

After Yale, I then became an executive trainee at R. H. Macy. I thought I would make a lot of money as a big merchant, big executive, and then would retire and write a book at age thirty. Well, I went through six months of it, and I was very popular with customers and fellow employees, but I didn't have that interest in making money, that punch, you know. I was really not a good salesman. I couldn't clinch the sale. The customers liked me but didn't buy. I was shopped several times. Comparison shoppers came to see how I was doing until I finally decided this was not for me. I couldn't even get a job in the advertising department. Then I finally got a job through a friend from Yale, Wilder Hobson, with the Luce organization. I became an editor with *Fortune*. I was on that staff for about six years. At one point they gave me a long vacation, and I spent it mostly in New York. I read for the most time, Marx and Trotsky, especially Marx. [Macdonald actually spent most of the time in Europe, in Majorca, doing this reading.] Then I became interested in Marxism. When I got back, I was quite a fellow traveler for a year or two. Until the Moscow Trials came along.

SB: *What was your position at* Fortune? *Were you an editor, or something special, or what?*
DB: I think they called us social editors. We weren't really editors, we were writers. There were about eight of us. Archibald MacLeish and Wilder Hobson, a friend of mine was another, and James Agee was there for a while. I got him a job there when he got out of Harvard. That was my position there. We wrote, we all wrote.

SB: *What kinds of things did you write?*
DB: We wrote all kinds of things. In the beginning we wrote only corporation stuff. Stories about the glories of business and so on. The first issue of *Fortune* came out about three or four months after the stock market crash, you know, Black Friday. We survived. In the first few years we wrote only about corporations, and business, big business. But, of course, the New Deal came along and then came the whole question of writing about the New Deal. People like MacLeish and myself were in favor of it and we also wanted to write about it. So there was a big hassle about that. But we all kept on writing, and Agee wrote what we used to call beautiful prose [obviously a reference to his articles that became *Let Us Now Praise Famous Men* dealing with southern sharecroppers], which was very modest but had nothing to do with business at all.

SB: *After you had read Marx and, to use a cliche, "seen the light of your position," how did this effect your writing at* Fortune?
DB: When I got back I was given the most important job in my life—to write a four-part article on the United States Steel Corporation. This was the crown of my career there. And then by an odd chance there was a fellow there who was their financial advisor—Charles Stillman. He was an advisor to Luce on

how to invest his millions. Stillman and I made an odd team because I was at that time a convinced Marxist and he was a convinced reactionary, a conservative, money guy. So we worked together on this series and he provided the financial savvy. He thought, we both thought, the steel corporation was a very bad example of capitalism, he from the point of view of capitalism and me from the point of socialism, because, you know, it paid bad wages to its employees. It wouldn't allow a union. It gave lousy dividends to its stockholders, and it charged high prices to its customers. The only group that was a positive force were the managers and they got very handsome salaries, huge bonuses, and so on. So we wrote this series together. I wrote the usual prose and he provided the factual data. When we got to the fourth installment, Luce groaned, because his organization was actually backed by J. P. Morgan and Company—the Morgan partners, especially Dwight Morrow, and somebody else, two Morgans. In any event, the Morgan people were very prominent in backing the original Luce *Time* Inc. So Luce gritted his teeth and published these things, then the final one, in which I really went to town, summarizing the thing, I began with a quotation from Lenin concerning monopoly capitalism: —Monopoly is the last stage of capitalism before socialism. I put that as an epigraph to the final article. Luce and his advisers drew the line there.

SB: *Did he publish it?*

DB: No, he didn't publish it. That is the point. He drew the line there, he wouldn't publish my final article. And he had a guy named Ralph Ingersoll, who was the managing editor of *Fortune*, rewrite it. He made it completely terrible, a mess of the whole thing. He took all of the truth out of it. At that point I decided I wanted to get out, and so I did resign from *Fortune* at the end of 1937, no, in the spring of 1936.

SB: *Well I think your departure from* Fortune *magazine is a good place for us to stop. And I want to thank you very much Mr. Macdonald for your generous interview and I want to thank Lillian Broudy, our technician on this tape.*

DB: I want to thank both of you—especially Shirley for a marvelous interview. Goodbye.

Index

Abel, Lionel, 140
Agee, James, 26–27, 55, 60, 64–65, 71, 143–44, 145–46, 173; *Let Us Now Praise Famous Men*, 91, 98, 118, 144, 145, 173
Algren, Nelson, 75
Allen, Woody, 70
American Writers Congress, 108
anarchism, 5, 6, 40, 75, 81, 88, 93–94, 114, 118, 164
Antonioni, Michelangelo, 15, 59, 61, 74, 95
Arendt, Hannah, 44, 97, 139–40; *Eichman in Jerusalem*, 140–42; *The Human Condition*, 43; *On Revolution*, 43; *The Origins of Totalitarianism*, 43, 140
Auden, W. H., 44
Augie March, 131
Austen, Jane, 39
auteurists, 60, 69

Barabbas, 15, 16–17
Barrett, Will, 126
Barth, John, 91
Barthelme, Donald, 92
Battle of Algiers, The, 64
Beatty, Warren, 53
Beauty and the Beast, 62
Beckett, Samuel, 28–29
Bek-Gran, Robert, 113
Bell, Daniel, 141
Bellow, Saul, 28, 46, 47, 92, 110, 131
Ben Hur (1926), 16
Ben Hur (1960), 13, 16

Benet, Stephen Vincent, 45
Bergman, Ingmar, 12, 15, 25, 46, 52, 61, 62, 74, 95, 100
Bettelheim, Bruno, 80, 92, 97
Birth of a Nation, 14, 19, 62, 147
Blind Husbands, 63
Blood of a Poet, 62, 69
Blow-Up, 50, 52, 55, 56, 74
Bogdanovich, Peter, 60–61
Bonnie and Clyde, 52–53, 54, 55, 56
Bottoms, Timothy, 60
Bourne, Randolph, 43
Brando, Marlon, 15
Breathless, 74
Breton, Andre, 109, 110
Brooks, Mel, 70
Broughton, Shirley, 159–73
Brustein, Robert, 27
bureaucratic collectivism, 133
Burke, Edmund, 88, 94
Burnham, James, 104, 108, 109, 122, 132–33, 160, 162–63

Cabell, James Branch, 41
Cabinet of Dr. Caligari, The, 62, 63, 69
Cabiria, 16
Cannon, James, 104–05, 106, 111, 122
Cantine, Holley, Jr., 113
Cape Fear, 56
Carnera, Primo, 17
Carry on Nurse, 11
Carter, James, 95, 96, 109, 164

175

Cavett, Dick, 58
Chamberlain, John, 107
Chandler, Raymond, 38
Chaplin, Charlie, 15, 19–20, 21, 25, 27, 61–62, 71, 144
Chase, Stuart, 44
Children of Paradise, 62
Citizen Kane, 9, 53, 62
City Lights, 61–62
Cleopatra, 14
Clockwork Orange, A, 54, 56, 59, 66, 74–75
Cocteau, Jean, 62
Cole, Lewis, 154
Coleridge, Samuel Taylor, 8–9
Commentary, 36–37, 40
Committee for Cultural Freedom and Socialism, 109–10
Communism, 78, 104, 108, 120, 121, 128, 135, 157, 164
Congress for Cultural Freedom, 110
Conrad, Joseph, 52
Cops, 70
Counts, George, 136
Cozzens, James Gould, *By Love Possessed*, 4, 71, 90–91, 104
Crowther, Bosley, 67
Cultural Freedom Committee, 110
culture. *See* Macdonald, Dwight, on culture

de Cleyre, Votairine, 114
De Laurentiis, Dino, 16
de Tocqueville, Alexis, 39, 43, 83, 164
de Wilde, Brandon, 60
Death in Venice, 66
DeMille, Cecil B., 16
Dickens, Charles, 41
Dickinson, Emily, 47
Dobbs, Farrell, 106
Douzhenko, Alexander, 26, 64
Downs, Hugh, 14
Dreiser, Theodore, 28
Dupee, Fred W., 23, 107–08, 110, 116, 128–29, 153–54, 170
Dutt, Palme, 39

Eastman, Max, 110
Eclipse, 50

8½, 20, 52, 55, 62, 98
Eisenhower, Dwight D., 6, 167
Eisenstein, Sergei, 14, 15, 26, 64, 69, 126, 147
Eliot, George, 39
Eliot, T. S., 28, 44
Elmer Gantry, 7–8
Encounter, 37, 40, 101–02
Engels, Friederich, 121
Evans, Rowland, 44
Evans, Walker, 121, 144–45, 146–47
Everson, William K., 19

Fadiman, Clifton, 44
Farrell, James T., 110–11
Fast, Howard, 137, 138
Faulkner, William, 28, 29
Fellini, Federico, 15, 26, 46, 59, 61, 74, 95, 98
Finney, Albert, 12
Fitzgerald, F. Scott, 28
Fonda, Henry, 16
Fonda, Jane, 56
Foolish Wives, 63
Ford, Gerald, 95, 96
Frank, Leon, 106
Frankenheimer, John, 60
French Connection, The, 56, 66
Friedman, Milton, 44, 165
Fritchey, Clayton, 44
Fuller, Buckminster, 102, 103

Gable, Clark, 15
Garis, Howard R., 40–41
General, The, 20
Getting Straight, 49–50
Gide, Andre, 129
Gill, Brendon, 91, 97
Ginsberg, Allen, 42
Gioni, John, 109
Go-Between, The, 66
Godard, Jean-Luc, 61, 74, 95
Gogol, Nikolai, 39
Gold Rush, The, 61
Goldman, Emma, 149, 150
Gombrich, Ernst, 44
Goodman, Paul, 68, 114, 165–66
Goodman, Percy, 165

Graduate, The, 56–57
Grand Illusion, 63
Greed, 63
Greenberg, Clement, 125, 126–27
Grey, Zane, 44
Griffith, D. W., 14–15, 19, 21, 25, 27, 56, 143

Hallelujah the Hills, 48
Harriott, Esther, 90–103
Hartmann, Paul, 16
Hawks, Howard, 60–61
Hawthorne, Nathaniel, 93
Hayden, Thomas, 151, 154
Hellman, Lillian, *Scoundrel Time*, 137, 138–39
Help!, 71
Hemingway, Ernest, 45
Henry, O., 41
Herndon, Angelo, 120
Herzen, Alexander, 39, 43, 67, 94
Hicks, Granville, 108
Higgins, Jimmy, 109
high culture. *See* Macdonald, Dwight, on culture
Hinz, Werner, 16
Hiroshima Mon Amour, 9, 10–11
Hobsbawm, Eric, 43
Hobson, Wilder, 23, 173
Hoffman, Abbie, 114
Hoffman, Dustin, 56–57
Hook, Sidney, 110, 135, 136
Hoover, Herbert, 95, 165
How to Murder Your Wife, 48
Howard, Trevor, 15
Howe, Irving, 109, 141
Hurst, Fanny, 44

I. F. Stone's Weekly, 35, 40
Ingersoll, Ralph, 174
Intolerance, 14, 19
It's a Mad, Mad, Mad, Mad World, 48

James, C. L. R., 105
James, Henry, 28, 52
John Reed Club, 170
Johnson, Lyndon B., 24

Joyce, James, 28, 44, 84
Jules and Jim, 20

Kael, Pauline, 64, 67, 71, 73, 100
Kauffman, Stanley, 56, 73
Kazan, Elia, 71
Keaton, Buster, 15, 19–20, 21, 25, 27, 62, 70, 71
Kennan, George, 166–67
Kennedy, John F., 24, 169–70
Kerr, Walter, 27
Khruschev, Nikita, 135, 169–70
Kipling, Rudyard, 41
Kirk, Grayson, 151, 157
Kiss Me Stupid, 48
Klute, 56, 58
Kropotkin, Peter, 40, 114, 149
Kubrick, Stanley, 50, 59, 74–75
Kurosawa, Akira, 15, 61, 95
Kurtz, Paul, 77–89

La Ronde, 62
Lagerkvist, Par, 16
Lancaster, Burt, 8
Lardner, Ring, 47
Last Picture Show, The, 66
Last Tango in Paris, 100
Last Year at Marienbad, 56, 62, 65
Laughton, Charles, 15
L'Avventura, 10, 50, 62
Lenin, Vladimir, 163
Leonard, John, 85
Lerner, Max, 44
Lester, Richard, 71
libertarianism, 82–83
Liebnecht, Karl, 171
Lolita, 92
Longest Day, The, 15, 16
Losey, Joseph, 60
Lowell, Cal, 136, 158
Lowell, Robert, 46
Luce, Henry, 173–74

Macdonald, Dwight: on acting, 56–57; on the American film industry, 12–13, 20–21, 26, 55–56, 60–61; on American foreign policy,

134–35, 166–70; on American politics, 77–83, 89; on anarchism, 5–6, 40, 75, 81, 82–83, 88, 93–94, 114, 118, 148–53, 161, 164–65; on art, 99; on auteurists, 60, 69; on being a critic, 97–98; biographical information, 22, 115; on book reviews, 24–25; on the British film industry, 11–12; on bureaucratic collectivism, 133; career, 4, 22–24, 71, 72, 90, 116–18, 172–74; on the Columbia University student uprising, 149–55; on comedy, 70–71; comments on specific films, 7–8, 9, 10–11, 12, 13, 14–17, 20, 48, 49–54, 56–57, 61–64, 65, 71, 73, 74; on Communism, 23, 78, 104, 108, 120, 121, 135, 164; on compromise, 124; on contemporary literature, 28–29, 91–92; on Cozzens' *By Love Possessed*, 4, 90–91; on the Cuban Missile Crisis, 169–70; on culture, 30–31, 44, 45–47, 57–58, 59, 61–62, 84–86, 98–99, 147–49; on the decline of the student movement, 155–56; education, 3, 22, 41–42, 115–16, 124; favorite films of, 62; on film, 14–16, 17, 25–26, 64, 94–95; on film criticism, 7–10, 18–19, 26–28, 42–43, 48–49, 51–52, 54–55, 58, 64–67, 68–69, 70–71, 72, 73–74, 100–01, 142–43; on good-bad films, 13, 20; on himself, 31–32; on his politics, 4, 23–24, 39–40, 49, 69, 72, 75, 81–82, 83, 88, 93–94, 95–96, 104–09, 119–22, 125–26, 147, 148, 161, 164, 165, 172; on his reading habits, 38–41, 42–44; on Israel, 125; on leaving *Fortune*, 23, 106, 117; on libertarianism, 82–83; on Marxism, 40, 43, 88, 120, 121, 156, 173, 174; at the *Militant*, 133; on the New Left, 78–80, 149; on newspapers, 33–37; on the novel, 91–92; opposition to World War II, 111–12, 125, 159–61, 171; on pacifism, 24, 113–14, 159, 161–62; and *Partisan Review*, 7, 23, 40, 57, 108, 109, 110, 111, 116–17, 118, 125, 126, 129, 130, 133, 140, 171; on Poe, 76, 80, 92–93; and *Politics*, 23–24, 40, 68, 71, 81, 84, 93, 96, 111, 113, 116, 119, 132, 133–34, 135, 140, 161, 162, 171–72; on poverty, 24, 78; on race, 6, 24, 79; on rebelliousness, 123–24; on religion, 86, 87–88, 96; on revolution, 135, 161–64; on revolutionary defeatism, 170–72; on Russian film, 64, 143; on science, 86–87; on slavery reparations, 142; on Socialism, 81–82; on the Soviet Union, 6, 134–35, 162–64, 166–70; and Students for a Democratic Society, 39, 148–49, 154; on teaching, 103, 117; on television, 15, 84, 102–03; on Trotskyism, 40, 66–67, 78, 81, 88, 104–09, 110–11, 116, 118, 119, 120, 121–22, 132–33, 137, 162, 164, 171; on voluntary associations, 83, 164; on the war in southeast Asia, 39, 79, 94, 95, 156–57, 168; on writing and editing, 96–97, 103; on Yale, 3, 4, 5, 116

Works: *Against the American Grain: Essays on the Effects of Mass Culture*, 14, 143; Amateur Journalism (essay), 72; *Discriminations: Essays and Afterthoughts*, 102; *Dwight Macdonald on Movies*, 61, 68, 74, 90; Fellini's Obvious Masterpieces (review), 55; *Masscult & Midcult*, 45, 47, 57–58, 59, 71; *My Past and Thoughts: The Memoirs of Alexander Herzon* (editor), 67, 94; *Parodies: An Anthology from Chaucer to Beerbohm—and After*, 4, 22, 24, 90; *Politics Past: Essays in Political Criticism* (*Memoirs of a Revolutionist*), 22, 39, 67–68, 119; A Theory of Popular Culture (essay), 84

Macdonald, Nancy, 106, 108, 112, 113, 130, 133
Macklin, F. Anthony, 48–69
MacLeish, Archibald, 173; *J. B.*, 45
Magnificent Ambersons, The, 62
Mailer, Norman, 28, 46–47, 59–60, 91, 92, 93, 131–32, 136–37, 158
Malamud, Bernard, 132
Malaquais, Jean, 136
Mangan, Sherry, 109
Mankiewicz, Joseph, 53
Markel, Lester, 25, 33–34, 85
Marshall, Margaret, 129
Marx, Karl, 39, 40, 121, 156, 163, 164, 173
Marxism, 40, 43, 88, 120, 121, 156, 173, 174
MASH, 100
mass culture. *See* Macdonald, Dwight, on culture

masscult. *See* Macdonald, Dwight, on culture
Mastroianni, Marcello, 56
Mathiesson, F. O., 108
Mayer, Louis B., 21
McCabe and Mrs. Miller, 53–54, 56, 58
McCarthy, Mary, 39, 99, 107, 108, 129–30, 136, 140, 157
McGovern, George, 77, 155
McLuhan, Marshall, 102–03
Mekas, Adolphus, 54
Mencken, H. L., 41
Mickey One, 53
midcult. *See* Macdonald, Dwight, on culture
Midnight Cowboy, 57
Mills, C. Wright, 112
Mission to Moscow, 145–46
Modern Times, 62
Monsieur Verdoux, 55, 144
Morris, George L. K., 23, 110, 116, 127, 128, 129, 170–71
Morris, Ivan, 152
Morrow, Felix, 109
Moses, Robert, 5, 6
Murnau, Friedrich, 25
Mutiny on the Bounty, 15–16
Myrdal, Jan, 43

Nabokov, Vladmir, 44, 91, 92
Nader, Ralph, 164
Naked Night, 62
Nation, The, 36
Navigator, The, 20
New Leader, The, 36
New Republic, The, 36
New York Herald-Tribune, 25
New York Post, 34–35
New York Review of Books, 25, 34
New York Times, 33–34
New York Times Book Review, 24–25, 85
New Yorker, The, 36
Newquist, Roy, 22–32
Newsweek, 35–36
Nixon, Richard M., 73, 75, 77, 78, 79, 89, 94, 95, 134
Novak, George, 108, 109
Novak, Robert, 44

Olivier, Laurence, 57
On the Waterfront, 71
O'Neill, Eugene, 118
Ophuls, Max, 62
Organizer, The, 63–64
Ozu, Yasujiro, 73, 95

Pabst, Georg Wilhelm, 25
pacifism, 24, 113–14, 159, 161–62
Packages for Europe, 112
Partisan Review, 40, 57, 110, 111, 116–17, 118, 125, 126, 129, 130, 132, 133, 140, 170–71
Peacemakers, 113
Peckinpah, Sam, 54
Penn, Arthur, 53
Persona, 74
Phelps, William Lyon, 42, 124
Phillips, William, 23, 108, 110, 116, 125, 127, 128, 129, 140, 170
Picasso, Pablo, 28
Poe, Edgar Allan, 38–39, 46, 67, 76, 80, 92–93
Polanski, Roman, 50
Politics, 23–24, 40, 68, 71, 81, 83, 93, 113, 116, 119, 132, 133- 34, 140, 161, 162, 171
Pollack, Jackson, 127
popular culture. *See* Macdonald, Dwight, on culture
Potemkin, 14, 62, 147
Powell, Anthony, 43
Preminger, Otto, 74
Proudhon, Pierre-Joseph, 40
Proust, Marcel, 28
Pudovkin, Vsevolod, 26, 64, 69
Pynchon, Thomas, 92

Quinn, Anthony, 16–17

Rahv, Phillip, 23, 107, 108, 110, 116, 127, 128, 129–30, 170
Ray, Satyajit, 95
Reader's Digest, 85
Reagan, Ronald, 164, 165, 167
Red Desert, 50
Reich, Wilhelm, 131
Reisz, Karel, 12
Renoir, Jean, 26, 63

180 Index

Repulsion, 50
Resnais, Alain, 10, 12, 15, 61, 62, 95
Revised Standard Version of the Bible, 98
Richardson, Dorothy, 39
Richardson, Tony, 60
Riefenstahl, Leni, 8
Rimbaud, Arthur, 28
Robbins, Harold, 44
Roosevelt, Franklin D., 23, 78, 117–18, 146, 165
Rosemary's Baby, 50, 56
Rosenfeld, Isaac, 130–31
Roskolenko, Harry, 109
Roth, Philip, 46, 47, 91
Rubin, Jerry, 114
Rudd, Mark, 42, 154
Rules of the Game, 63
Ryan, Robert, 16

Sarris, Andrew, 73
Saturday Night and Sunday Morning, 11, 12
Satyricon, 74
Sawdust and Tinsel, 62
Schlesinger, John, 57
Schwartz, Delmore, 126
Sennett, Mack, 15, 21, 27, 71
Seventh Seal, The, 52
Shachtman, Max, 105, 106, 108, 111, 122
Shadows, 9
Shampoo, 100
Shaw, George Bernard, 31, 54–55
Shawn, William, 97, 117
Sherlock, Jr., 20, 76, 70, 71
Shostakovich, Dmitri, 136
Sight and Sound, 9
Silent Movie, 70
Simmons, Jean, 8
Simon, John, 27, 56, 64–65, 66, 68, 73, 74, 99–100
Smith, Al, 165
Socialist Workers Party, 106, 109
Solow, Herbert, 109
Spanish Refugees Aid, 112
Splendor in the Grass, 71
Stalin, Josef, 26, 135, 143, 163, 169

Stevenson, Robert Louis, 41, 42
Stillman, Charles, 173–74
Strachey, John, 39
Stravinsky, Igor, 28, 44
Straw Dogs, 56, 57
Stroheim, Erich von, 15, 25, 63, 143
Students for a Democratic Society (SDS), 78, 148–49, 151
Suddenly Last Summer, 13
Sundowners, The, 13
Suskind, David, 58–59
Swados, Harvey, 109

Tati, Jacques, 27
Taylor, Harold, 151
Taylor, Myron C., 23
television, 15, 84, 102–03
Ten Commandments, The, 16
Ten Days That Shook the World, 62, 147
Thackeray, William Makepeace, 41
Thalberg, Irving, 21
Thomas, Jeffrey, 3–4
Time, 35–36, 85
Tokyo Story, 73, 95
Tracey, Mike, 7–14
Trilling, Diana, 115–58
Trilling, Lionel, 99, 118, 125
Triumph of the Will, 8
Trotsky, Leon, 39, 40, 66, 106, 107, 108, 109, 110, 120, 122, 162, 163, 171, 173
Trotsky Defense Committee, 104, 109, 116, 122, 164
Trotskyism, 40, 66–67, 78, 81, 88, 104–09, 110–11, 116, 118, 119, 120, 121–22, 132–33, 137, 162, 164, 171
Truffaut, Francois, 15, 26, 61, 95
Tunes of Glory, 13
2001: A Space Odyssey, 50–51, 52, 56

Untermeyer, Louis, 136
Updike, John, 28, 92, 99

Veysey, Laurence, 114
Village Voice, The, 36
Vitti, Monica, 50

Voight, Jon, 57
Vonnegut, Kurt, 92

Waldorf Conference (1949), 135–38
War Resisters League, 113, 161
Warshow, Robert, 55, 143
Wayne, John, 16
We Are the Lambeth Boys, 11
Webster's New International Dictionary, 98
Weekend, 74
Weil, Simone, 43
Welles, Orson, 53
What's New Pussycat, 48
Wheelwright, John, 109
Wicki, Bernard, 16

Wild Strawberries, 12
Wilde, Oscar, 41
Wilder, Thornton, *Our Town*, 45, 99
Wills, Garry, 137
Wilson, Colin, 71
Wilson, Edmund, 27, 29, 91, 99, 107, 118, 129–30
Wolfe, Bernard, 109
Woolf, Virginia, 39
Wuthering Heights, 57

Yglesias, Jose, 43

Zabriskie Point, 74
Zanuck, Darryl, 16, 21
Zazie, 48